Excel 365 Basics

A Quick and Easy Guide to Boosting Your Productivity with Excel

Nathan George

Excel 365 Basics: A Quick and Easy Guide to Boosting Your Productivity with Excel

Published 2022.

Published by GTech Publishing.

ISBN: 978-1-915476-04-3

https://www.excelbytes.com

Contents

Introduction

Excel 365 Basics covers all you would need to successfully create workbooks that provide solutions for your data. Starting from the basics, you learn how to create, edit, format, and print your worksheets. You learn how to carry out different calculations with formulas and functions, work with Excel tables, summarize data from different perspectives with pivot tables, and visually analyze your data with different charts.

This book is concise and to the point, as you don't need to wade through a wall of text to learn how to quickly carry out a task in Excel. Hence you will not see the unnecessary verbosity and filler text you may find in some other Excel books in this book. The aim is to take even a complete beginner to someone skilled in Excel within a few short hours.

Who Is This Book For?

Excel 365 Basics starts from the basics, so it is suitable for you if you're new to Excel or spreadsheets in general. This book is also for you if you have some Excel skills and want to expand on that by learning the new features in Excel.

The necessary topics have been covered to give you a solid foundation and the tools to create solutions for your data. However, the topics have been kept at a level to not be overwhelming if you're completely new to Excel and interested in a quick course without getting bogged down with the more advanced topics.

If you need something more advanced, like What-If Analysis, macros, advanced functions, in-depth pivot tables, etc., then this book is not for you. It might be a good idea to examine the table of contents to see if it covers your requirements.

This book is aimed at readers with Excel for Microsoft 365 or Excel 2021 (the current standalone version). However, many of the core Excel features remain the same for earlier versions of the software, like Excel 2019, 2016, and 2013. So, you would still find many lessons in this book relevant even if you have an earlier version of Excel.

As much as possible, I point out the features new in Excel when covered. Note, however, that if you're using an earlier version of Excel, some of the dialog boxes displayed in this book may differ from your version.

How to Use This Book

This book can be used as a step-by-step training guide or a reference manual that you come back to from time to time. You can read it cover to cover or skip to certain parts that cover topics you want to learn. Although the chapters have been organized logically, the book has been designed to enable you to read a chapter as a standalone tutorial to learn how to carry out a certain task.

There are many ways to perform the same task in Excel. So, for brevity, this book focuses on the most efficient way of carrying out a task. However, alternative ways to perform a task are also provided occasionally.

As much as possible, the menu items and commands mentioned are bolded to distinguish them from the other text. This book also includes many screenshots to illustrate the covered features and tasks.

Assumptions

When writing this book, the software assumptions are that you already have Excel for Microsoft 365 (or Excel 2021) installed on your computer and that you're working on the Windows 10 (or Windows 11) platform.

If you are using an older version of Excel, you can still use this book (as long as you're aware that some of the covered features may not be available in your version). Alternatively, you can get my *Excel 2019 Basics* book, the previous edition of this book.

If you are using Excel on a Mac, simply substitute any Windows keyboard commands mentioned in the book for the Mac equivalent. All the features within Excel remain the same for both platforms.

If you're using Excel on a tablet or touchscreen device, simply substitute any keyboard commands mentioned in the book with the equivalent on your touchscreen device.

Excel Versions

Excel for Microsoft 365 (2022 update) is the version of Excel that comes with a Microsoft 365 subscription while Excel 2021 is the latest standalone (perpetual license) version of Excel. In the last few years, Microsoft has adopted a release cycle where new features are released for Microsoft 365 products as they become available. Conversely, standalone versions get new features approximately every 2-3 years when a new version of Office is released.

This book covers the latest version of Excel for Microsoft 365 (2022 update) and Excel 2021.

Practice Files

Downloadable Excel files have been provided to save you time if you want to practice in Excel as you follow the examples in the book. All examples are fully detailed in the book, and these files have simply been provided to save you some typing, so they're optional.

You can practice by changing the data to view different results. Please note that practice files have only been included for chapters where the examples use a sizable amount of sample data. Click the link below to go to the download page:

https://www.excelbytes.com/excel-365-dl

Notes:

- Type the URL in your Internet browser's address bar, and press Enter to navigate to the download page. If you encounter an error, double-check that you have correctly entered all the URL characters.

- The files have been zipped into one download. Windows 10 (or Windows 11) has the functionality to unzip files. If your OS does not have this functionality, you'll need to get a piece of software like WinZip or WinRAR to unzip the file.

- The files are Excel files, so you will need to have Excel installed on your computer to open and use these files (preferably Excel 2013 and above).

- If you encounter any problems downloading these files, please contact me at **support@excelbytes.com**. Include the title of this book in your email, and the practice files will be emailed directly to you.

Chapter 1

Getting Started with Excel

To start Excel, click the Windows Start icon and enter "Excel" in the search bar. Windows displays the Excel app in the results below. Click Excel to start the application.

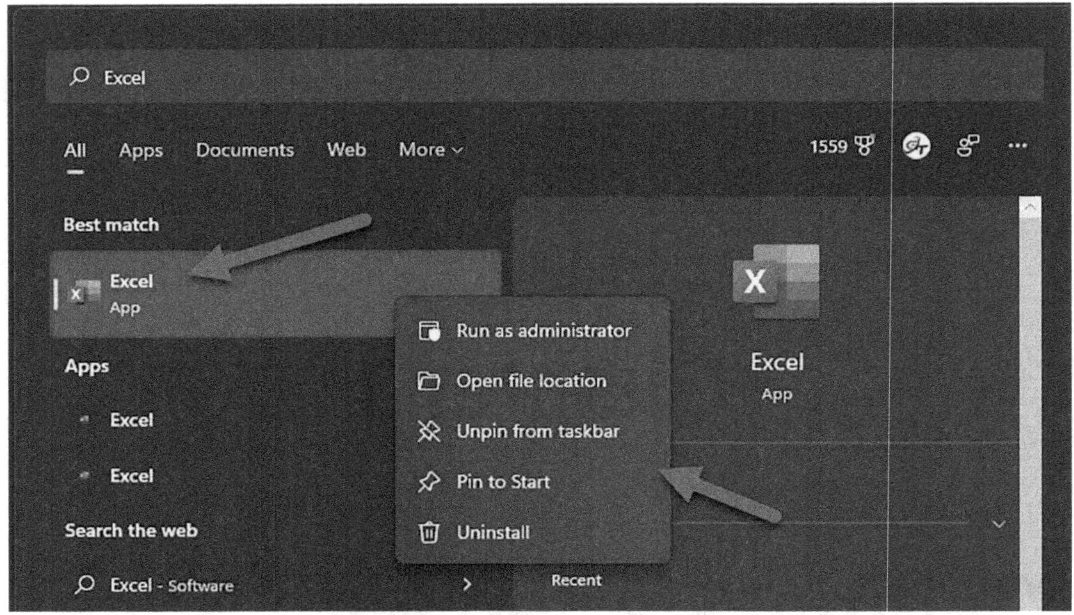

To access Excel faster next time, you can pin it to the **Start menu, taskbar**, or place a shortcut on your **desktop**.

Do the following to pin Excel to your **Start menu**:

1. Click the Windows **Start** icon.
2. On the Start menu, enter "Excel" in the search bar.
3. On the results list below, right-click **Excel** and select **Pin to Start**.

Do the following to pin Excel to your **taskbar:**

1. Click the Windows **Start** icon.
2. On the Start menu, enter "Excel" in the search bar.
3. Right-click **Excel** and select **Pin to taskbar**.

To place a copy of Excel's shortcut on your **desktop**, do the following:

1. Click the Windows **Start** icon.
2. On the Start menu, enter "Excel" in the search bar.
3. Right-click **Excel** and select **Open file location** on the shortcut menu.

   Windows will open the shortcut folder location of Excel in Windows Explorer.
4. In the folder, right-click **Excel**, and select **Copy** on the shortcut menu.
5. On your desktop, right-click any area and select **Paste**.

Creating a New Excel Workbook

Launch Excel from the Start menu or the shortcut you have created on your taskbar or desktop.

Excel will open and display the **Home** screen. The Excel start screen enables you to create a new blank workbook or open one of your recently opened workbooks. You also have a selection of predefined templates that you can use as the basis of your workbook.

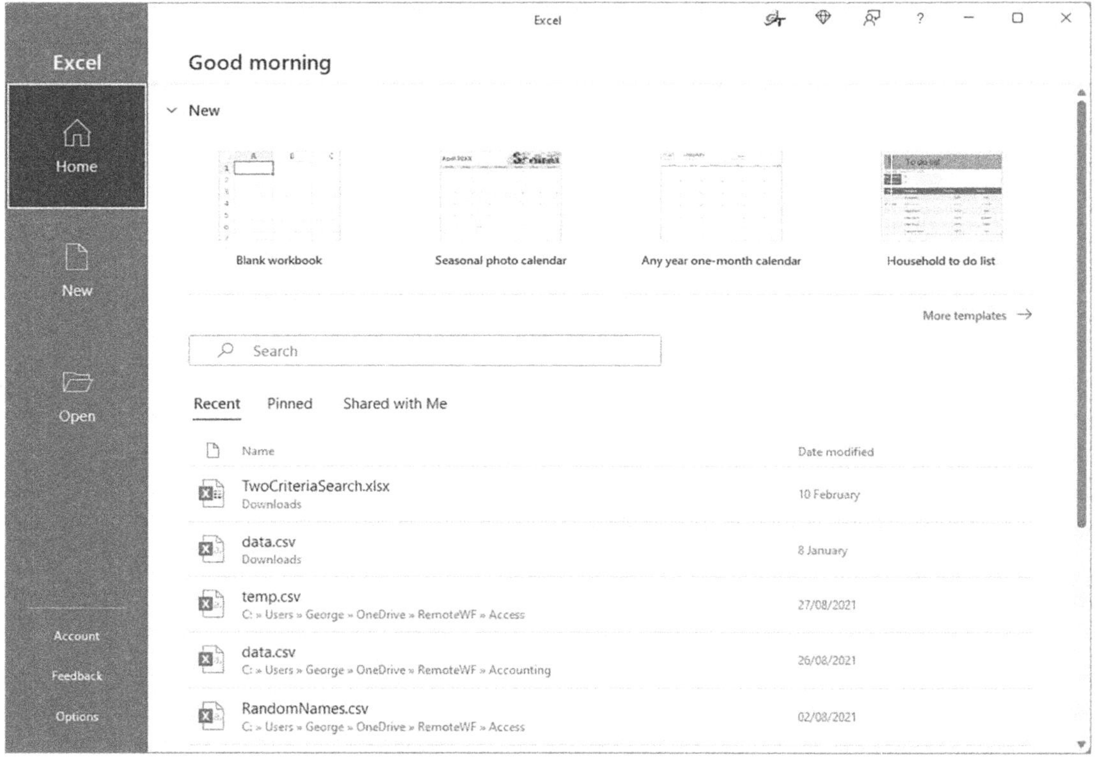

To create a new workbook, click **Blank workbook**. Excel creates a new workbook with a worksheet named **Sheet1**.

Tip To quickly create a new workbook when you already have a workbook open, press **Ctrl + N** on your keyboard.

Creating A Workbook Based on A Template

To create a new workbook based on one of Excel's predefined templates, open Excel and click the **New** button on the left navigation pane to display the New screen. The categories of available templates are listed under the search bar next to **Suggested searches**.

You can narrow down the displayed templates by clicking one of the listed categories: Business, Personal, Planners and Trackers, Lists, Budgets, Charts, or Calendars.

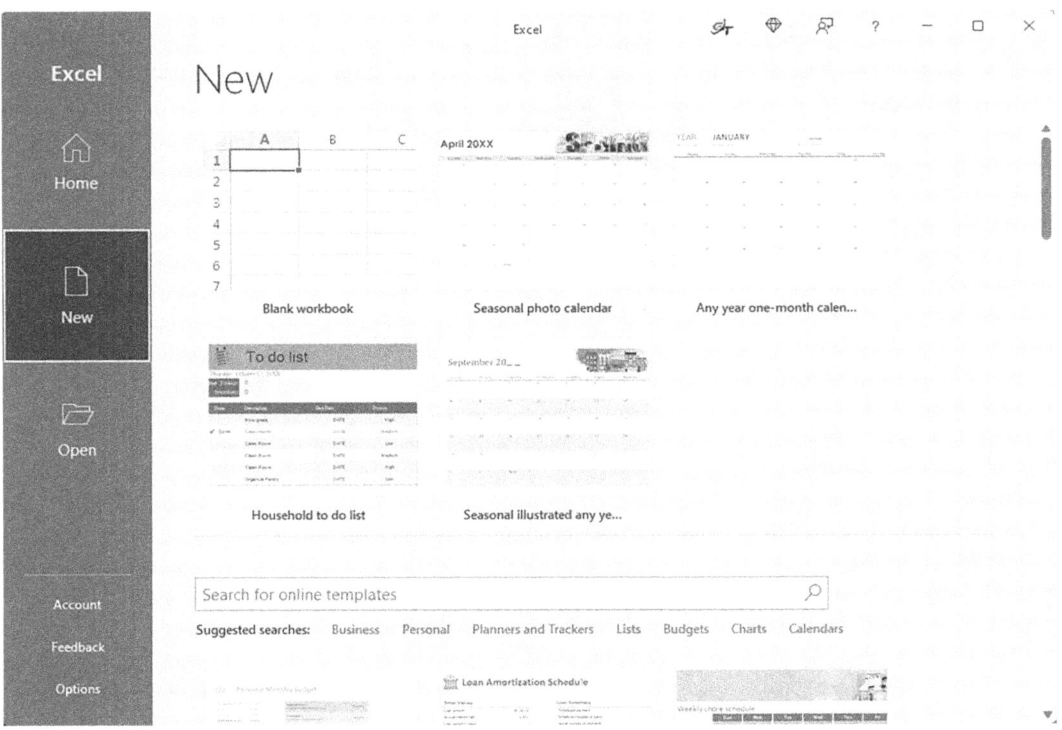

Once you identify the template you want to use, double-click the thumbnail to create a new worksheet based on it.

Saving Your Excel Workbook

To save your workbook for the first time:

1. Click the **File** tab to go to the Backstage view.
2. In the Backstage view, click **Save As** (you'll see **Save a Copy** if your file has been previously saved to OneDrive).
3. On the next screen, click **OneDrive – Personal** (if you're using OneDrive) or **This PC** (if you're not saving it to OneDrive).
4. You get a text box to enter the file name on the right side of the window. Enter the name of your worksheet here.
5. To save the file to an existing folder, navigate to the folder using the list displayed below on the lower-right of the screen. Double-click a folder name to navigate to that folder.

   You can also create a new folder by clicking the **New Folder** button.
6. Click the **Save** button to save the workbook.

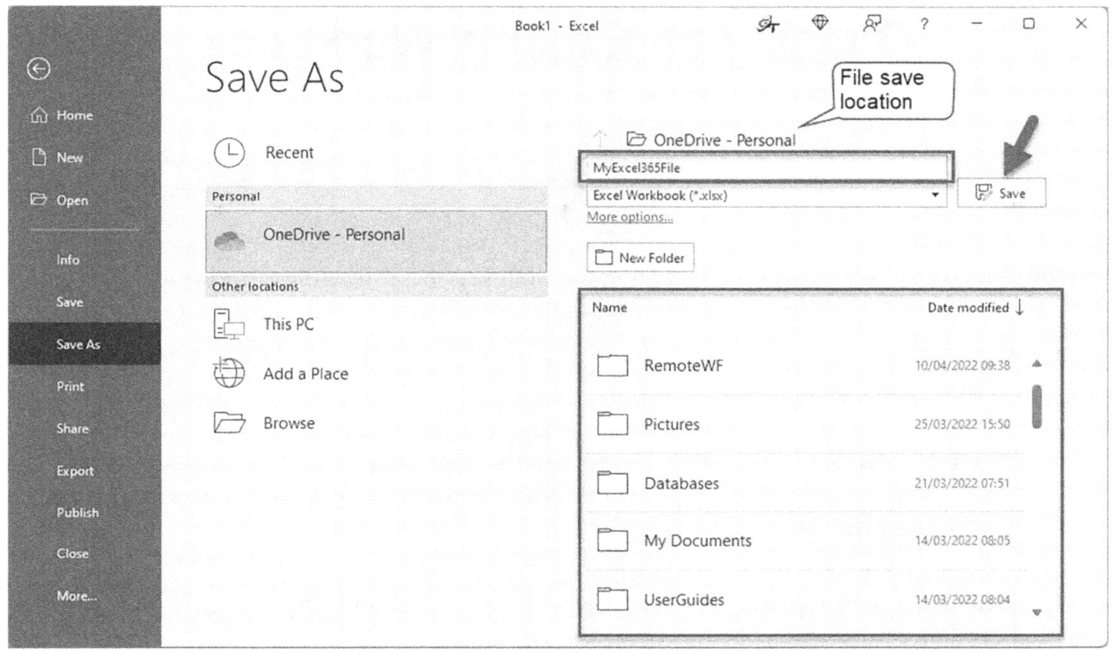

Excel returns you to the **Home** tab after it saves the file.

Note If your workbook has been previously saved to OneDrive or SharePoint, and **AutoSave** is set to on, you'll have **Save a Copy** in place of **Save As**. You can use Save a Copy to save your workbook as a different file.

When you save a file, you overwrite the previous version of the file. If you want to keep an old version of the file while working on it, you need to use **Save As** (or **Save a Copy**). Excel saves the workbook you're working on as a new file while the old version remains unchanged.

Tip To save your workbook quicker, you can use the **Ctrl+S** shortcut after the first save. For a list of the most frequently used shortcuts in Excel, see the Appendix in this book.

Opening an Existing Workbook

Click the **File** menu button to display the Backstage view, and then click **Open** or press **Ctrl+O**.

On the **Open** screen of the Backstage view, you'll see the following options:

- **Recent**: To open a recent workbook, select **Recent** and click the workbook you want to open on the right.

- **Shared with me**: Select this tab to see the files that others have shared with you. Files can be shared through outlook email attachments, a link in an email, a link in Teams, or other methods.

- **OneDrive - Personal**: To open a workbook saved on OneDrive, click OneDrive - Personal and select your file from the right.

Note If you're not in the root folder of OneDrive, you can use the blue up-arrow to navigate to the folder that contains your workbook.

- **This PC**: To open a workbook from the Documents local folder on your PC, click **This PC** to display the Documents folder. Navigate to the folder containing your workbook. Click the file to open it.

- **Browse**: To browse for a file on your computer, click the **Browse** button and use the Open dialog box to locate the file you want to open. Then, select the file and click the **Open** button.

Closing a Workbook

Ensure you've saved the workbook (if you want to keep the changes).

Click **File** to display the Backstage view, and then click **Close**.

Or

Press the **Ctrl+W** shortcut keys to close the workbook.

The Excel User Interface

This section provides an overview of the Excel user interface to familiarize you with the names of various parts of the interface mentioned throughout the book.

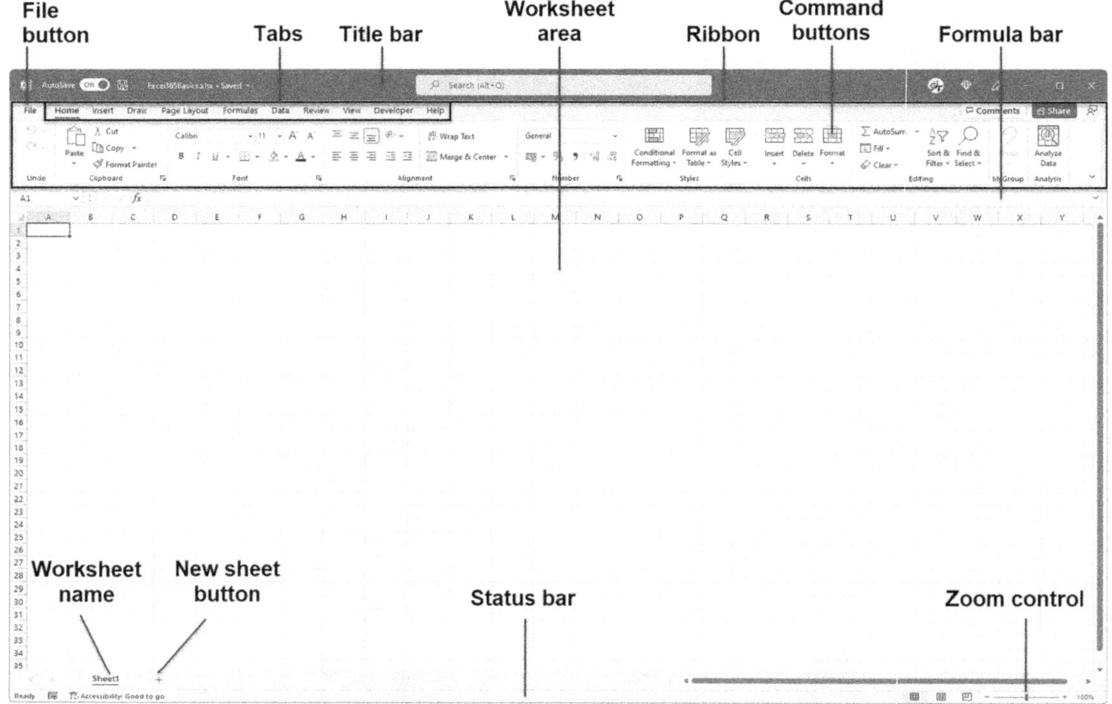

The **Ribbon** contains the bulk of the commands in Excel arranged into a series of tabs from Home to Help.

The **File** button/tab opens the Backstage view when clicked. The Backstage view has several menu options, including Home, New, Open, Info, Save, Save As, Print, Share, Export, Publish, and Close. You have the Account menu option at the bottom of the list to view your user information. You also have Options where you can change many of Excel's default settings.

Note that if your Excel workbook is saved on OneDrive and **AutoSave** is set to **On**, you'll not see the **Save As** menu option. Instead, you'll have **Save a Copy** in its place.

To exit the Backstage view, click the back button (the left-pointing arrow at the top-left of the page).

The **Home** tab provides the most used set of commands. The other tabs provide command buttons for specific tasks like inserting objects into your spreadsheet, formatting the page layout, working with formulas, working with datasets, reviewing your spreadsheet, etc.

The **Worksheet area** contains the cells that will hold your data. The row headings are numbered, while the column headings have letters. Each cell is identified by the combination of the column letter and row number. For example, the first cell on the sheet is A1, the second cell in the first row is B1, and the second cell in the first column is A2. You use these references to identify the cells on the worksheet.

A **workbook** is the Excel document itself. A **worksheet** is a sheet inside a workbook. Each workbook can have several worksheets. You can use the tabs at the bottom of the screen to name, move, copy, and delete worksheets. The plus (+) button next to the name tab enables you to add a new worksheet.

The **Formula bar** displays the contents of the active cell, including any formula.

The **Status bar** provides information on the current display mode. You can zoom in and out of your spreadsheet by clicking the plus (+) and minus (-) signs at the bottom-right of the status bar.

The **Dialog Box Launcher** is a button with a diagonal arrow in the lower-right corner of some groups. When clicked, Excel opens a dialog box containing additional command options related to that group. So, if you cannot see a command on the Ribbon for a task you want to perform, click the small dialog box launcher to display more options for that group.

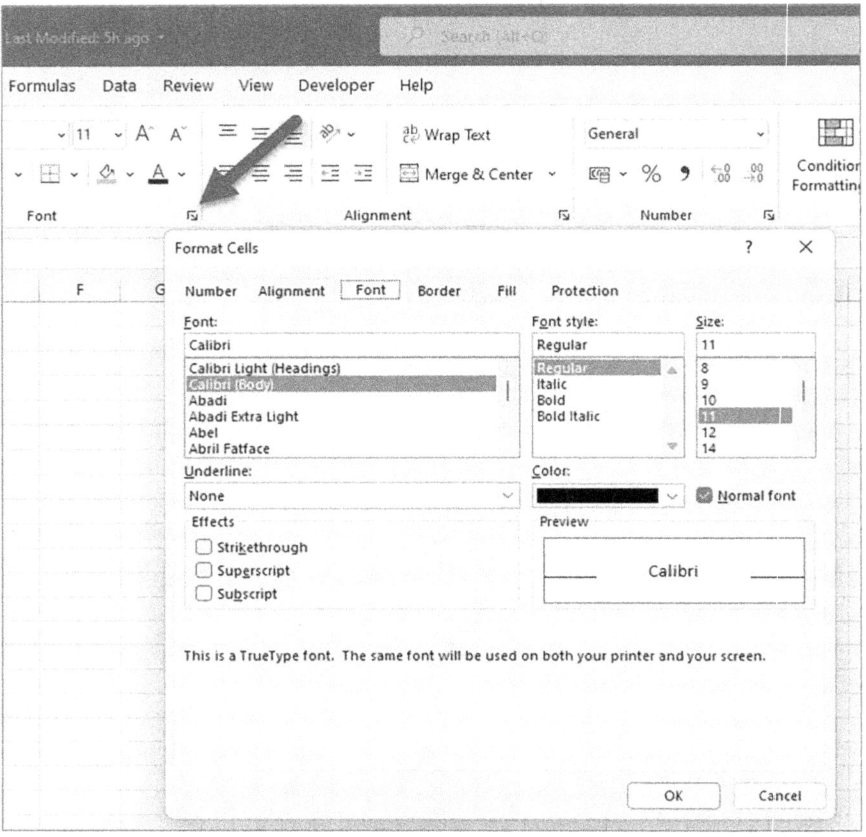
Last Modified: 5h ago
Search (Alt+Q)
Formulas
Data
Review
View
Developer
Help
Wrap Text
Merge & Center
General
Conditional Formatting
Font
Alignment
Number
Format Cells
Number
Alignment
Font
Border
Fill
Protection
Font:
Calibri
Calibri Light (Headings)
Calibri (Body)
Abadi
Abadi Extra Light
Abel
Abril Fatface
Font style:
Regular
Regular
Italic
Bold
Bold Italic
Size:
11
8
9
10
11
12
14
Underline:
None
Color:
Normal font
Effects
Strikethrough
Superscript
Subscript
Preview
Calibri
This is a TrueType font. The same font will be used on both your printer and your screen.
OK
Cancel

Using AutoSave

AutoSave is a feature on the top-left of the title bar that is enabled when a file is stored on OneDrive or SharePoint. It automatically saves your changes every few seconds as you are working. The main advantage of AutoSave is that if your PC were to crash for any reason, your changes right up to the point it crashed would have been saved to disk. So, you'll hardly lose any work.

With AutoSave on, the **Save As** menu option in the Backstage view is replaced by **Save a Copy**. If you're making changes to your workbook and you normally use **File** > **Save As** to avoid changing the original file, it is recommended that you use **File** > **Save a Copy** before making your changes. That way, AutoSave will not overwrite the original file with the changes but the copy.

If like me, you're in the habit of just closing a workbook without saving it, if you do not want to keep the changes, then AutoSave becomes an issue. In such a case, you can turn off AutoSave before you make any changes and then save your workbook manually if you want to keep the changes.

With **AutoSave** set to On, if you make a mistake that you want to undo, ensure you use the **Undo** button on the **Home** tab to undo the changes before closing the workbook.

Turning off AutoSave

Switching off AutoSave is not recommended. However, if you want to be able to just close Excel and discard all changes whenever you wish, you could turn off AutoSave for that particular file and manually save your workbook.

The default setting for AutoSave is On for files on the cloud (OneDrive or SharePoint). However, if you set AutoSave to Off for a particular workbook, Excel will remember the setting and keep it off every time you reopen it. If you switch it back to On, it will remember to keep it on for that workbook.

Restoring a Previous Version of your Workbook

You can also restore a previous version of your workbook from the Version History.

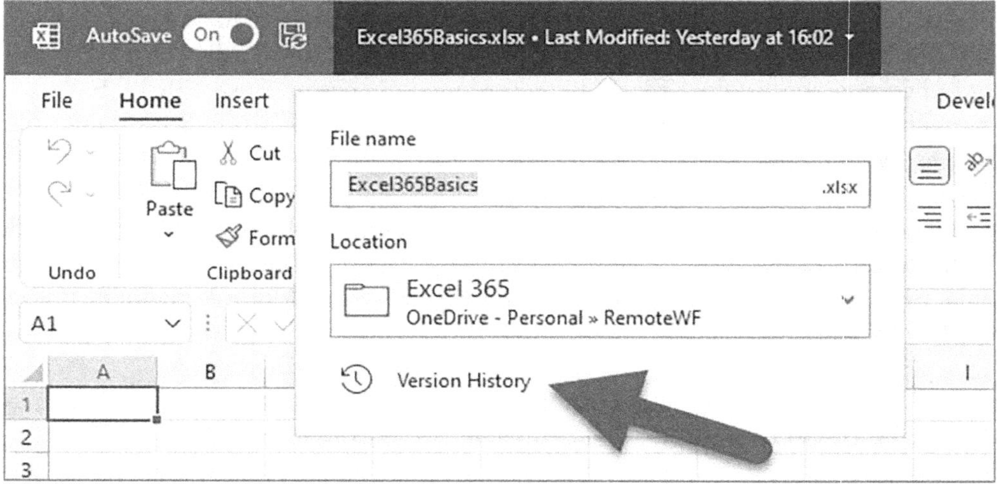

To restore an older version from the Version History list, do the following:

1. Click the file name on the title bar.

2. Click **Version History**.

   Excel displays the **Version History** pane on the right side of the window. The Version History pane shows you the different versions of your document, including the date and time they were saved. The versions are grouped under the date the file was saved. Look at the dates and times to find the version you want to restore.

3. Double click the version you want to restore, and Excel will open the workbook in a second window.

4. Click the **Restore** button displayed just under the Ribbon to revert to this version.

Renaming Your Workbook

You can rename a previously saved workbook from the pop-up menu displayed when you click the file name on the title bar. In the **File Name** box, you can enter a new name for the workbook and press Enter to rename the workbook.

Customizing the Ribbon

The area of the window containing the tabs and command buttons is called the **Ribbon**. You can customize the Ribbon to your liking by adding or removing tabs and command buttons.

To customize the Ribbon, right-click anywhere on the Ribbon, below the tabs, and select **Customize the Ribbon** from the pop-up menu.

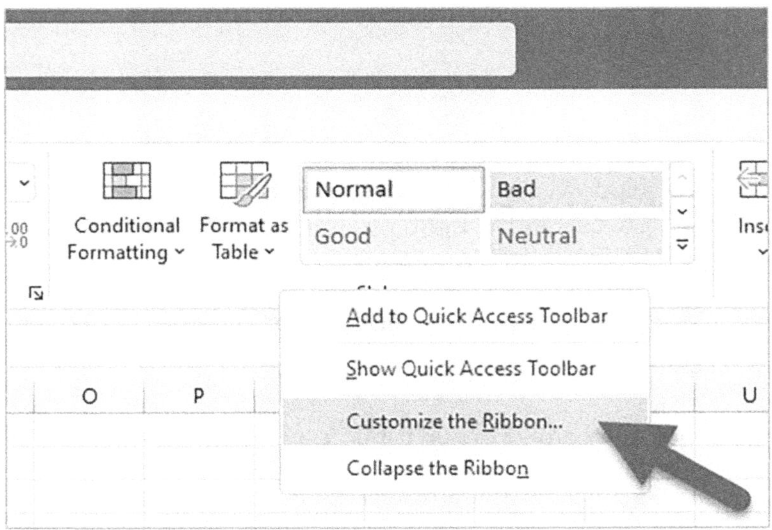

Excel opens the **Excel Options** window.

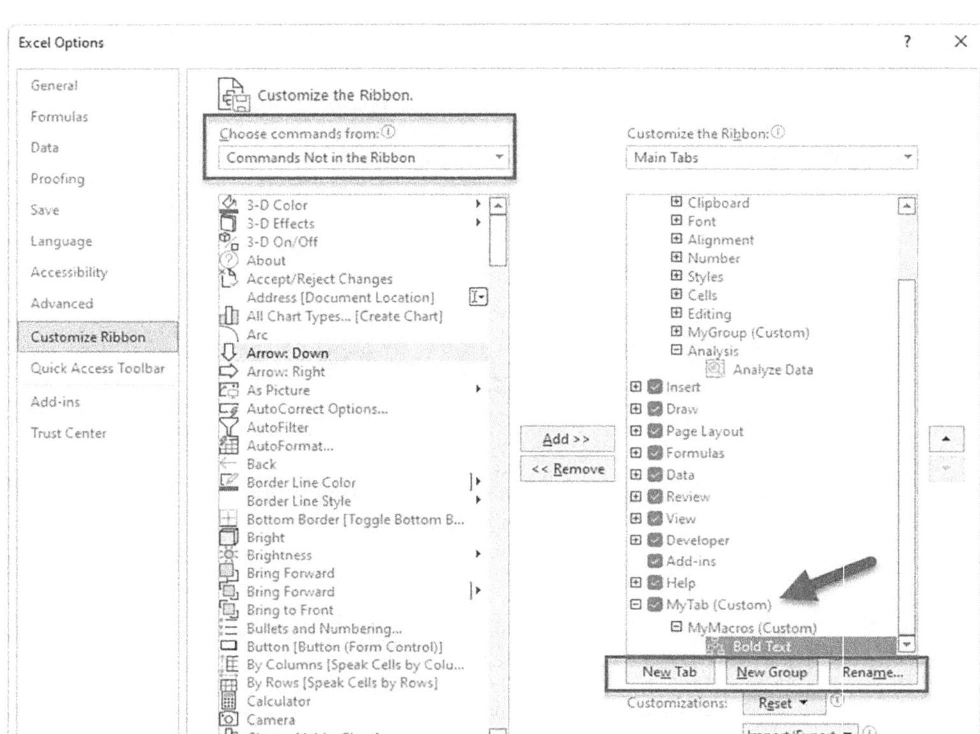

In the **Excel Options** window, the **Customize Ribbon** tab will be selected, and on that tab, you have two main boxes. On the right, you have the box that shows your current tabs - **Main Tabs**. On the left, you have the command buttons that you can add to the Ribbon.

To expand a group in the **Main Tabs** box, click the plus sign (+) to the left of an item. To collapse a group, click the minus sign (-).

To find commands not currently on your Ribbon, click the drop-down arrow on the left box (**Choose commands from)** and select **Commands Not in the Ribbon** from the drop-down list.

You will see a list of commands not on your Ribbon, which is useful as it filters out the commands already on your Ribbon.

Note You can't add or remove the default commands on the Ribbon, but you can uncheck them on the list to prevent them from being displayed. Also, you can't add command buttons to the default groups. You must create a new group (called a custom group) to add a new command button.

To create a new tab, do the following:

Click the **New Tab** button to create a new tab. Inside the tab, you must create at least one group before you can add a command button from the list of commands in the box on the left side of the Excel Options dialog box.

To create a custom group, do the following:

1. Select the tab in which you want to create the group. It could be one of the default tabs or the new one you've created.
2. Click the **New Group** button (located at the bottom of the dialog box, under the Main Tabs list). Excel will create a new group within the currently selected tab.
3. Select the new group and click **Rename** to give the group your preferred name.

You now have a custom group in which you can add commands.

To add commands to your custom group, do the following:

1. Select your custom group in the box on the right side of the screen.
2. Select the new command you want to add from the box on the left side of the screen and click the **Add** button to add it to your custom group.

   To remove a command from your custom group, select the command in the right box and click the **Remove** button.
3. Click **OK** to confirm the change.

When you view the customized tab on the Ribbon, you'll see your new group and your added command buttons.

The Quick Access Toolbar

The Quick Access Toolbar is no longer displayed by default in Microsoft 365 because the most used commands on it are now on the Ribbon by default. These commands are **Save**, **Undo**, and **Redo**.

You can skip this section if you seldom use the Quick Access Toolbar and don't need to display it.

To display the Quick Access Toolbar, right-click any blank area of the Ribbon and select **Show Quick Access Toolbar** from the pop-up menu.

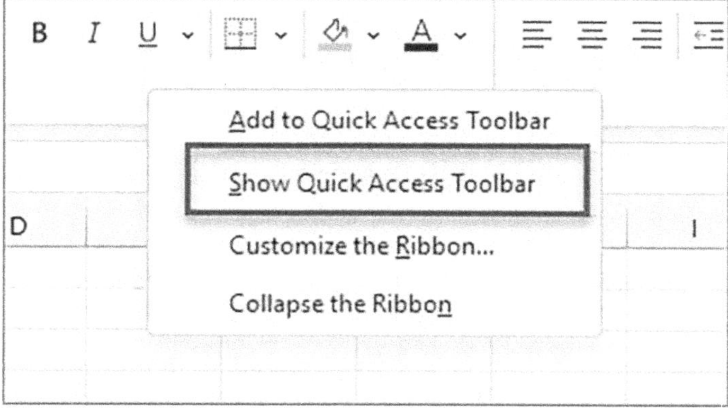

Excel will display the Quick Access Toolbar on a bar below the Ribbon by default. You can switch the toolbar to the title bar by right-clicking anywhere on the bar and selecting **Show Quick Access Toolbar Above the Ribbon**.

Note If you hide and redisplay the Quick Access Toolbar, Excel will remember where it was last positioned and display it there again.

The Quick Access Toolbar is a customizable toolbar with commands independent of the active tab on the Ribbon. The Quick Access Toolbar allows you to add commands you often use in Excel.

To customize the Quick Access Toolbar, click its drop-down arrow to display a drop-down menu.

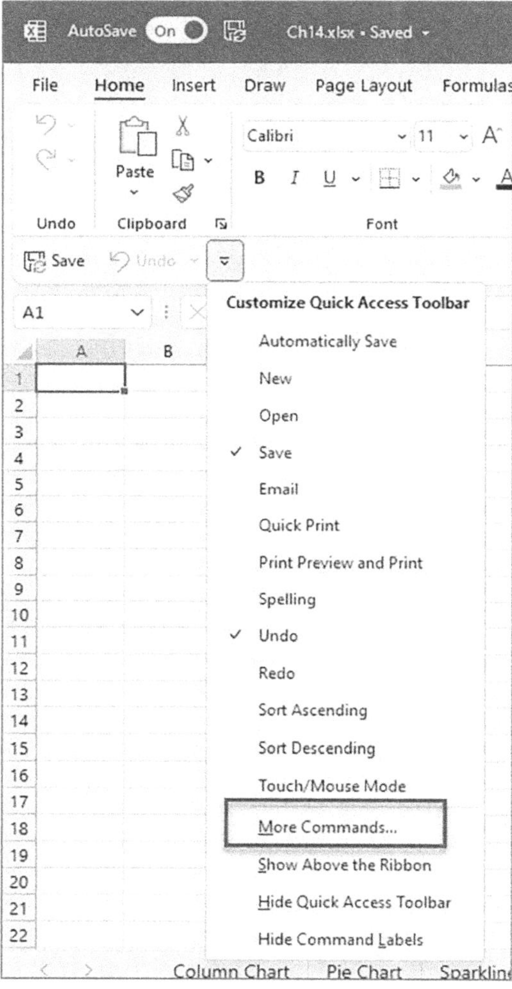

Select items on the menu you want to add to the Quick Access Toolbar and deselect the items you want to remove.

To add commands to the Quick Access Toolbar that you can't find on the menu, do the following:

1. Click the **More Commands** menu option. Excel will open the Quick Access Toolbar pane in Excel Options.

2. In the drop-down list named **Choose commands from**, select **All Commands**.

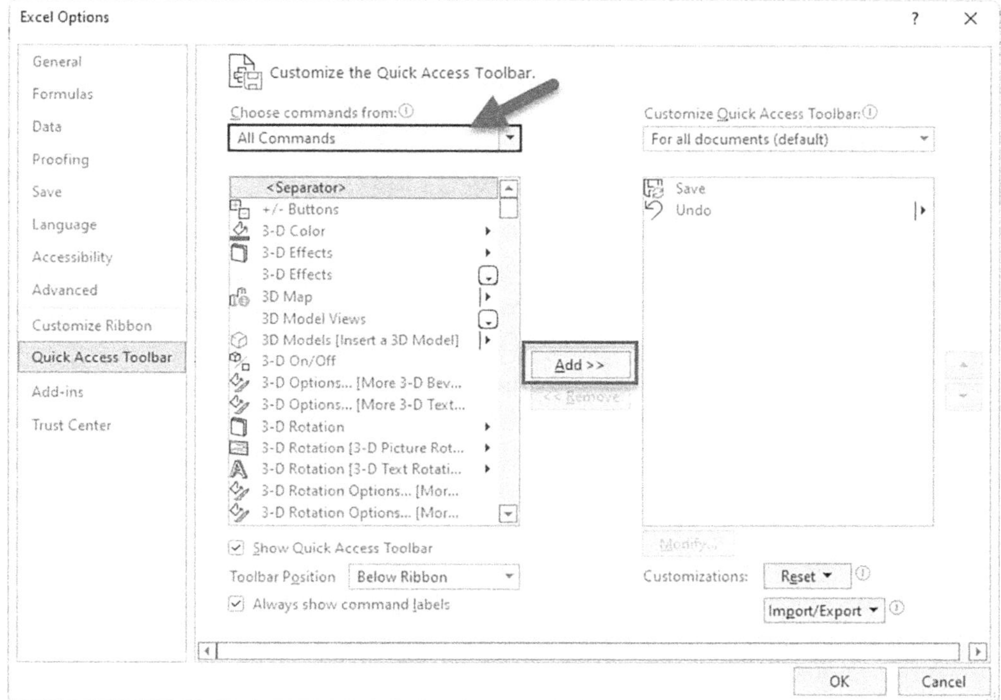

3. From the list of commands on the left, select a command you would like to add to the Quick Access Toolbar and click the **Add** button to add it to the list on the right. Do this for every command you want to add to the list.

4. To change the order of commands on the Quick Access Toolbar, select an item on the list on the right and use the up and down arrows to change its position.

5. Click **OK** when you are done.

Getting Help in Excel

To access help in Excel, click the Help tab and then the Help command button on the Ribbon. Excel displays the Help pane on the right side of the screen. You can use the search box in the Help pane to search for the topic for which you want help.

A quick way to access help is to press the **F1** key on your keyboard (while Excel is the active window) to display the Help pane on the right side of the screen.

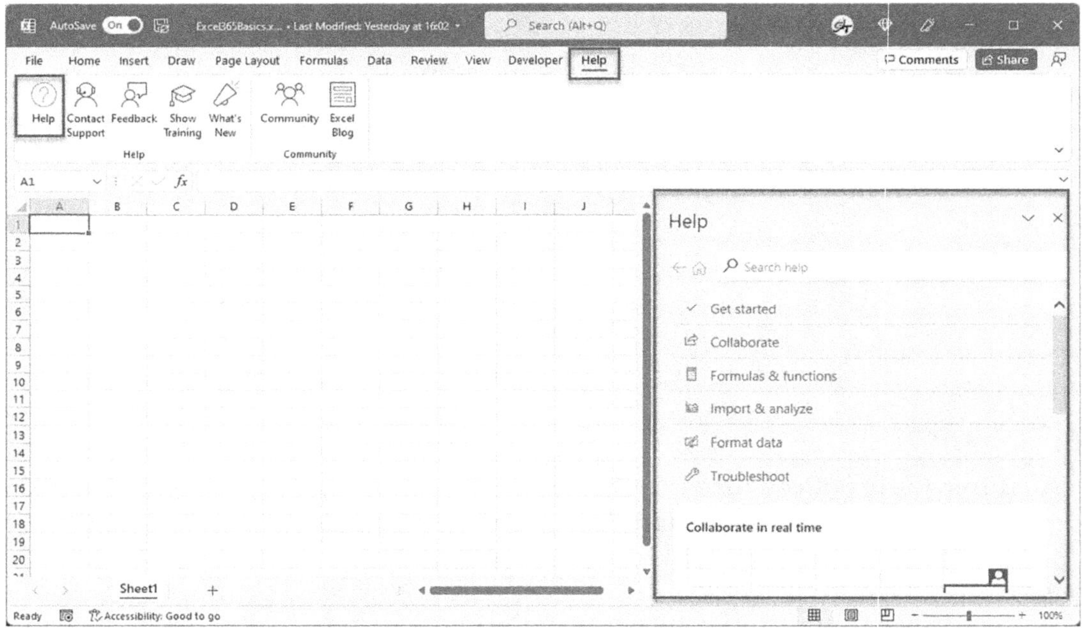

Using Search

Another way to get help in Excel is to use the Search box on the title bar. Click the Search box or press **ALT+Q** to activate the search box.

Before you type anything, the search box will display a drop-down list of help topics related to your recent actions and other suggestions based on what you appear to be doing. If any of the suggestions is related to the topic for which you're seeking help, select it from the list. Otherwise, you can enter words or phrases regarding actions you want to perform or a topic for which you want further information.

Depending on the topic or how direct your question is, Excel will either list the steps needed to complete the task, take you to the appropriate dialog box, or display information related to the topic in the Help pane.

Chapter 2

Entering and Editing Data

This chapter will cover how to enter and edit data in your Excel worksheet, including using automated features like AutoFill and Flash Fill.

Entering and Editing Data Manually

Entering data:

Click a cell in the worksheet area, and a rectangular box will appear around the cell. This box is the **cell pointer** or the active cell. You can move the cell pointer with the left, right, up, or down arrow keys on your keyboard.

To enter data, simply type it directly into the cell, or you can click in the formula bar and type the data in there. To enter a formula, you need to prefix your entry with the equal sign (=). We will cover this later in the chapter on formulas.

Editing data:

When typing in the worksheet area, use the BACKSPACE key to go back and not the left arrow key if you want to make a correction. The arrow keys move the cell pointer from cell to cell. To use the arrow keys when editing data, select the cell, then click in the formula bar to edit the data there.

To overwrite data, click the cell to make it the active cell and just type in the new value. Your entry will overwrite the previous value.

If you only want to edit parts of the data in a cell, for example, a piece of text, then select the cell and click in the formula bar to edit the contents there.

Deleting data:

Select the data and hit the Delete key to delete data from your worksheet.

Default content alignment:

In Excel, numbers and formulas are right-aligned in the cell by default. Everything else is left-aligned by default. So, you can tell if Excel recognizes an entry as a number or text value.

Using AutoFill

The Autofill feature in Excel lets you fill cells with a series of sequential dates and numbers. It enables you to automate repetitive tasks as it is smart enough to figure out what data goes in a cell (based on another cell) when you drag the fill handle across cells.

Entering Dates with AutoFill

You may have a worksheet where you need to enter dates. You can enter *January* in one cell and use the AutoFill feature to automatically enter the rest of the months.

The **Fill Handle** is the small black square at the lower right of the cell pointer. When you hover over the lower right corner of the active cell, a black plus sign (+) appears. This change is an indication that when you drag the selection down (or to the right), Excel will either copy the contents of the first cell to the selected cells or use it as the first entry in a consecutive series.

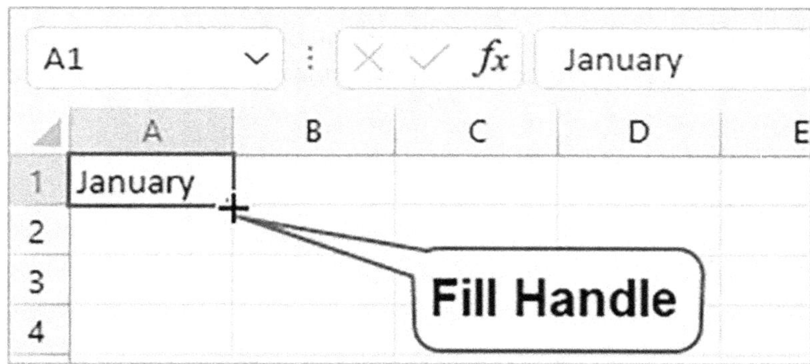

So, you first need to click the cell to select it and then hover over the bottom right corner to display the small plus sign (+).

To AutoFill dates, enter *January* or any other starting month in one cell, then grab the small fill handle and drag it across the other cells.

AutoFill also works with abbreviations, but they must be three letters. For example, if you enter Jan and then drag down, Excel will fill the cells with Feb, Mar, Apr, May, etc.

Let's say you want to enter the seven days of the week as your row headings. In the first cell of your range, enter *Monday* or *Mon*. Then drag the autofill handle down over the remaining six cells. Excel will AutoFill the remaining cells with Tuesday to Sunday.

Excel keeps the filled days selected, giving you a chance to drag the handle back if you went too far or to drag it further if you didn't go far enough.

You can also use the **AutoFill Options** drop-down menu to refine your fill options further. To access the AutoFill options, you will see a drop-down button that appears on the last cell with the cells still selected. When you click it, Excel displays a list of options that enable you to choose whether you want to copy the data across the cells, fill the series, copy formatting only, ignore the formatting, flash fill, etc.

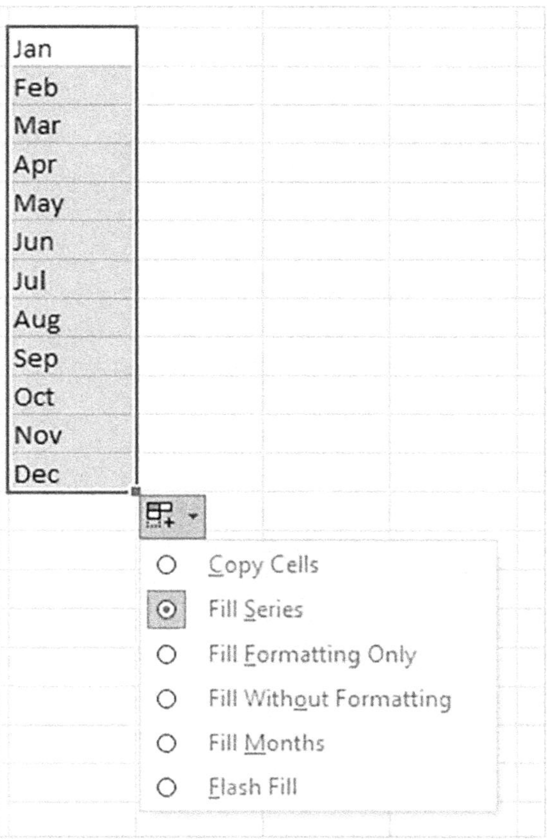

Note If you don't see a button that enables you to access the AutoFill Options drop-down menu (shown in the image above) after an autofill, it is most likely because the option hasn't been enabled in Excel Options.

To enable AutoFill Options, do the following:

1. On the Ribbon, click **File** > **Options** > **Advanced**.
2. Under the **Cut, copy, and paste** section, select the checkbox for **Show Paste Options button when content is pasted**.

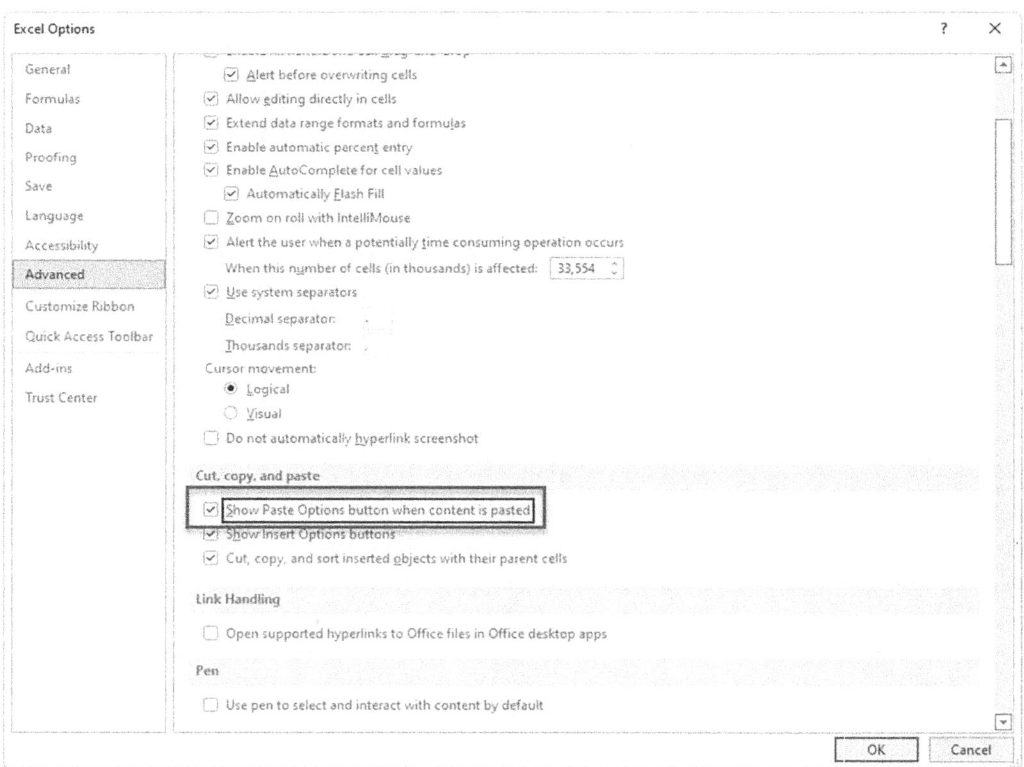

AutoFill Incremental Values

To AutoFill other incremental values, you need to first let Excel know the difference. Thus, you would need to enter values in at least two cells before dragging the fill handle across the other cells.

For example, let's say you want to enter dates that increment by seven days, i.e., a weekly interval. You would need to enter two dates (for example, 01/10/22 and 01/17/22). Then you select both cells and drag across the empty cells to autofill the other cells with dates having an interval of seven days.

You can do the same with other numbers. If you enter number 1 and drag down the fill handle, the number 1 will just be copied to the other cells. However, if you enter numbers 1 and 2 in two cells and then select both cells and drag the fill handle down (or to the right), you will get 3, 4, 5, 6, etc.

AutoFill Formulas

To AutoFill a formula across several cells, enter the formula in the first cell and drag the fill handle over the other cells in the range. If the cell references are relative, then the references will also change to match the position of the active cell.

For example, if the first cell of your formula is = *A1* + *B1*, when you drag this formula down to the other cells, the formula in the other cells will be, *=A2+B2*, *=A3+B3*, *=A4+B4,* and so on.

Another way to use AutoFill is to click the **Fill** button in the **Editing** group on the **Home** tab.

Note If the cell references in your formula are absolute, then the cell references will not change when you use AutoFill to copy it to other cells. See the difference between relative and absolute cell references in chapter 6 in this book.

AutoFill the Same Values

To AutoFill the same value across a series of cells, enter the value in the first cell, then hold down the **Ctrl** key while dragging the fill handle across the other cells.

For example, if you want to fill a range of cells with January:

1. Enter **January** in the first cell.

2. Hold down the **Ctrl** key.

3. Hover over the fill handle (small square in the lower-right of the cell pointer), click and then drag it across the other cells.

   Excel will enter January in all the selected cells.

Using Flash Fill

Flash Fill is a feature introduced in Excel 2013 that enables you to split and rearrange data automatically. In the past, you would need to combine several Excel text functions like LEFT and MID to get the same results that you can now get with the Flash Fill command.

Example 1

In this example, we have a name field (made up of the first name and last name) that we want to sort by **Last Name**. To sort by Last Name, we need to re-enter the names in another column with the last name first. This change is required because Excel starts sorting with the field's first character, then the next, etc.

With Flash Fill, you can insert a new column next to the name column and enter the first value starting with the last name. When you enter the second value, Excel will figure out what you're trying to do and automatically Flash Fill the other cells in the format it predicts you want to enter the data. This automation will save you a lot of time as you only need to enter two cells to have the rest automatically completed for you.

B3 | fx | West, Peter

	A	B	C	D
1	Employee		Month1	Month2
2	Jane Smith	Smith, Jane	$1,453.00	$1,946.00
3	Peter West	West, Peter	$1,713.00	$1,251.00
4	Derek Brown	Brown, Derek	$1,467.00	$1,582.00
5	Jason Fields	Fields, Jason	$1,356.00	$1,097.00
6	Mark Powell	Powell, Mark	$1,919.00	$1,118.00
7	Julie Rush	Rush, Julie	$1,282.00	$1,437.00
8				
9				

Steps in Flash Fill:

1. Enter the value in the first cell in the new format.
2. Start entering the second value in the next cell.
3. You'll see a preview of the rest of the column displaying the suggested entries.
4. Press **Enter** to accept the suggestions.

Excel populates the other cells in the column with the data in the new format.

Another way to use Flash Fill is to use the **Flash Fill** command button in the **Data Tools** group on the **Data** tab.

To use the Flash Fill command button for the same example above, do the following:

1. Enter the value the way you want it in an adjacent cell and press enter.
2. On the **Data** tab, in the **Data Tools** group, click the **Flash Fill** button.

Excel automatically enters the rest of the values in the same format as the first cell.

Example 2

To quickly split a full name field up into first name and last name fields, do the following:

1. Assuming the full name is in column A2, enter the first name in B2 and press enter.
2. On the **Data** tab, in the **Data Tools** group, click **Flash Fill**.

   Excel populates the other rows in column B with the first name from column A.
3. Enter the last name from A2 in C2 and apply the Flash Fill command.

   Excel populates the other rows with the last name from column A.

C2 | fx | Smith

	A	B	C	D
1	**Name**	**First name**	**Last name**	
2	Jane Smith	Jane	Smith	
3	Peter West	Peter	West	
4	Derek Brown	Derek	Brown	
5	Jason Fields	Jason	Fields	
6	Mark Powell	Mark	Powell	
7	Julie Rush	Julie	Rush	
8				

Chapter 3

Design and Organize Workbooks

This chapter will cover various tasks to do with organizing your workbook.

In this chapter, we will cover:

- Adding and removing worksheets.
- Moving, copying, hiding, and deleting worksheets.
- Freezing rows and columns.
- Applying themes to your worksheets.

Adding New Worksheets

We covered creating a new workbook in Chapter 1. When you first create a workbook, you'll have one worksheet named **Sheet1**.

To add a new sheet to your workbook, click the plus sign (+) at the bottom of the worksheet area, to the right of Sheet1, and it will create a new worksheet named Sheet2. You can add more worksheets to your workbook this way.

The number of worksheets you can have in a workbook is unlimited. You're only limited by your computer resources like RAM and hard disk space. However, try not to have too many sheets in one workbook as the file can become very large, and taking longer to open.

Naming a Worksheet

To name your worksheet, double-click the name tab at the bottom of the screen, and the name will become editable. For example, if you double-click *Sheet1,* the name will be selected with the cursor blinking, allowing you to type in the new name.

Moving and Copying Worksheets

You can move and reorder your worksheets by clicking the name and dragging it to the left or right. You can also move a sheet by right-clicking the name and selecting **Move or Copy** from the pop-up menu.

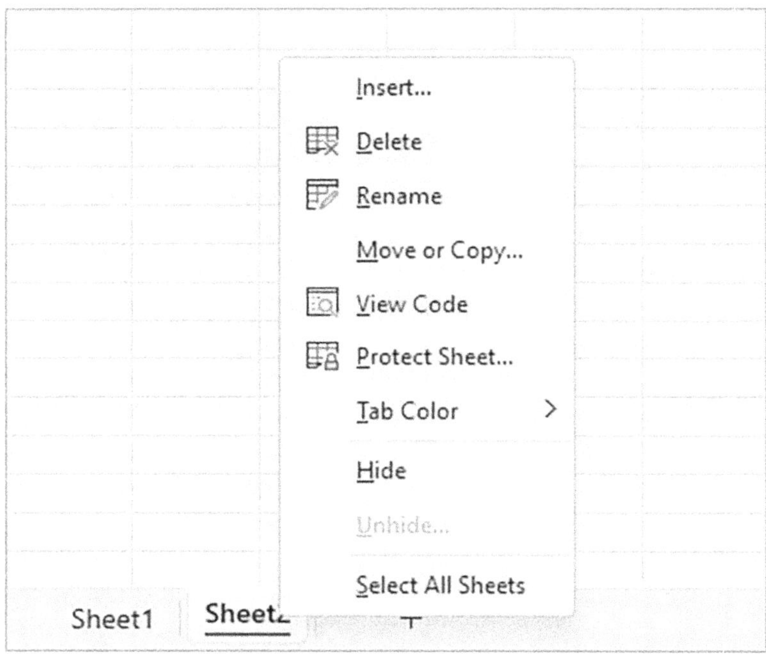

On the **Move or Copy** screen, select a name from the list and click OK. The selected worksheet will be moved to the front of the sheet selected.

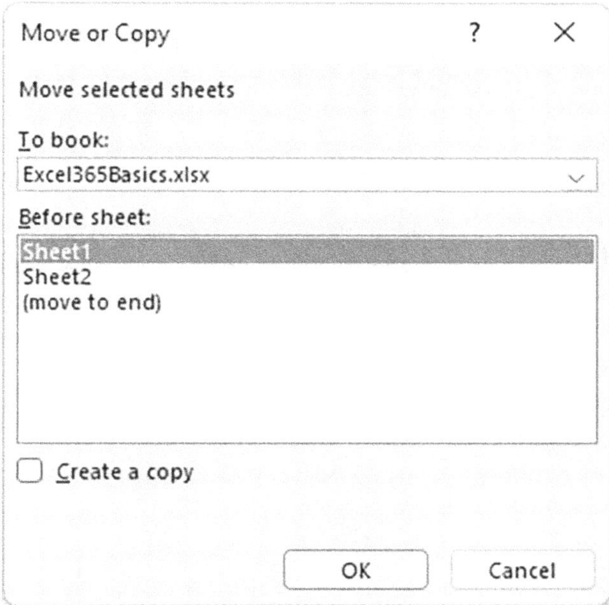

If you want the worksheet copied instead of moved, select the **Create a copy** checkbox before clicking OK. A copy will be placed in front of the selected sheet.

Removing a Worksheet

On the Sheet tab, right-click the sheet you want to remove and click **Delete**.

If the sheet is empty, it will be deleted right away. If the sheet has data, Excel will prompt you with a message asking you to confirm the deletion. Click **Delete** to confirm the deletion.

Hiding and Unhiding Worksheets

To **hide** a worksheet, right-click the name tab of the sheet you want to hide and select **Hide** on the pop-up menu.

To **unhide** a worksheet, right-click any of the sheet name tabs. The **Unhide** option will be enabled on the pop-up menu if a sheet is hidden. Select **Unhide** to display a window listing the hidden sheets. You can select any sheet on the list and click **OK** to show it again.

Freezing Rows and Columns

When you have a large worksheet with lots of data, you may want your data headers (row and/or column) to remain visible as you scroll down or to the right of the page.

To make your column headings always visible, you can freeze them on the page so that scrolling down does not take them out of view.

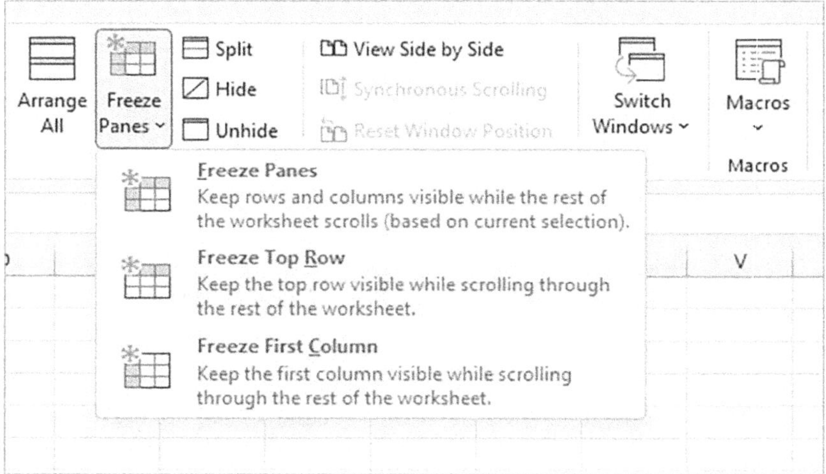

To quickly freeze the top row of your worksheet:

1. Click the **View** tab on the Ribbon.
2. In the Window group, click **Freeze Panes** and select **Freeze Top Row.**

When you now scroll down the page, the top row will always remain visible.

To quickly freeze the first column of your worksheet:

1. Click the **View** tab on the Ribbon.
2. In the Window group, click **Freeze Panes** and select **Freeze First Column.**

When you now scroll to the right of the page, the first column will always remain visible.

On some occasions, you may want to freeze rows and columns other than the first ones.

To freeze any row of your choosing:

1. Place the cell pointer directly under the row you want to freeze to make it the active cell.
2. Click the **View** tab.
3. In the Window group, click **Freeze Panes** and select **Freeze Panes** from the pop-up list.

To freeze any column of your choosing:

1. Select a cell on the first row of the column that's to the right of the one you want to freeze. For example, if you want to freeze *column B,* then you would select cell *C1*.
2. Click the **View** tab.
3. In the Window group, click **Freeze Panes** and select **Freeze Panes** from the pop-up list.

Other examples:

- If you want to freeze the first row and first column of your worksheet, select cell **B2** and then select **View** > **Freeze Panes > Freeze Panes**.
- If you want to freeze only rows 1 and 2, select cell **A3** and select **View** > **Freeze Panes > Freeze Panes**.
- If you want to freeze only columns A and B, click cell **C1** and select **View** > **Freeze Panes > Freeze Panes**.

Unfreeze panes:

To unfreeze any frozen row or columns, click **View** > **Freeze Panes** and select **Unfreeze Panes** from the pop-up menu.

Applying Themes to Your Worksheet

A theme is a predefined formatting package that you can apply to your worksheet that may include colors for headers, text fonts, the size of cells, etc.

There are several themes in Excel that you can apply to your whole worksheet.

To change the look and feel of your worksheet with themes, do the following:

1. Click the **Page Layout** tab on the Ribbon.
2. In the Themes group, click the **Themes** button to display a drop-down list with many themes you can apply to your worksheet.
3. You can hover over a theme on the list to get an instant preview of how your worksheet would look with that theme without selecting it.
4. When you find a theme you want, click it to apply it to your worksheet.

Removing a Theme

If you apply a theme, you don't like, simply click the **Undo** button on the Home tab to undo the changes and return your worksheet to its previous state.

Chapter 4

Organizing Your Data

In this chapter, we will cover some essential tasks to do with organizing your data in Excel.

This chapter covers:

- Copying and pasting data.
- Moving data.
- Inserting/deleting rows and columns.
- Finding and replacing data.
- Sorting data.
- Filtering data.

Copying, Moving, and Deleting Data

Selecting a Group of Cells

Method 1

1. Click the first cell of the area.
2. Ensure your mouse pointer is a white plus sign.
3. Click and drag over the other cells in the range you want to include in the selection.

Method 2

1. Click the top-left cell in the range, for example, A2.
2. Hold down the Shift key and click the bottom-right cell in the range, for example, D10.

Excel selects range A1:D10.

Deselecting Cells

Sometimes, you might accidentally select more cells than you intended when selecting several cells or ranges. With the deselect feature, you can deselect any extra cells within the selected range.

To deselect cells within a selection, hold down the **Ctrl** key, then click (or click and drag) to deselect any cells or ranges within the selection.

If you need to reselect any cells, hold down the **Ctrl** key and click the cells to select them again.

Copying and Pasting Data

Quick Copy and Paste

To quickly copy and paste values in a range, do the following:

1. Select the range that you want to copy.
2. On the **Home** tab, in the **Clipboard** group, click **Copy**.

   You will see a dotted rectangle around the area, which is called a bounding outline.
3. Click the first cell of the area where you want to paste the contents.
4. Click **Paste**.

   The bounding outline remains active to let you know that you can carry on pasting the copied content if you wish to paste it in multiple areas. To get rid of the bounding outline, hit the **ESC** key.

Using the Shortcut Menu

Another way to copy or move data is to use commands on the shortcut menu:

1. Select the source range.
2. Right-click the source range and select Copy (or Cut) from the shortcut menu.
3. Right-click the first cell of the destination range and select the Paste icon (the first icon under Paste Options) on the shortcut menu.

Other Pasting Options

To access other pasting options, after copying data, click the drop-down arrow on the **Paste** command button to display a drop-down menu with several paste options.

You can hover over each icon on the menu for a tip on what each one does. You'll also see a preview of the paste action on your worksheet.

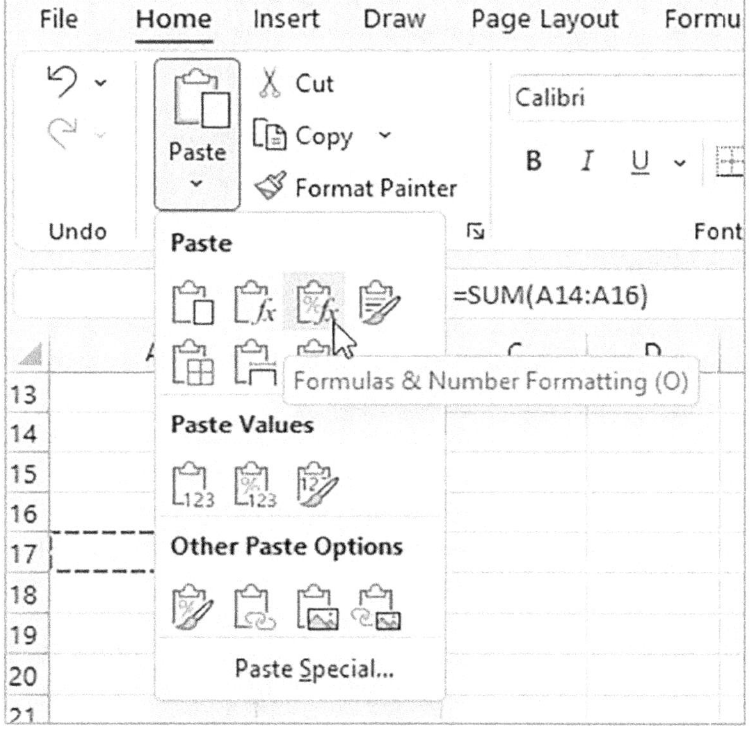

Hover over an icon for a description of what it does

For example, to copy and paste a range while maintaining the column widths, do the following:

1. Select and copy the source range.

2. In the destination worksheet, click the down-arrow on the **Paste** button and select the option that says **Keep Source Column Widths (W)**. This icon is on the second row of the menu.

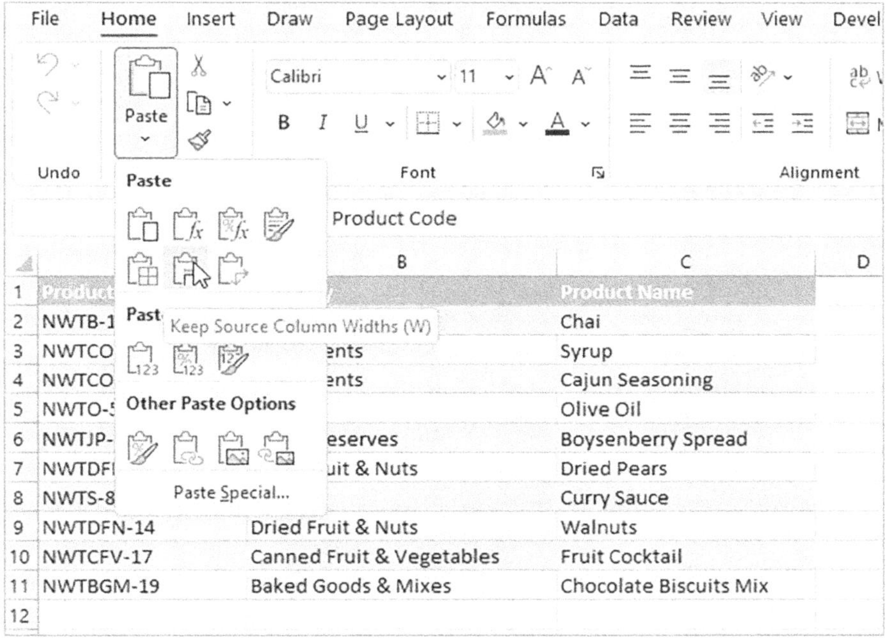

3. Select that option to paste the data and the cell formatting and column width.

4. Once done, remove the bounding outline around the source range by hitting the ESC key. Pressing ESC tells Excel you've completed the copying action.

Using Paste Special

Another way to copy and paste values is to use the **Paste Special** command. Paste Special provides more paste options, including basic calculations like addition, subtraction, and multiplication with the paste operation.

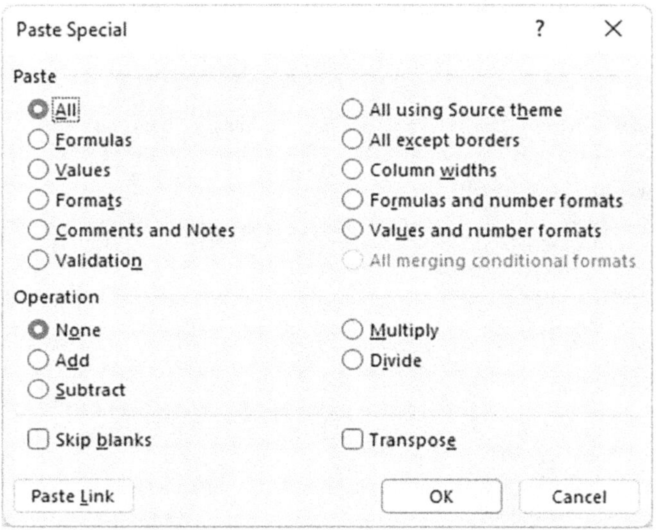

In the following example, we want to convert a list of negative values to positive values. We can use the **Multiply** operation in the Paste Special dialog box to help us perform this action.

To convert a range of negative numbers to positive values, do the following:

1. In any cell in your worksheet, enter **-1**.
2. Copy the value to the clipboard.
3. Select the range of cells with the negative numbers you want to convert.
4. On the Home tab, in the Clipboard group, select **Paste** > **Paste Special**.

   Excel displays the Paste Special dialog box.

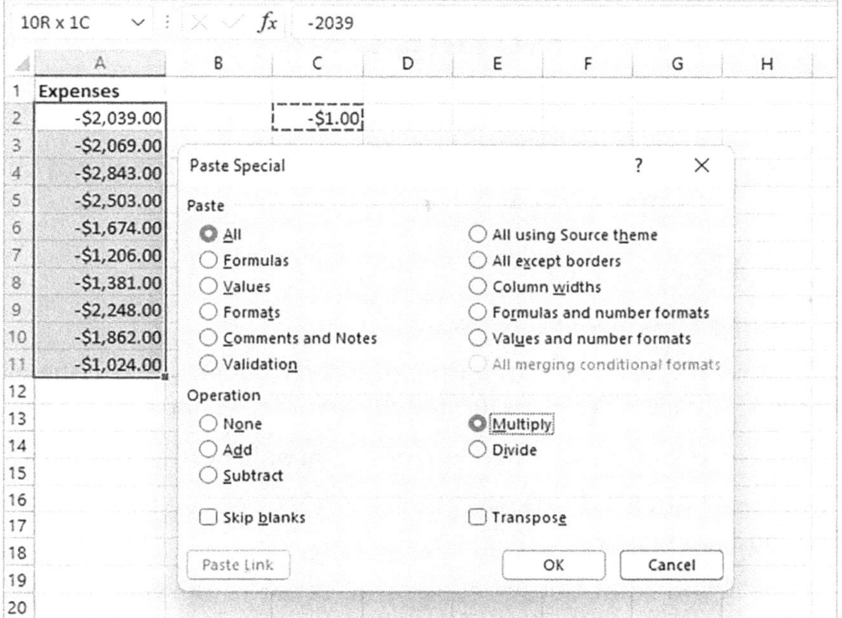

5. In the Paste Special dialog box, select **All** and **Multiply**.
6. Click **OK**.

Excel converts the values in the range to positive numbers by multiplying them by -1 during the paste action.

Moving Data

To move content, you follow a similar set of actions as we did with copying, but you would **Cut** the data instead of **Copy** it.

To move content, do the following:

1. Select the range you want to move.
2. On the Home tab, click the **Cut** button (this is the command with the scissors icon). A bounding outline will appear around the area you've chosen to cut.
3. Click the first cell of the destination range. You only need to select one cell.
4. On the Home tab, click **Paste**. Excel will move the content from its current location to the destination range.

The copy & paste action automatically copies the format of the cells across, but not the width. So, you need to adjust the width of the cells if necessary.

Insert or Delete Rows and Columns

To insert a column, do the following:

1. Click the column letter immediately to the right of the column where you want to insert the new column. For example, select column B if you want to insert a column between columns A and B.
2. On the **Home** tab, in the **Cells** group, click the **Insert** button.

Excel will insert a new column to the left of the column you selected, and the new column will now be B.

Inserting a new column by using the pop-up menu:

1. Click the column letter to the right of the insertion point to select the whole column.
2. Right-click and select **Insert** from the pop-up menu to insert the new column.

Inserting a new row by using the pop-up menu:

1. Click the row number directly below the insertion point to select the whole row.
2. Right-click and select **Insert** from the pop-up menu to insert a new row directly above the selected row.

You could also insert new rows and columns with the **Insert** command button on the **Home** tab.

Inserting multiple rows or columns:

1. Hold down the Ctrl key.
2. One by one, select the rows up to the number you want to insert. For example, if you want to insert four rows, select four rows directly under the insertion point.
3. Click **Home** > **Insert** (or right-click and select **Insert**).

Excel will insert four new rows above the insertion point.

Finding and Replacing Data

A worksheet can have over a million rows of data, so it may be difficult to locate specific information in a large worksheet. Excel provides a Find and Replace feature to quickly find and replace data in your worksheet if required. If you have used the Find function in other Microsoft 365 applications, you should be familiar with this feature.

To find text or numbers in your worksheet, do the following:

1. On the **Home** tab, in the **Editing** group, click **Find & Select > Find**. Alternatively, press **Ctrl+F**.

   Excel displays the Find tab of the **Find and Replace** dialog box.

Note By default, Excel displays a dialog box with Options hidden (if it wasn't expended when previously used). Click the **Options >>** button to expand the dialog box, as shown below.

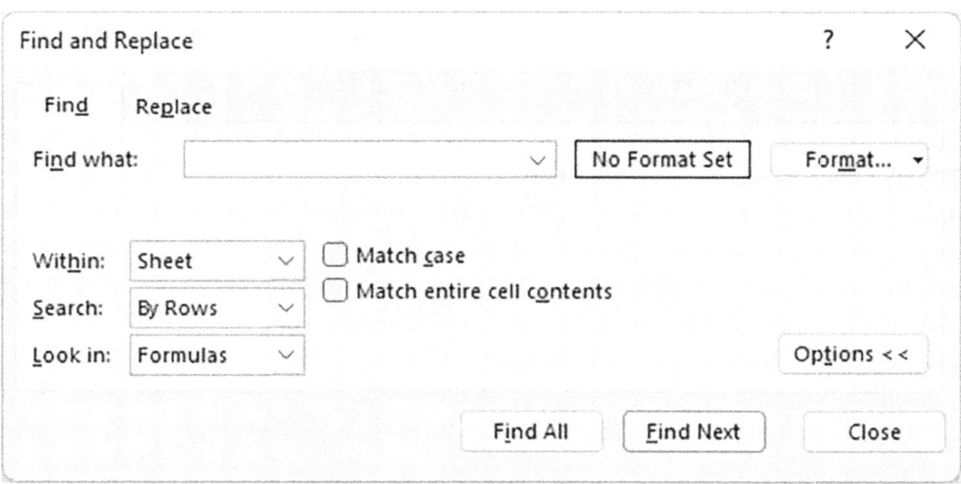

2. In the **Find what** box, enter the text or number you want to find.

   You can also click the down-arrow on the **Find what** box and select a recent item you've searched for.

Click **Find All** (to find all instances of your criteria) or **Find Next** (to find them one by one).

Note When you click **Find All**, Excel lists every instance of your criteria. Click a column heading to sort the results by that column. Click an item on the list to select its cell in the worksheet.

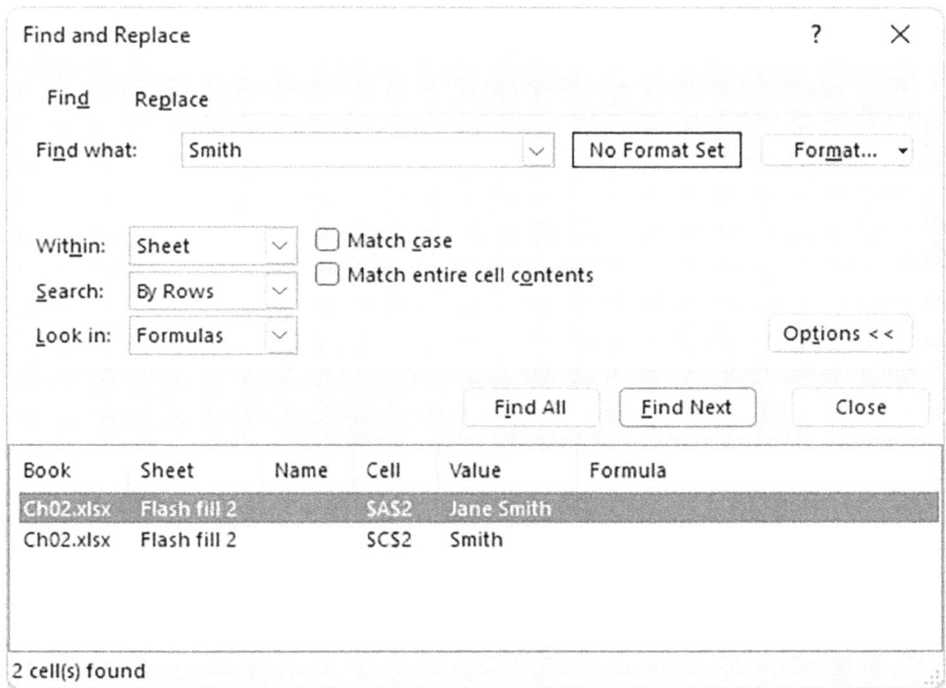

3. The expanded dialog box (when you click **Options >>**) gives you the following additional search options:

    - **Format:** This option allows you to select the data format you're searching for.
    - **Within:** Allows you to search the current worksheet or the whole workbook.
    - **Search:** Allows you to search by rows (default) or columns.
    - **Look in:** Enables you to search for Formulas, Values, Notes, or Comments.

The default is Formulas.

Select **Values** here if the search area has formulas, but you want to find the values derived from those formulas. Otherwise, leave this setting as the default.

- **Match case:** This option enables you to only find values that match the case of the entry in the **Find what** box.
- **Match entire cell contents:** Select this option to only find values that match the exact value in the **Find what** box.
- **Options**: The **Options >>** button expands the dialog box with more options to refine your search.

Replacing Data

To replace text or number in your worksheet, go to **Home** > **Editing** > **Find & Select** > **Replace**. Alternatively, press **Ctrl+H**.

If the Find dialog box is already open, click the **Replace** tab.

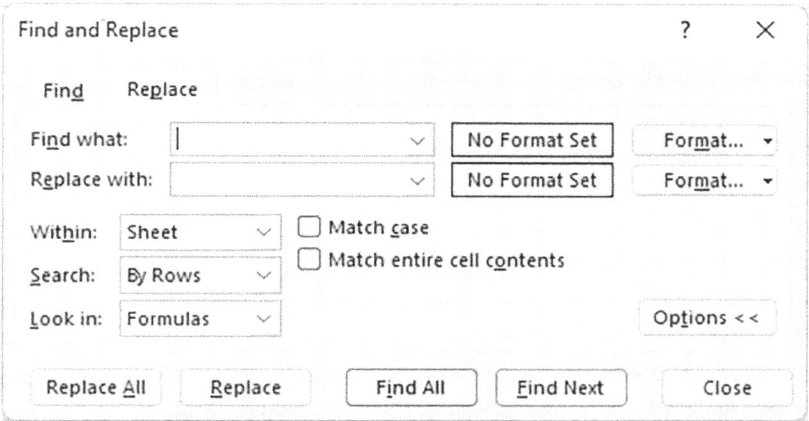

In addition to the options on the Find tab (described above), the Replace tab has the following options:

- **Replace with**: Use this box to specify an alternative value to replace any values found in your worksheet that match the criteria specified in **Find what**.
- **Replace All**: Automatically replaces all instances found with the value in **Replace with**.
- **Replace**: Replaces only the next one found.

All the other options on the dialog box remain the same on this tab as described for Find.

Tip If you use **Replace/Replace All** to change data by mistake, use the **Undo** button on the Home tab to reverse your changes.

Sorting Data

Excel offers various methods to sort your data, from a quick and basic sort to more complex sorts using your own custom list. We will be covering the popular methods in this section.

Quick Sort

To quickly sort data in Excel, do the following:

1. Select any single cell in the column you want to sort.

2. Right-click the cell. From the pop-up menu, select **Sort A to Z** (for ascending) or **Sort Z to A** (for descending).

   If your column is a number field, you'll have **Sort Smallest to Largest** (for ascending) and **Sort Largest to Smallest** (for descending).

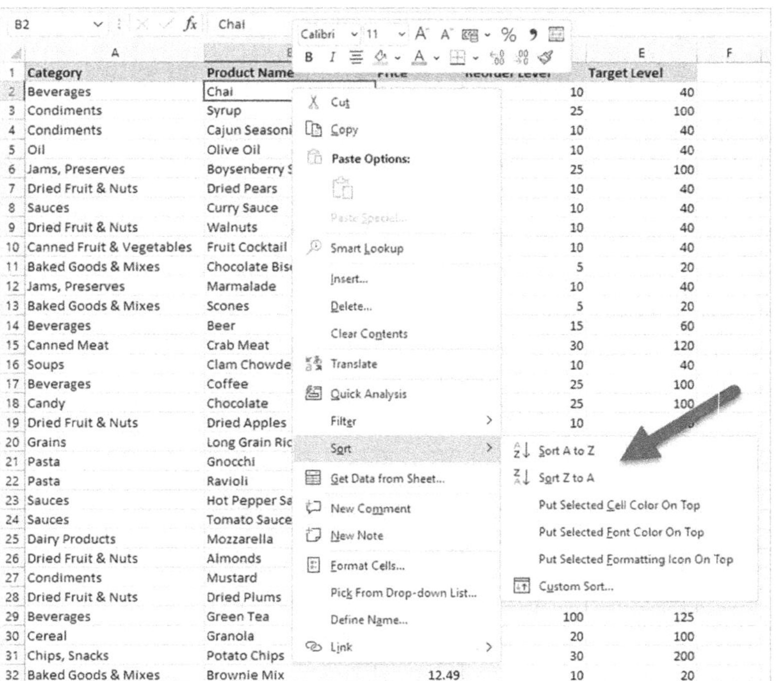

The Sort action does not change your data in any way. It simply reorders your rows according to your chosen sort order and column.

Custom Sort

In the example above, we sorted using just one column. However, you can sort using multiple columns. For example, in the data shown below, we may want to sort by *Category* and *Product Name*. We would use the Custom Sort command on the Ribbon in this case.

	A	B	C
1	Category	Product Name	Price
2	Beverages	Chai	18.00
3	Condiments	Syrup	10.00
4	Condiments	Cajun Seasoning	22.00
5	Cereal	Granola	4.00
6	Chips, Snacks	Potato Chips	1.80
7	Baked Goods & Mixes	Brownie Mix	12.49
8	Baked Goods & Mixes	Cake Mix	15.99
9	Beverages	Tea	4.00
10	Canned Fruit & Vegetables	Pears	1.30
11	Canned Fruit & Vegetables	Peaches	1.50
12	Canned Fruit & Vegetables	Pineapple	1.80
13	Canned Fruit & Vegetables	Cherry Pie Filling	2.00
14	Canned Fruit & Vegetables	Green Beans	1.20
15	Canned Fruit & Vegetables	Corn	1.20
16	Canned Fruit & Vegetables	Peas	1.50
17	Canned Meat	Tuna Fish	2.00
18	Canned Meat	Smoked Salmon	4.00
19	Cereal	Hot Cereal	5.00
20	Soups	Vegetable Soup	1.89
21	Soups	Chicken Soup	1.95
22			

To apply a Custom Sort, do the following:

1. Select a single cell anywhere in the data.

2. On the **Home** tab, in the **Editing** group, click **Sort & Filter**, then select **Custom Sort** from the pop-up menu.

   Excel displays the **Sort** dialog box.

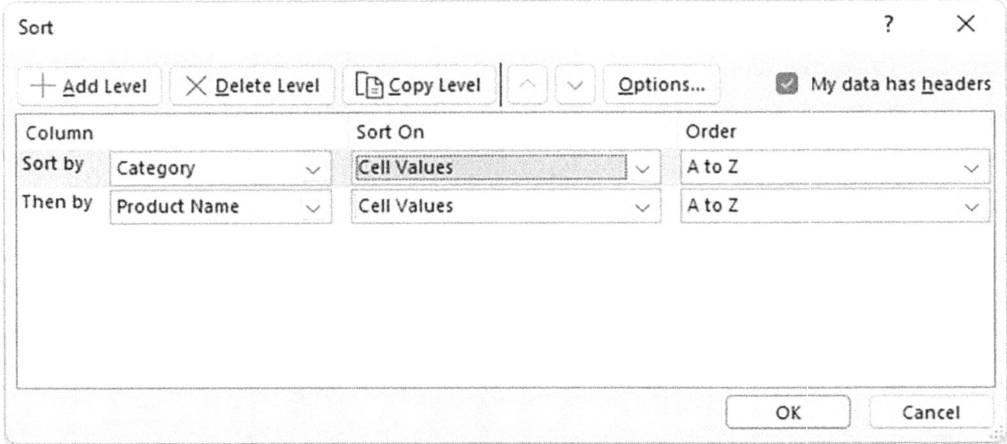

3. In the **Sort by** list, select the first column you want to sort.

4. In the **Sort On** box, you can select Cell Values, Cell Color, Font Color, or Conditional Formatting Icon. If you're sorting by value, select **Cell Value**.

5. In the **Order** list, select the order for the sort. For a text column, you can choose **A to Z** (ascending order) or **Z to A** (descending order).

   For a number column, you can choose **Smallest to Largest** or **Largest to Smallest**.

6. Click **OK** when you're done.

Your data will now be sorted according to the criteria you've entered.

Sorting with a Custom List

In the Sort dialog box, the **Order** drop-down list has an option named **Custom List**, which enables you to sort data by days of the week or months.

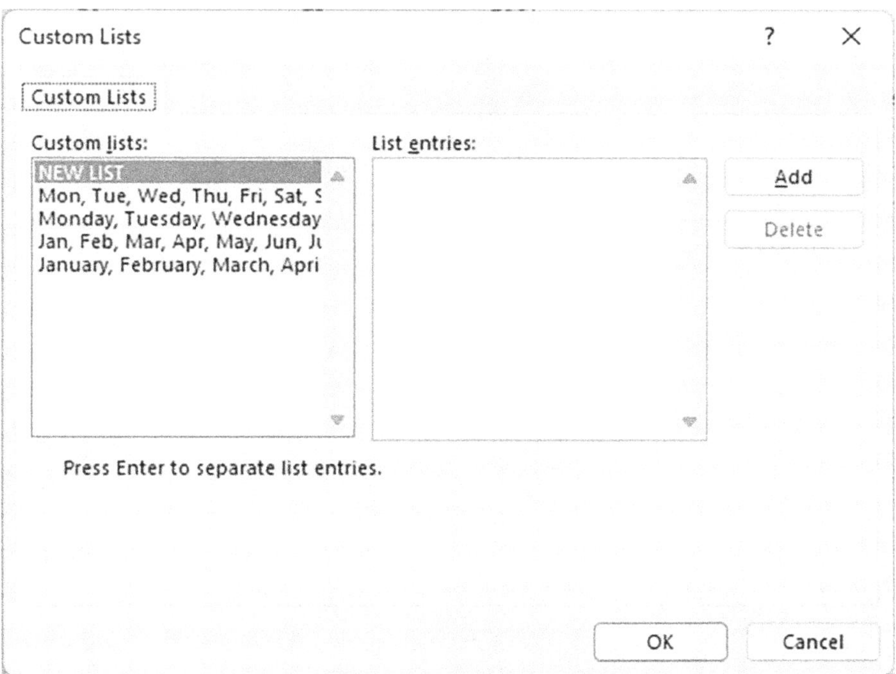

You can add a custom list if none of the pre-defined custom lists meet your needs. Creating your custom list is useful for sorting with an order different from the standard ascending or descending.

For example, if we wanted to sort our data by *employee grade,* we could enter the grades in our list in the order we want the data sorted.

To add a new custom list, do the following:

1. Select NEW LIST in the **Custom lists** box.
2. In the **List entries** box (on the right), enter your list items, one item per line. Press Enter to go to the next line.

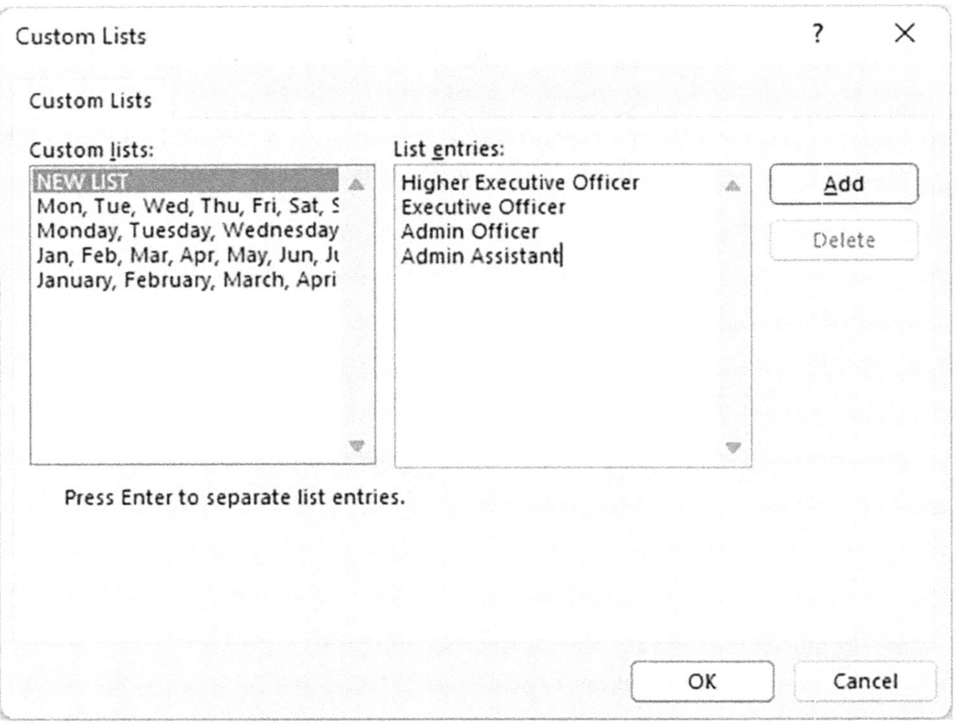

3. When you're done, click the **Add** button to add the list.
4. You can now select the list under **Custom lists** and click **OK** to use it for your sort.

Your custom list will now be available to all Excel workbooks on the PC.

Filtering Data

Excel worksheets can hold a lot of data, and you might not want to work with all the data at the same time. For example, you might want to only display a category of products or products within a certain price range.

Excel provides several ways to filter your data so that you can view only the data you want to see. Filters provide a quick way to work with a subset of data in a range or table. When you apply a filter, you temporarily hide some of the data so that you can focus on the data you need to work with.

Excel tables have column headings by default, but if your data is just a range, ensure you have column headings like Category, Product Name, Price, etc. Column headings makes filtering and sorting much easier.

	B	C	D	E	F
1	Category	Product Name	Price	Reorder Level	Target Level
2	Beverages	Chai	18.00	10	40
3	Condiments	Syrup	10.00	25	100
4	Condiments	Cajun Seasoning	22.00	10	40
5	Oil	Olive Oil	21.35	10	40
6	Jams, Preserves	Boysenberry Spread	25.00	25	100
7	Dried Fruit & Nuts	Dried Pears	30.00	10	40
8	Sauces	Curry Sauce	40.00	10	40

Column headings

You can add column headings to your data by inserting a new row at the top of your worksheet and entering the headings. Column headings are important because Excel will use the first row for the filter arrows.

Quick Filter

To filter data, do the following:

1. Select any cell within the data that you want to filter.
2. Select **Home** > **Editing** > **Sort & Filter** > **Filter**.

   Alternatively, select **Data** > **Sort & Filter** > **Filter**.

   You will get a **filter arrow** at the top of each column, also called an **AutoFilter**. Note that in Excel tables, filter arrows are turned on by default.
3. Click the AutoFilter of the column you want to filter. For example, Price.
4. Uncheck **Select All** and check the values you want to use for the filter.
5. Click **OK**.

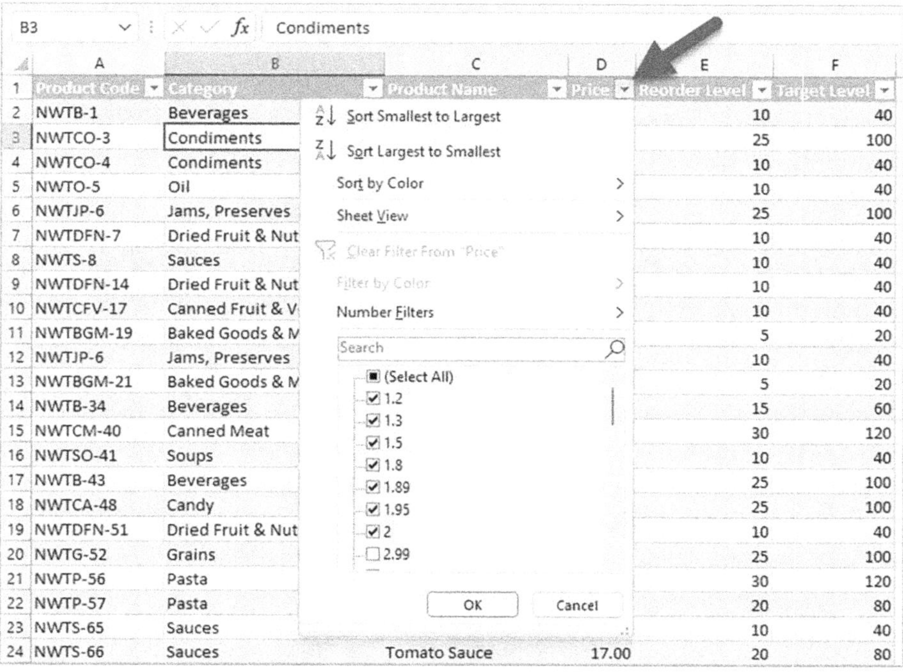

The AutoFilter changes to a funnel icon to show that the column is filtered. If you look at the row heading numbers, you'll see that they're now blue, indicating which rows are included in the filtered data.

Custom Filter

You can create a custom filter if the default options do not meet your needs. To access the **Custom Filter** command, click the **AutoFilter** of the column you want to use to filter the data.

You'll get the following options depending on the data type of the selected column:

- **Text Filters**: Available when the column is a text field or has a mixture of text and numbers. The filter options available include, Equals, Does Not Equal, Begins With, Ends With, or Contains.

- **Number Filters**: This option is available when the column contains only numbers. The filter options available include, Equals, Does Not Equal, Greater Than, Less Than, or Between.

- **Date Filters**: This option is available when the column contains only dates. The filter options available include, Last Week, Next Month, This Month, and Last Month.

- **Clear Filter from [Column name]:** This option is only available if the column already has a filter. Select this option to clear the filter.

When you select an option related to any of the three options above, Excel displays the **Custom AutoFilter** dialog box, where you can specify your custom filter criteria.

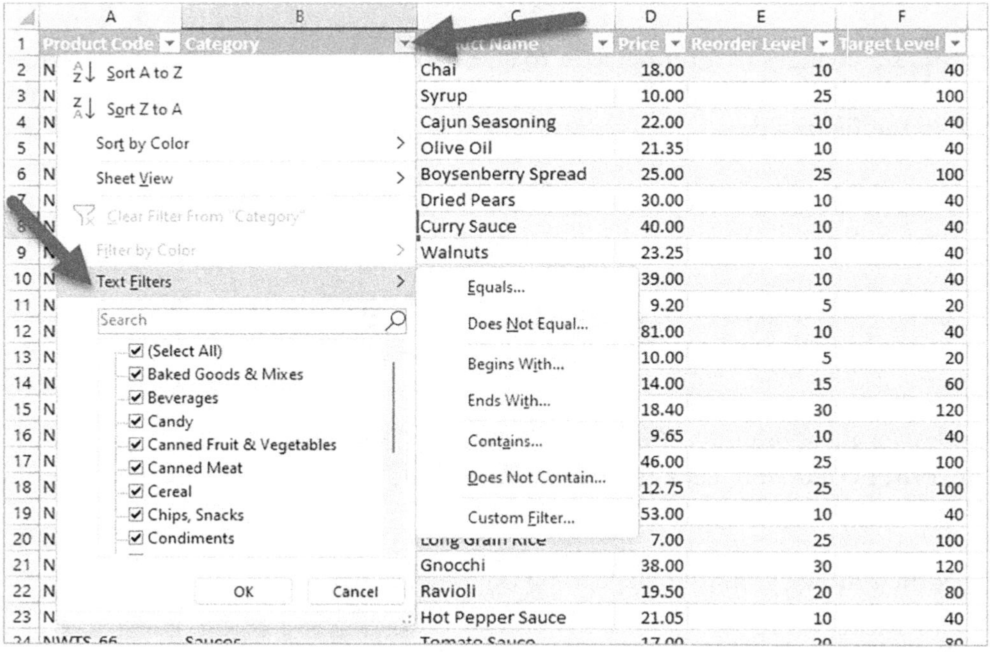

Example

Let's say we wanted to display only data with a price range between $2 and $10.

Follow the steps below to filter the data for the chosen criteria:

1. Click the AutoFilter on the **Price** column, and on the dropdown menu, select **Number Filters** > **Between**.

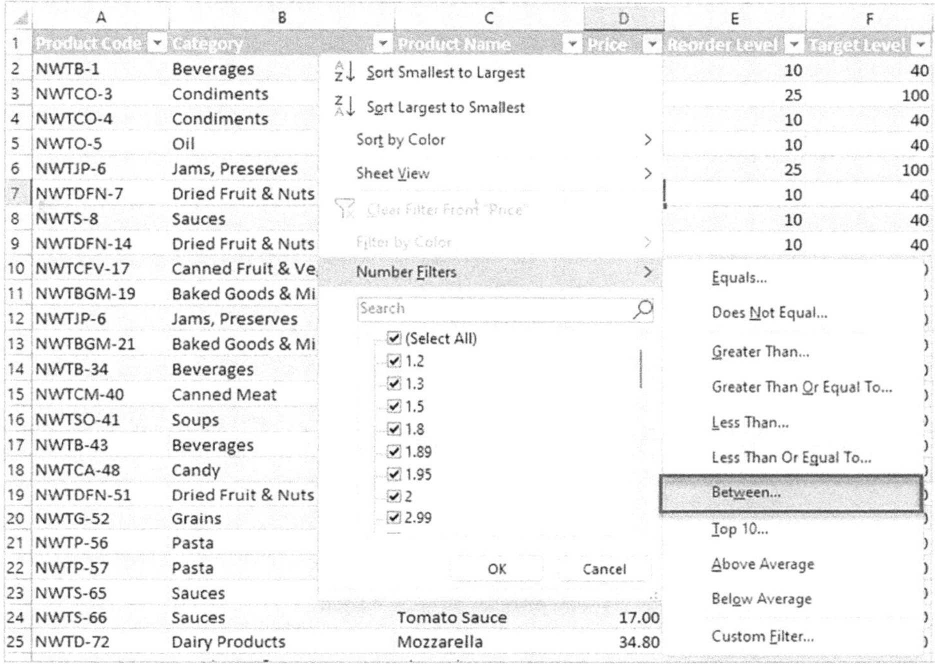

The **Custom AutoFilter** dialog box allows you to enter the criteria and specify the condition.

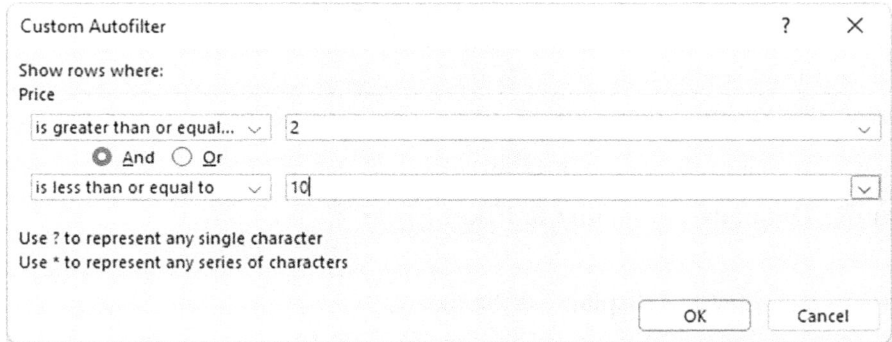

2. Enter the values you want to use for the filter. In our example, the values would be 2 and 10.

3. Select the logical operator. In this case, we will need **And**, as both conditions must be true.

Price >= 2 And <= 10.

If only one of the conditions needs to be true, select **Or**.

4. Click **OK** when done.

Excel filters the data to only show records where the Price is between $2 and $10.

Changing the Sort Order of a Filtered List

To change the sort order of the filtered results, click the **AutoFilter** icon on the column used for the filter.

Select either **Sort Smallest to Largest** or **Sort Largest to Smallest**. For a text column, it would be **Sort A to Z** or **Sort Z to A.**

Removing a Filter

To remove a filter, do the following:

1. Select any cell in the range or table.
2. On the **Data** tab, in the **Sort & Filter** group, click **Clear**.

Excel removes the filter and displays all the data.

Another way to remove a filter is to click the AutoFilter of the filtered column and select **Clear Filter From "[Column name]"** to display all the data.

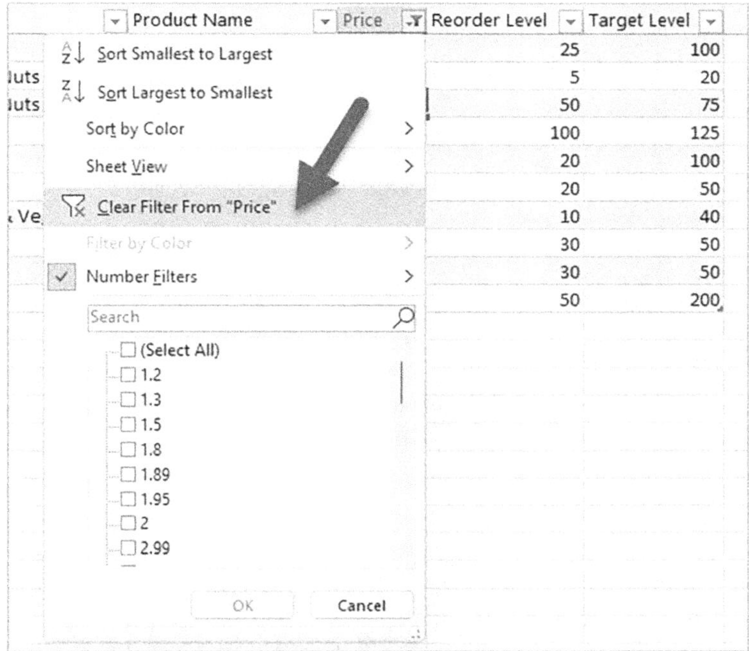
Product Name
Price
Reorder Level
Target Level
Sort Smallest to Largest
Sort Largest to Smallest
Sort by Color
Sheet View
Clear Filter From "Price"
Filter by Color
Number Filters
Search
(Select All)
1.2
1.3
1.5
1.8
1.89
1.95
2
2.99
OK
Cancel
25 100
5 20
50 75
100 125
20 100
20 50
10 40
30 50
30 50
50 200

Chapter 5

Formatting Cells

In this chapter, we will cover various methods to format and resize cells in your worksheet to present your data in your desired format.

This chapter covers:

- Resizing cells, rows, and columns.
- Hiding and unhide rows and columns.
- Merging cells and aligning data.
- Hiding and unhiding worksheets.
- Applying predefined cell styles.
- Applying different types of number formats to cells.
- Creating and applying custom cell formats.
- Applying conditional formatting to add visual representations to your data.

Arrange Cells, Rows, and Columns

Resizing Rows and Columns

You can resize rows and columns with your mouse or use the **Format** command on the toolbar.

To resize a **column**, do the following:

1. Click any cell in the column.
2. Click the right edge of the column letter and drag it to the right to widen the column.

To resize a **row**, do the following:

1. Click any cell in the row.
2. Click the bottom edge of the row number, then drag it down to increase the row's height.

Resizing Cells with the Cells Format Command

You can increase the column width and row height of a range of cells simultaneously by using the **Format** command on the **Home** tab of the Ribbon.

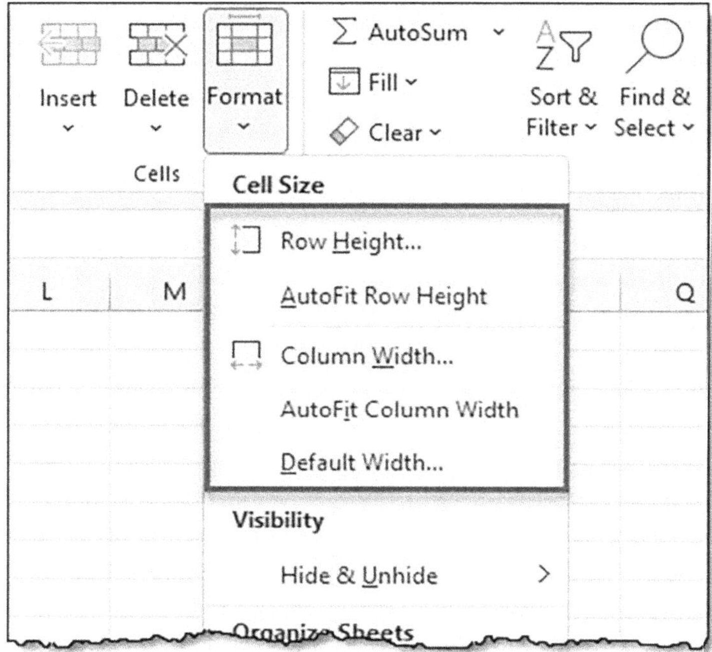

For example, to increase the widths of columns A to E, do the following:

1. Hover over the header for column A until you see a downward pointing arrow.
2. Click **A** to select the column and drag to column **E** to select columns A to E.

Tip Another way to select a range of columns is to select the first column, hold down the **Shift** key, and select the last column.

---

3. Click **Home** > **Format** > **Column Width**.
4. Enter the **Column width** in the box.

5. Click **OK**.

To increase the height of rows 1 to 14, do the following:

1. Hover over the header of row 1 until you get an arrow pointing right.
2. Click to select the whole row.
3. Hold down the Shift key and click the header of row 14.
4. Go to **Home** > **Cells** > **Format** > **Row Height…**
5. The default row height is 15. Thus, you can enter any number higher than 15 to increase the height of the selected rows.
6. Click **OK**.

Automatically adjust columns to fit your data using AutoFit:

1. Select the columns you want to adjust.
2. On the **Home** tab, in the **Cells** group, select **Format** > **AutoFit Column Width**.

Excel adjusts each column to fit the length of all entries.

Automatically adjust row heights to fit your data using AutoFit:

1. Select the rows to which you want to apply AutoFit.
2. On the **Home** tab, in the **Cells** group, select **Format** > **AutoFit Row Height**.

Excel adjusts each column to fit the height of all entries. This setting is particularly useful if you have **Wrap Text** enabled, and some cells have more than one line of text.

Set the default column width for the whole workbook:

1. On the **Home** tab, in the **Cells** group, select **Format** > **Default Width**.
2. Enter the new default value in the **Standard column width** box.

Hide Rows and Columns

Sometimes, with very large worksheets, you may want to hide some rows or columns to make it easier to access the data with which you want to work.

To hide rows:

1. Select the rows you want to hide.
2. Go to **Home** > **Cells** > **Format**.
3. On the pop-up menu, under **Visibility**, select **Hide & Unhide**, and then click **Hide Rows**.

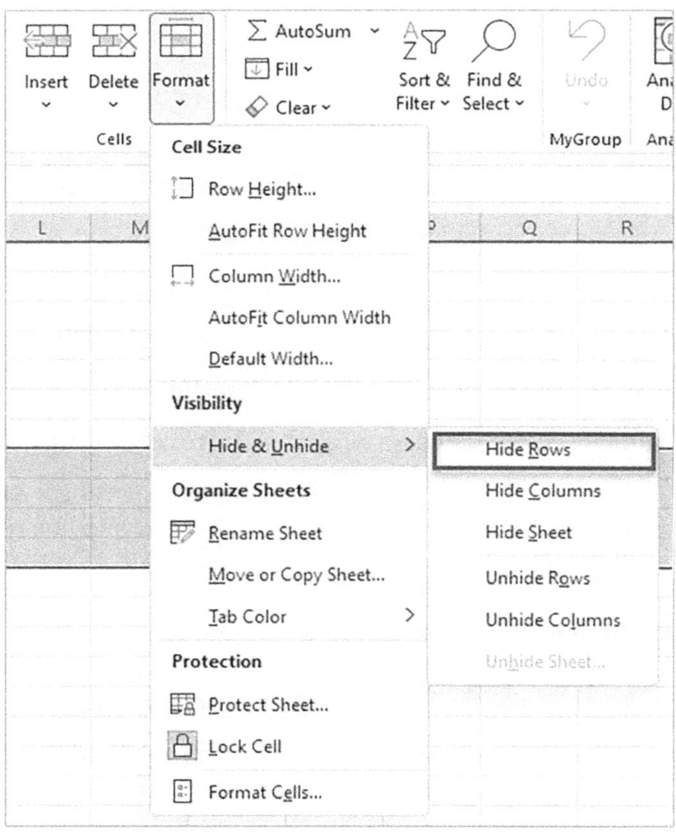

To hide columns:

1. Select the target columns
2. Go to **Home** > **Cells** > **Format**.
3. On the pop-up menu, under **Visibility**, select **Hide & Unhide** and then click **Hide Columns**.

To unhide rows and columns:

Go to **Home** > **Cells** > **Format** > **Hide & Unhide** and then select **Unhide Columns** to display hidden columns (or **Unhide Rows** to display hidden rows).

Hide and Unhide a Worksheet

You can use two methods to Hide a worksheet:

- **Method 1:** Right-click the worksheet's name tab and select **Hide** from the pop-up menu.
- **Method 2:** Ensure the worksheet you want to hide is the active one, then on the Ribbon, select **Home** > **Cells** > **Format** > **Hide & Unhide** > **Hide Sheet**.

To hide multiple worksheets simultaneously, do the following:

1. Select the first worksheet's name tab.
2. Hold down the **Ctrl** key and click any additional worksheet tabs you want to hide.
3. Right-click any of the worksheet tabs and select **Hide** on the shortcut menu.

There are two ways to Unhide a worksheet:

- **Method 1**:
  1. Right-click any of the tabs at the bottom of the workbook and select **Unhide** on the shortcut menu.
  2. Select the worksheet name in the **Unhide** dialog box and click **OK**.

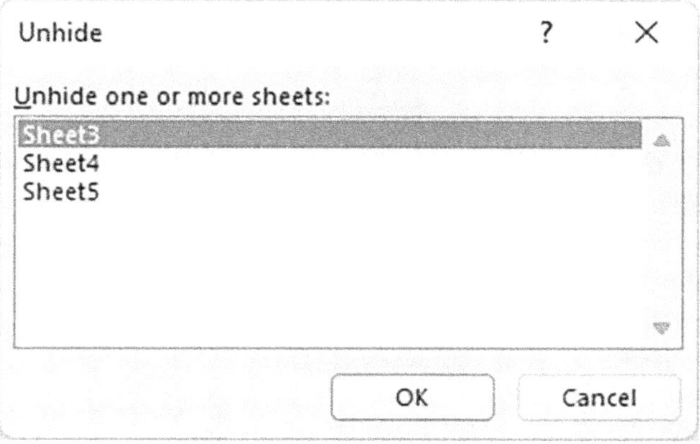

- **Method 2**:
    1. On the Ribbon, go to **Home** > **Cells** > **Format** > **Hide & Unhide** > **Unhide Sheet**.
    2. Select the worksheet name in the **Unhide** dialog box and click **OK**.

Note To unhide more than one worksheet, hold down the **Ctrl** key and select any additional worksheets you want to unhide in the Unhide dialog box.

Applying Cell Styles

You can select a predefined color format for your cells from a wide selection of styles from the **Styles** group on the **Home** tab.

To format a cell or range with a different style:

1. Select the cell or range that you want to format.
2. On the **Home** tab, in the **Styles** group, click the **More** dropdown arrow to expand the style gallery.

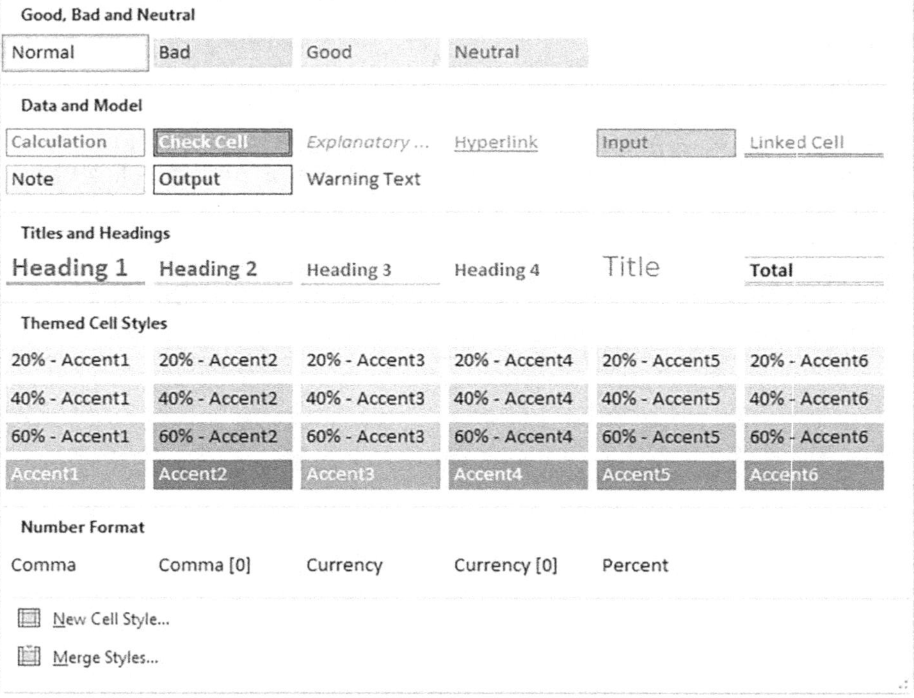

   You can hover over the different styles for a preview on your worksheet before selecting one.

3. Select a style on the gallery to apply it to your worksheet.

Merging Cells and Aligning Data

To **merge** cells on your worksheet, select the cells you want to merge. On the **Home** tab, click **Merge & Center**. Alternatively, you can click the drop-down button for Merge & Center and choose other merge options from the drop-down menu.

To **unmerge** cells, select the merged cells, then on the **Home** tab, click the drop-down button for **Merge & Center**. Select **Unmerge Cells** from the drop-down menu.

Text Alignment and Wrapping

To align text in a cell, select the cell and click one of the alignment options in the **Alignment** group on the **Home** tab. You can also wrap text and merge cells from the command options available.

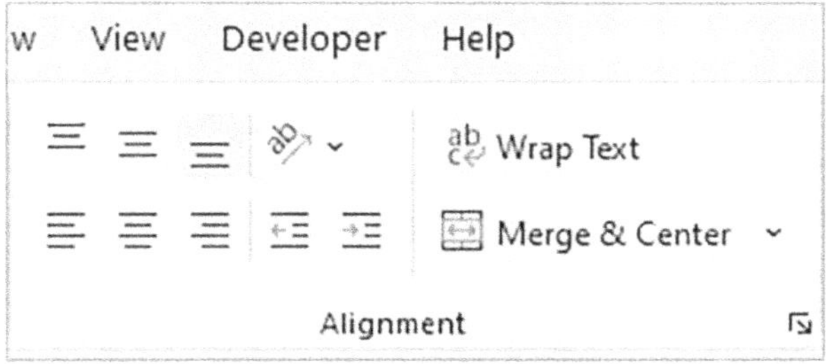

Shrink to Fit and Text Direction

The **Format Cells** dialog box provides additional formatting options like **Shrink to fit** and **Text direction**. To open the dialog box, click the dialog box launcher on the bottom-right of the **Alignment** group.

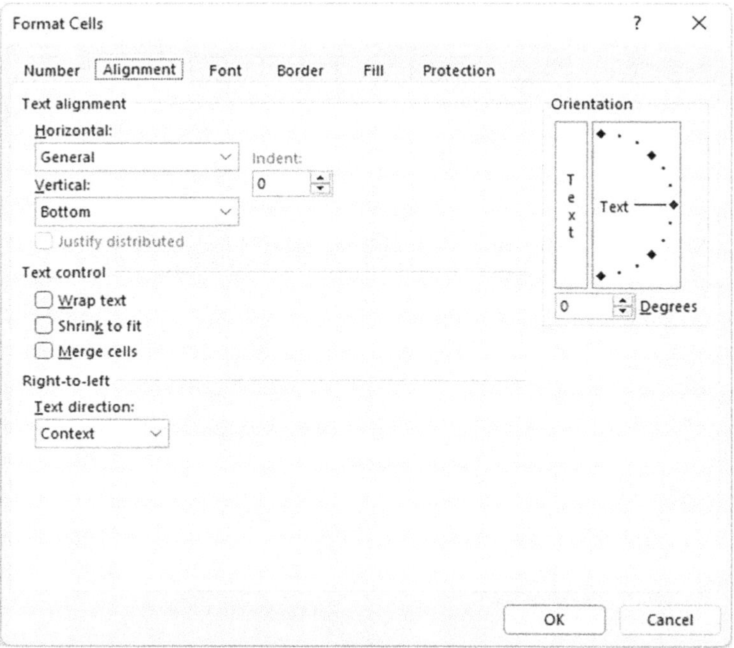

On the Alignment tab, you can:

- Align text in your cells vertically and horizontally.
- Wrap text to go to a new line in a cell instead of continuing into other cells to the right.
- Shrink text to fit one cell.
- Merge cells.

Applying Number Formats

To quickly set the format for a range of cells:

1. Select the range of cells that you want to format.
2. On the **Home** tab, in the **Number** group, click the dropdown arrow on the **Number Format** box.
3. Select the format you want from the dropdown menu.

The selected cell/range will now be formatted in the format you selected.

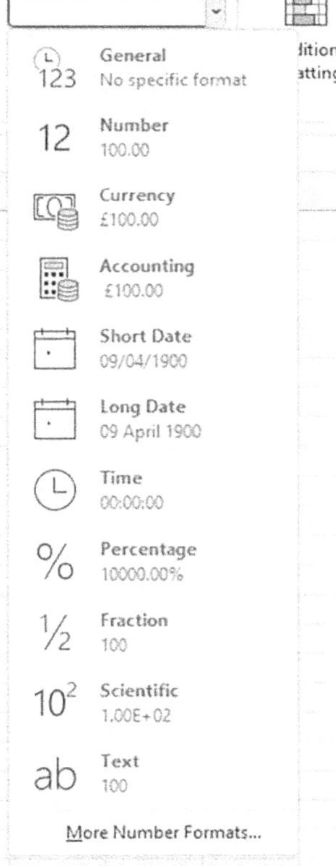

Number Format dropdown menu.

Accessing More Formats

To access formats not available on the **Number Format** dropdown menu, open the **Format Cells** dialog box.

For example, if you're in the US and you want to change currency formats in your worksheet to UK pounds, do the following:

1. Select the range of cells that you want to format.

2. On the **Home** tab, in the **Number** group, click the dropdown arrow on the **Number Format** box, and select **More Number Formats**.

   Excel displays the **Number** tab of the **Format Cells** dialog box.

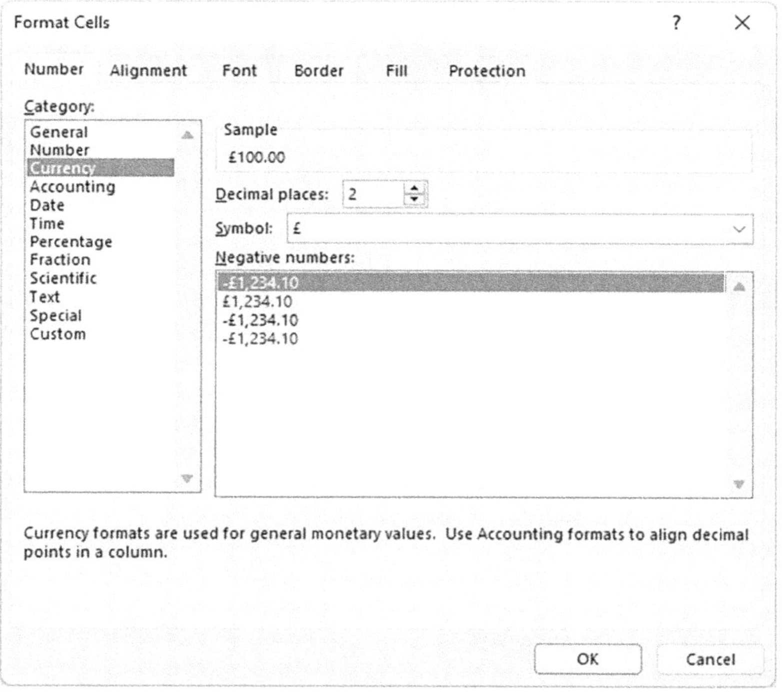

Tip Another way to display the Format Cells dialog box is to click the dialog box launcher in the **Number** group on the **Home** tab.

3. On the left side of the dialog box, under **Category**, select **Currency**.
4. Click the **Symbol** field to display a dropdown list. Select the British pound sign (£) from the list.

   You can also set the number of decimal places and the format you want for negative numbers on this tab. The **Sample** box displays how the selected format will look on your worksheet.
5. Click **OK** to confirm your changes when done.

Creating Custom Numeric Formats

Excel has many predefined number formats you can select and then amend to create your own custom format if none of the predefined formats meets your needs.

For example, imagine that you have a column in your worksheet that you use to record a set of numbers. It could be product serial numbers, unique product IDs, or even telephone numbers. You may want the numbers to appear in a certain format regardless of how they've been entered.

In some applications like Microsoft Access, this would be called a *format mask*.

In Excel, you can create a custom format for a group of cells so that every entry is automatically formatted with your default format.

To create a custom format, follow the steps below:

1. Select the range of cells to be formatted.

2. Right-click any area in your selection and select **Format Cells** from the pop-up menu.

   Alternatively, on the **Home** tab, in the **Number** group, click the dialog box launcher to open the **Format Cells** dialog box.

3. Under **Category,** select **Custom**.

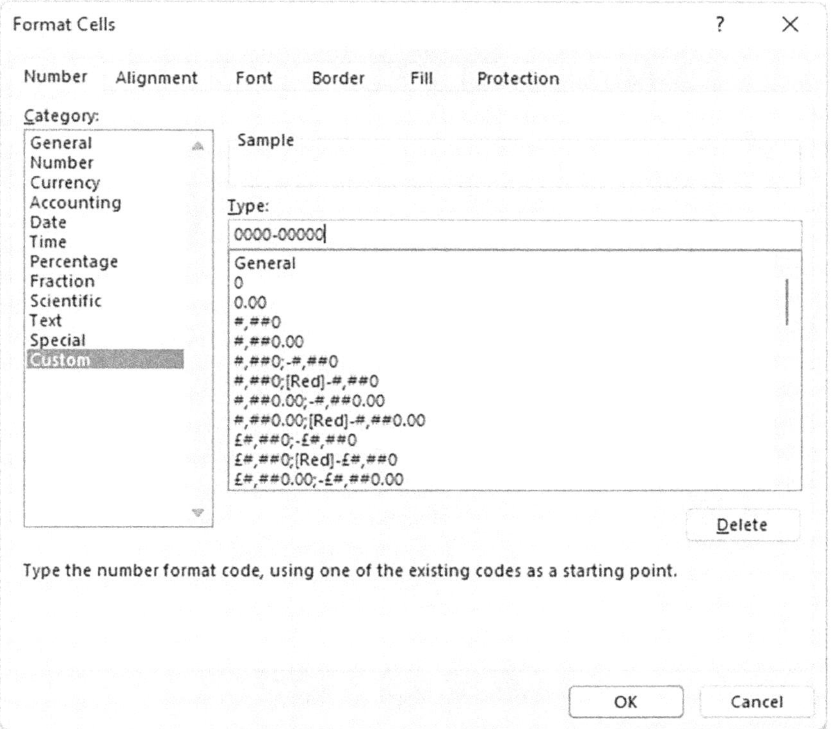

4. In the **Type** box, select an existing format close to the one you would like to create.

Note If you find a format on the list that meets your needs, you can select that one and click OK.

---

5. In the **Type** box, enter the format you want to create. For example, *0000-00000.*

6. Click **OK**.

	A	B	C
1	**Serial Number**		
2	234401107	2344-01107	
3	234434589	2344-34589	
4	234466123	2344-66123	
5	234455692	2344-55692	
6	234234500	2342-34500	
7	234410976	2344-10976	
8	232310978	2323-10978	
9	234093419	2340-93419	
10	230923100	2309-23100	
11	234109035	2341-09035	
12	234102345	2341-02345	
13	234109093	2341-09093	
14			

In the image above, column A has a set of numbers. Column B shows the same numbers with a custom format (*0000-00000*) now applied to them.

Copy Cell Formatting

A quick way to format a cell or group of cells based on another cell in your worksheet is to use the **Format Painter** in the **Clipboard** group on the **Home** tab. The Format Painter can be a time saver as you only create the format once and copy it to other cells in your worksheet.

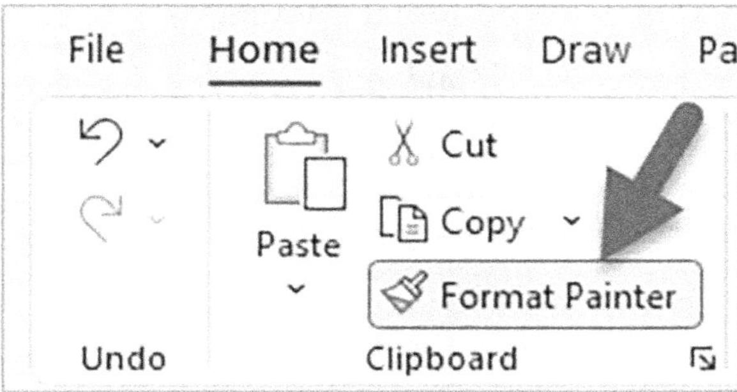

To copy cell formatting with the **Format Painter**, do the following:

1. Select the cell with the format you want to copy.
2. On the **Home** tab, in the **Clipboard** group, click **Format Painter**. The mouse pointer will turn into a plus sign (+) and a brush icon.
3. Click and drag over the cells to which you're applying the format.

The destination cells will now have the same format as the source cell.

Tip When clicked once, the **Format Painter** is enabled for only one use and then turned off. If you want to apply the same format to multiple ranges, double-click the Format Painter to turn it on for multiple uses. It remains enabled until you click it again to turn it off.

Example:

In the following example, we want to copy the **Currency** format in cell **A2** and apply it to range **A3:A14**.

Follow the steps below to copy the format using the Format Painter:

1. Click cell *A2* to select it.
2. Select **Home** > **Clipboard** > **Format Painter**.
3. In the worksheet area, click *A3* and drag to *A14*.

Excel applies the currency format in *A2* to the range A3:A14.

Clearing the Cell Format

To remove formatting from a cell or range, do the following:

1. Select the cells you want to clear.
2. Select **Home** > **Editing** > **Clear**.

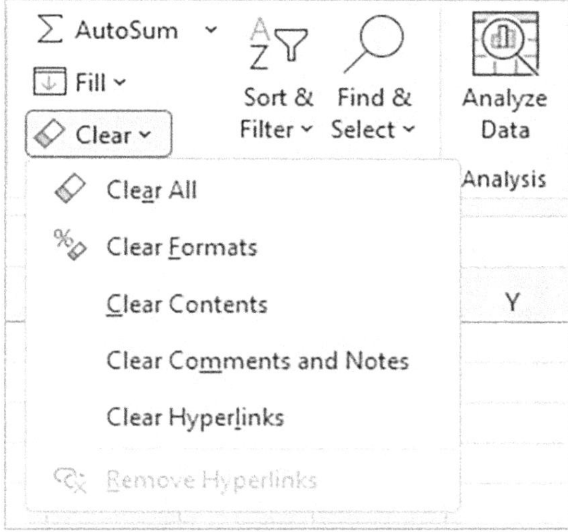

3. Excel displays a dropdown menu with several options - Clear All, Clear Formats, Clear Contents, Clear Comments and Notes, and Clear Hyperlinks.

4. To clear just the format and not the values, click **Clear Formats**.

Excel returns the format of the selected cells to **General,** which is the default.

Conditional Formatting

You can format your data based on certain criteria to display a visual representation that helps to spot critical issues and identify patterns and trends. For example, you can use visual representations to clearly show the highs and lows in your data and the trend. This type of formatting is called conditional formatting in Excel.

In the example below, we can quickly see the trend in sales and how they compare to each other.

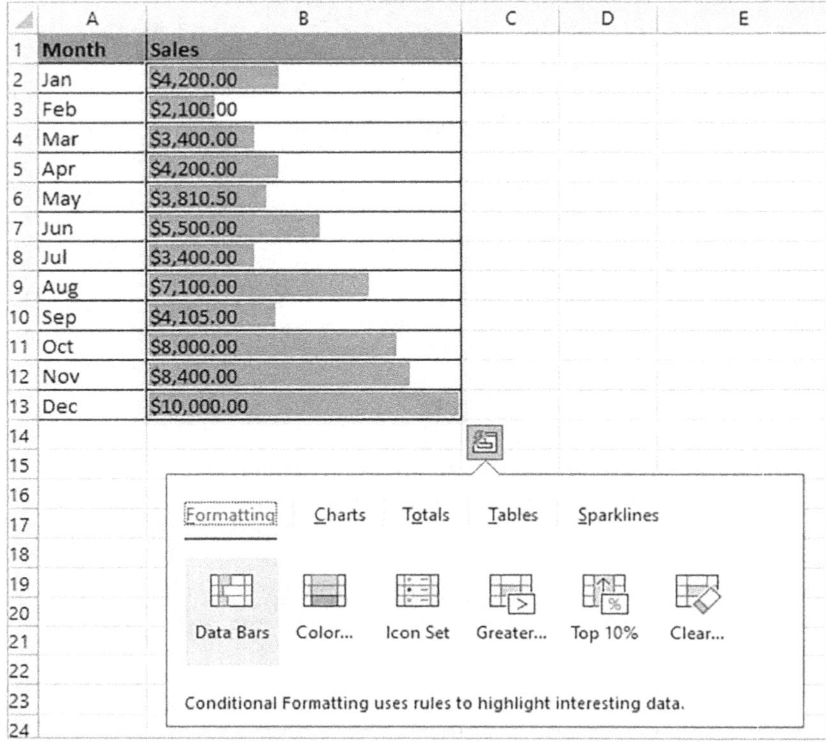

A
B
C
D
E
Month
Sales
Jan
$4,200.00
Feb
$2,100.00
Mar
$3,400.00
Apr
$4,200.00
May
$3,810.50
Jun
$5,500.00
Jul
$3,400.00
Aug
$7,100.00
Sep
$4,105.00
Oct
$8,000.00
Nov
$8,400.00
Dec
$10,000.00
Formatting
Charts
Totals
Tables
Sparklines
Data Bars
Color...
Icon Set
Greater...
Top 10%
Clear...
Conditional Formatting uses rules to highlight interesting data.

To quickly apply a conditional format:

1. Select the range of cells you want to format. The quick analysis button will be displayed at the bottom-right of the selection.

2. Click the Quick Analysis button, and use the default **Formatting** tab.

3. Hover over the formatting options on the Formatting tab to see a live preview of what your data will look like when applied.

4. Click **Data Bars** to apply the formatting to your data.

You now have a visual representation of the data that's easier to analyze.

Use Multiple Conditional Formats

You can apply more than one conditional format to the same group of cells. Select the cells, click the Quick Analysis button, and click another format option, for example, **Icon Set**. The arrows illustrate the upper, middle, and lower values in the set of data.

Formatting Text Fields

You can apply conditional formatting to text, but the formatting options for text are different from that of numbers.

For example, to highlight all the rows with "Sauce" in the name, do the following:

1. Select the range.
2. Click the Quick Analysis button.
3. Select **Text** on the Formatting tab.
4. In the **Text That Contains** dialog box, enter "Sauce" in the first box and select the type of formatting from the drop-down list.

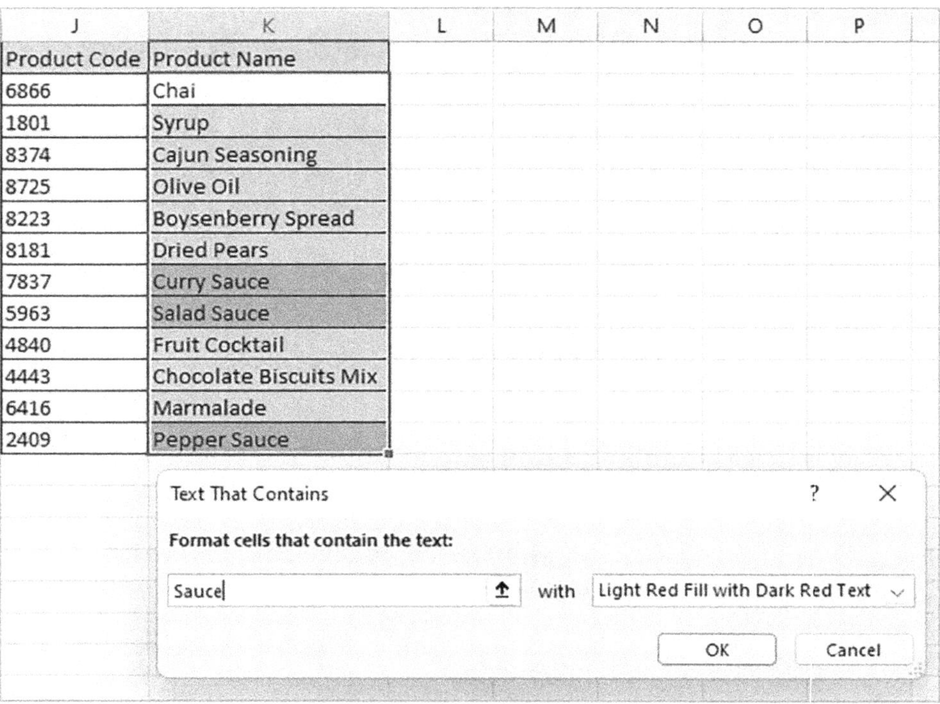

J
K
L
M
N
O
P
Product Code
Product Name
6866
Chai
1801
Syrup
8374
Cajun Seasoning
8725
Olive Oil
8223
Boysenberry Spread
8181
Dried Pears
7837
Curry Sauce
5963
Salad Sauce
4840
Fruit Cocktail
4443
Chocolate Biscuits Mix
6416
Marmalade
2409
Pepper Sauce
Text That Contains
?
Format cells that contain the text:
Sauce
with
Light Red Fill with Dark Red Text
OK
Cancel

You can explore the formatting options for different data types by selecting the data to be formatted and clicking the Quick Analysis button.

Conditionally Formatting Time

Let's say we had a list of projects, and we wanted to see which projects are overdue, that is, the ones with a due date before today.

To highlight the overdue projects, do the following:

1. Select the cells in the *Due date* column.
2. Click the Quick Analysis button, and then click Less Than.
3. Type in **=TODAY()**

You could type in today's date, but that would mean updating the conditional formatting daily, which would get tedious fast and even introduce errors! The TODAY function will always return today's date.

4. Select the formatting you'll like to use from the drop-down list.

5. Click **OK**.

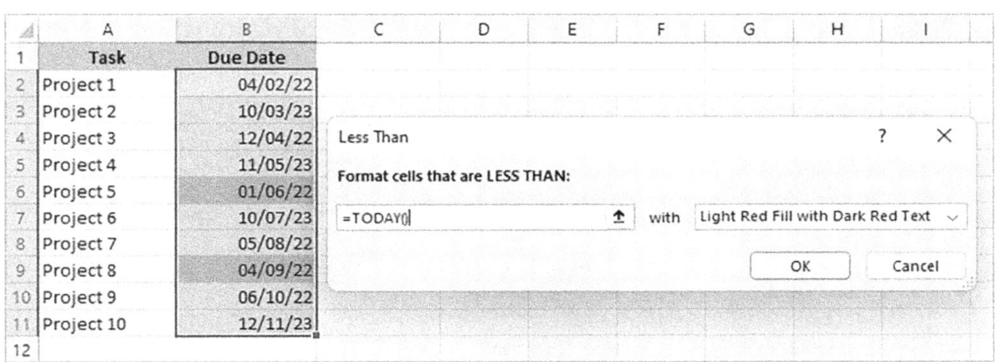

Task
Due Date
Project 1
04/02/22
Project 2
10/03/23
Project 3
12/04/22
Project 4
11/05/23
Project 5
01/06/22
Project 6
10/07/23
Project 7
05/08/22
Project 8
04/09/22
Project 9
06/10/22
Project 10
12/11/23
Less Than
Format cells that are LESS THAN:
=TODAY()
with
Light Red Fill with Dark Red Text
OK
Cancel

The overdue projects now stand out on the list and are easy to identify immediately. The date format used here is **mm/dd/yy**.

Note You can also sort the data in this example to figure out the overdue projects, but depending on your data, sorting is not always an available option.

Creating Conditional Formatting Rules

An alternative way to create conditional formatting is by creating **Rules** in Excel.

To launch the **New Formatting Rule** dialog box:

1. Select the range to which you want to apply the conditional formatting.
2. On the Ribbon, go to **Home** > **Styles** > **Conditional Formatting** > **New Rule**.

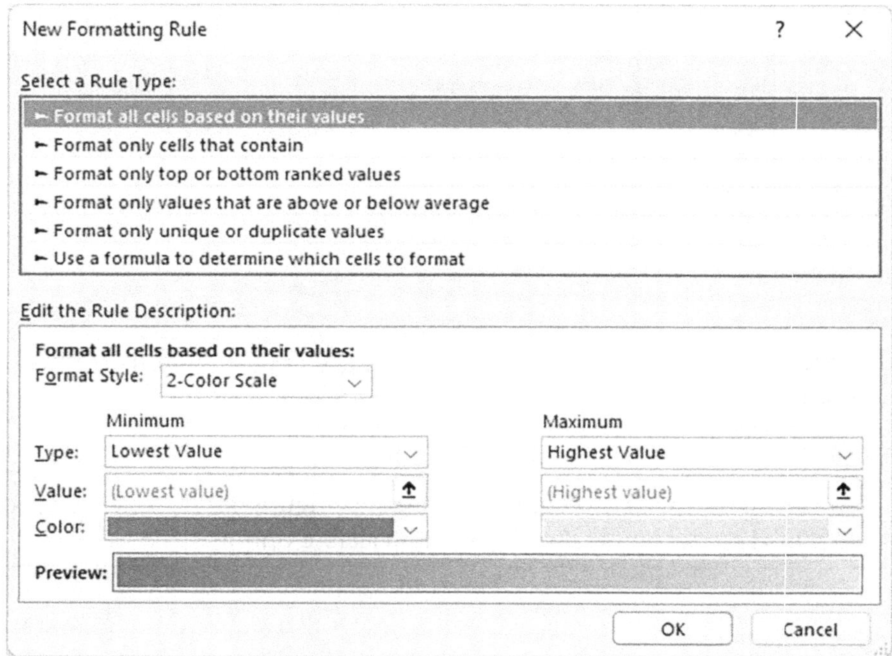

You can use the New Formatting Rule dialog box to create more complex rules using a series of conditions and criteria.

You can select a rule type from the following options:

- Format all cells based on their values.
- Format only cells that contain.
- Format only top or bottom ranked values.
- Format only values that are above or below average.
- Format only unique or duplicate values.
- Use a formula to determine which cells to format.

The bottom section of the dialog box, labeled **Edit the Rule Description**, gives you different fields to define your rule for each rule type.

Example:

Let's say you had a list of products, and you want to format the whole row grey if one of the fields, the product Stock, fell below 10.

Follow the steps below to create a conditional formatting rule for the above scenario:

1. Select the range you want to conditionally format, that is, A2:C18. Note that A2 is the active cell.
2. On the Ribbon, select **Home** > **Styles** >**Conditional Formatting** > **New Rule**.
3. In the **New Formatting Rule** dialog, select **Use a formula to determine which cells to format**.

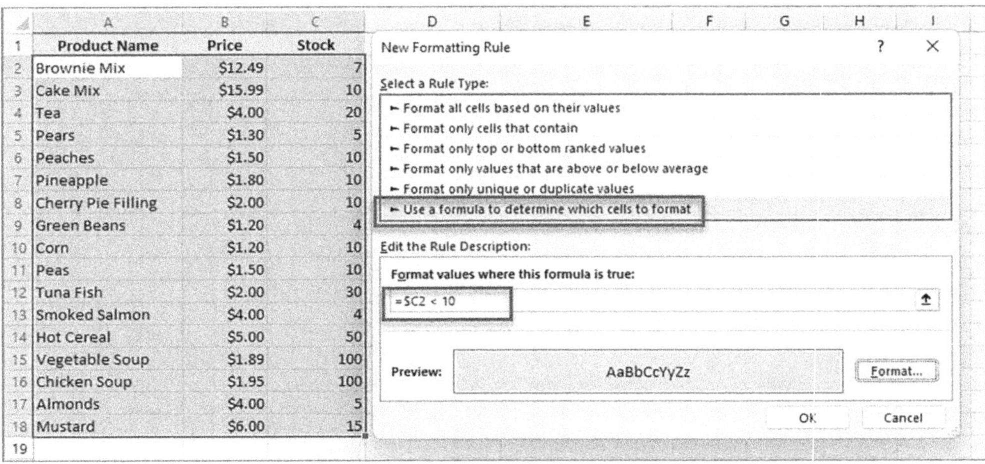

Product Name
Price
Stock
Brownie Mix $12.49 7
Cake Mix $15.99 10
Tea $4.00 20
Pears $1.30 5
Peaches $1.50 10
Pineapple $1.80 10
Cherry Pie Filling $2.00 10
Green Beans $1.20 4
Corn $1.20 10
Peas $1.50 10
Tuna Fish $2.00 30
Smoked Salmon $4.00 4
Hot Cereal $5.00 50
Vegetable Soup $1.89 100
Chicken Soup $1.95 100
Almonds $4.00 5
Mustard $6.00 15
New Formatting Rule
Select a Rule Type:
Format all cells based on their values
Format only cells that contain
Format only top or bottom ranked values
Format only values that are above or below average
Format only unique or duplicate values
Use a formula to determine which cells to format
Edit the Rule Description:
Format values where this formula is true:
=$C2 < 10
Preview:
AaBbCcYyZz
Format...
OK
Cancel

Since A2 is the active cell, you need to enter a formula that is valid for row 2 and will apply to all the other rows.

4. Type in the formula ***=$C2 < 10***.

   The dollar sign before the C means it is an **absolute reference** for column C ($C). The value in column C for each row is evaluated and used to determine if the format should be applied.

Note The difference between an absolute reference and a relative reference is covered in chapter 6.

---

5. For the fill color, click the **Format** button, select the fill color you want, and click **OK**, and **OK** again to apply the rule.

   The rows with Stock below 10 will now be filled with grey.

	A	B	C
1	**Product Name**	**Price**	**Stock**
2	Brownie Mix	$12.49	7
3	Cake Mix	$15.99	10
4	Tea	$4.00	20
5	Pears	$1.30	5
6	Peaches	$1.50	10
7	Pineapple	$1.80	10
8	Cherry Pie Filling	$2.00	10
9	Green Beans	$1.20	4
10	Corn	$1.20	10
11	Peas	$1.50	10
12	Tuna Fish	$2.00	30
13	Smoked Salmon	$4.00	4
14	Hot Cereal	$5.00	50
15	Vegetable Soup	$1.89	100
16	Chicken Soup	$1.95	100
17	Almonds	$4.00	5
18	Mustard	$6.00	15
19			

Chapter 6

Carrying out Calculations with Formulas

Excel provides tools and features that enable you to perform different types of calculations, from basic arithmetic to complex engineering calculations using formulas.

This chapter covers:

- Operator precedence in Excel and its effect on calculations.
- How to enter formulas in Excel.
- How to calculate percentages, dates, and time.
- How to use the AutoSum feature for automated calculations.
- The difference between relative and absolute cell references.
- How to access data in other worksheets in your formulas.

Operators in Excel

Arithmetic Operators

The following arithmetic operators are used to perform basic mathematical operations such as addition, subtraction, multiplication, or division.

Arithmetic operator	Meaning	Example
+ (plus sign)	Addition	=4+4
– (minus sign)	Subtraction	=4–4
	Negation	=-4
* (asterisk)	Multiplication	=4*4
/ (forward slash)	Division	=4/4
% (percent sign)	Percent	40%
^ (caret)	Exponentiation	=4^4

Comparison Operators

Comparison operators allow you to compare two values and produce a logical result, that is, TRUE or FALSE.

Comparison operator	Meaning	Example
=	Equal to	=A1=B1
>	Greater than	=A1>B1
<	Less than	=A1<B1
>=	Greater than or equal to	=A1>=B1
<=	Less than or equal to	=A1<=B1
<>	Not equal to	=A1<>B1

Operator Precedence

If you combine several operators in a single formula, Excel performs the operations in the following order.

Operator	Description
: (colon) (single space) ,(comma)	Reference operators
–	Negation (as in –1)
%	Percent
^	Exponentiation
* and /	Multiplication and division
+ and –	Addition and subtraction
&	Connects two strings of text (concatenation)
= <> <= >= <>	Comparison

At a basic level, you just need to remember that Excel performs multiplication and division before addition and subtraction. If a formula contains operators with the same precedence, for instance, multiplication and division, Excel will evaluate the operators from left to right.

Parentheses and Operator Precedence

You can change the order of evaluation by enclosing parts of your formula in parentheses (). The part of the formula in parentheses will be calculated first.

For example, the following formula produces 75 because Excel calculates multiplication before addition. So, Excel multiplies 7 by 10 first before adding 5 to the result.

=5+7*10

Answer = 75

In contrast, if we enclose 5+7 in parentheses, Excel will calculate 5 + 7 first before multiplying the result by 7 to produce 120.

=(5+7)*10

Answer = 120

In another example, we want to add 20% to 300. The parentheses around the second part of the formula ensure Excel calculates the addition first before the multiplication to produce 360.

=300 * (1 + 0.2)

Answer = 360

Entering a Formula

To enter a formula in a cell, always start your entry with an equal sign (=) in the formula bar. The equal sign tells Excel that your entry is a formula, not a static value.

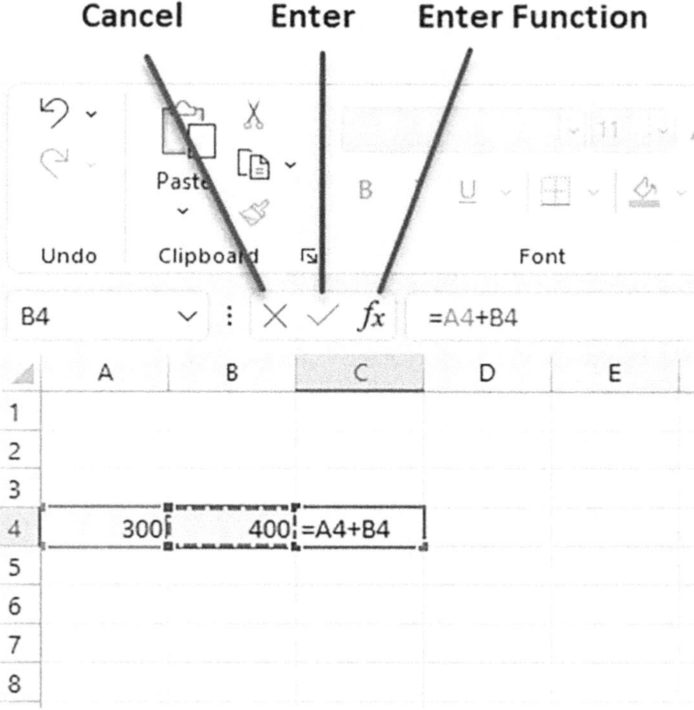

Next to the formula bar, you have the **Enter** command (checkmark) that you use to confirm your formula. You enter your formula in the formula bar and click **Enter** to confirm the entry. If you wish to cancel your entry, click **Cancel** to discard it.

For example, if you wanted to add two numbers, 300 + 400, you would do the following:

1. Enter 300 in cell **A4**.
2. Enter 400 in cell **B4**.
3. In cell C4, enter **= A4 + B4**.
4. Click **Enter**.
5. C4 will now have the sum of the two figures, 700.

Tip To minimize errors, avoid typing cell references directly into the formula bar as much as possible. After you type in the leading equal sign (=) in the formula bar, you can add cell references to your formula by selecting them on the worksheet with your mouse. Select the cell on the worksheet with your mouse to automatically enter its reference in the formula bar whenever you want to reference a cell.

Thus, for the basic calculation we performed above, the way you would enter it in the formula bar is as follows:

1. Enter 300 in cell **A4**, and 400 in cell **B4**.
2. Select **C4**.
3. Type "=" in the formula bar.
4. Select **A4**.
5. Type "+" in the formula bar.
6. Select **B4**.
7. Click **Enter**.

Excel displays the sum of the two cells, 700, in cell C4.

Calculating Percentages

In this example, we want to calculate 20% of a value and then add it to the total, the way sales tax is calculated in invoices.

The product price is $2,900, and the sales tax is 20%.

Note 100 percent is 1 in Excel. Anything less than 100 percent will be less than 1. Hence, 20 percent will be 0.2. Always enter a percent as a decimal place number unless it is 100% or greater.

For the **Sales tax,** we then enter 0.2 in cell B3.

We can format the cell as a **Percentage** data type (although this is not compulsory when calculating percentages in Excel). On the **Home** tab, in the **Numbers** group, click the % sign. Excel changes the 0.2 you entered in the cell to 20%.

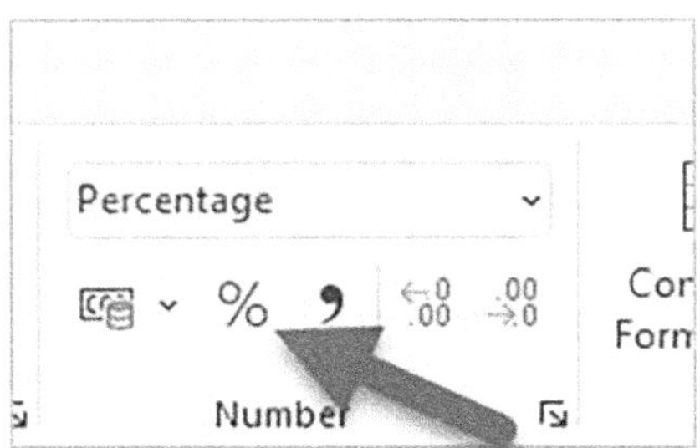

For the **Price**, enter $2,900.

For the Sales Tax formula, enter =*A6*B3* to calculate 20% of $2,900, which is $580.00.

For the **Total**, you can use the AutoSum tool to generate the sum, or you can enter the formula directly =*SUM(A6:B6)* to produce the total figure of $3,480.00.

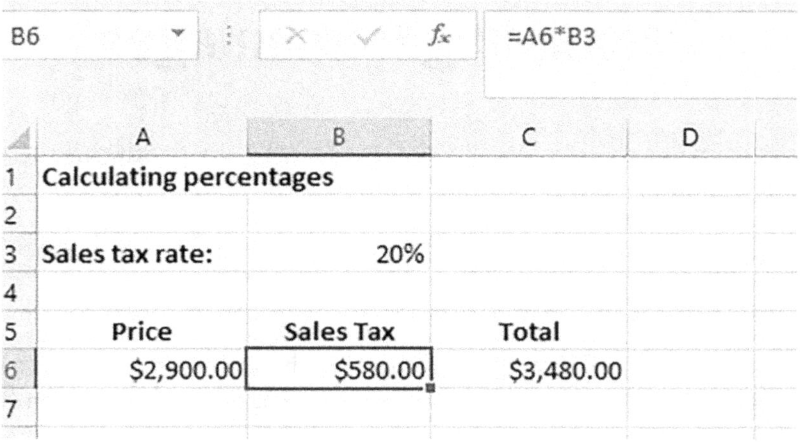

B6 | =A6*B3

	A	B	C	D
1	**Calculating percentages**			
2				
3	**Sales tax rate:**	20%		
4				
5	**Price**	**Sales Tax**	**Total**	
6	$2,900.00	$580.00	$3,480.00	
7				

You can use the same method above to subtract percentages. For example, to subtract the Sales Tax from the Price, enter =*A6-B6* in cell c6.

Using AutoSum

The AutoSum tool can be found on the **Home** tab, in the **Editing** group. It is the Greek Sigma symbol. AutoSum allows you to insert functions in your worksheet. The tool automatically selects the range to be used as your argument. You can use AutoSum with the SUM, AVERAGE, COUNT, MAX, and MIN functions.

AutoSum will default to the SUM function when clicked, but you can use a different function with AutoSum. Click the AutoSum drop-down button to display a pop-up menu of the other functions you can use. Select another function on the menu, for example, **Average**, to insert it as the function used with AutoSum.

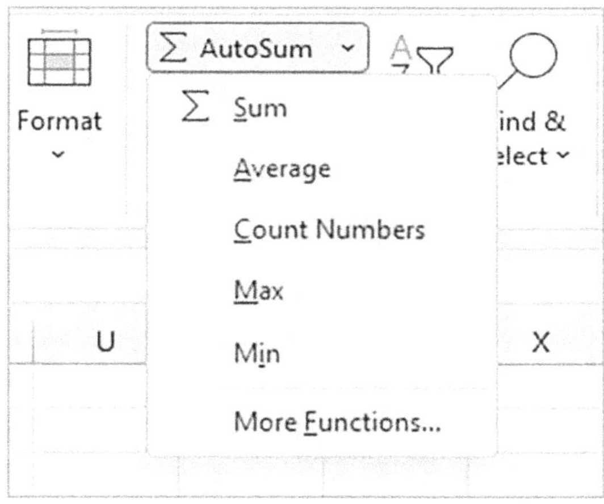

A *range* in Excel is a collection of two or more cells that contain the data with which you're working. See chapter 8 for more on ranges.

A function *argument* is a piece of data that a function needs to run. The SUM function, for example, can have one or more arguments for the input ranges to be summed.

=SUM(A2:A10)

=SUM(A2:A10, C2:C10)

The great thing about AutoSum is that it selects the most likely range of cells in the current column or row that you want to use. It then automatically enters them in the function's argument.

For the most part, it selects the correct range of cells and marks the selection with a moving dotted line called a bounding outline. For non-continuous data, AutoSum may not automatically select everything. In those cases, you can manually correct the range by dragging the selection (bounding outline) over the other cells you want in the formula.

Example

In the following example, we have figures in B2 to B14 that we want to sum up, and we can do this quickly with the AutoSum command.

Follow the steps below to apply AutoSum to a range of continuous data:

1. Click the cell where you want the total displayed. For this example, this would be **B14**.
2. Click the **AutoSum** command button (**Home** > **Editing** > **AutoSum**).
3. AutoSum will automatically select the range of cells with continuous data (above or to the side of the cell with the formula). In this case, it selects B2 to B13.
4. Click **Enter** (the checkmark button next to the formula bar) or hit the **Enter** key.

Cell B14 will now show the sum of the numbers.

SUM | =SUM(B2:B13)

	A	B	C	D
1	**Month**	**Expenses**		
2	Jan	$950.00		
3	Feb	$716.00		
4	Mar	$981.00		
5	Apr	$903.00		
6	May	$625.00		
7	Jun	$825.00		
8	Jul	$930.00		
9	Aug	$983.00		
10	Sep	$745.00		
11	Oct	$768.00		
12	Nov	$950.00		
13	Dec	$824.00		
14	**Sum**	=SUM(B2:B13)		
15		SUM(**number1**, [number2], ...)		
16				

Using AutoSum with Non-contiguous Data

A non-contiguous range has blank rows or columns in the data. AutoSum will only select the contiguous range next to the cell with the formula. So, you must manually drag the selection over the rest of the data.

To use AutoSum with non-contiguous data, do the following:

1. Click the cell where you want the total to be displayed.
2. Click the **AutoSum** command button.
3. AutoSum will automatically select the range of cells next to the cell with the formula.
4. Hover your mouse pointer over the right edge of the selection until it turns into a double-headed arrow. Then drag over the rest of the cells in your range.
5. Click the **Enter** button or hit the **Enter** key on your keyboard.

The formula cell will now show the sum of the numbers.

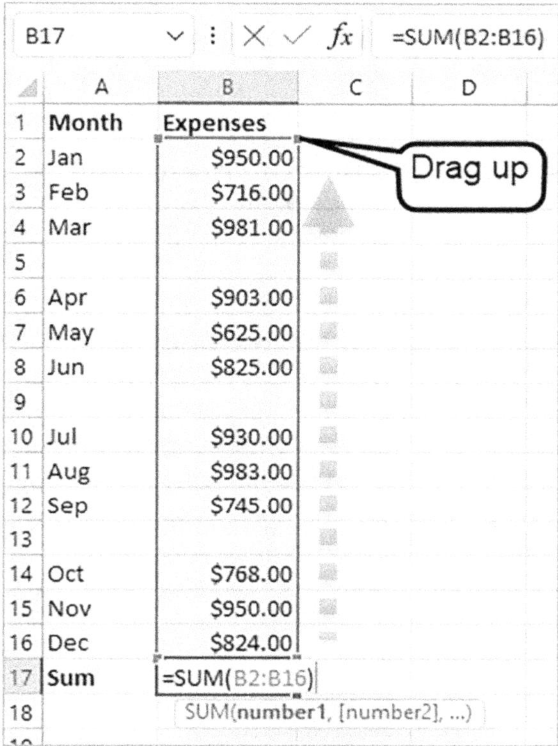
B17
=SUM(B2:B16)
A
B
C
D
1 Month Expenses
2 Jan $950.00
3 Feb $716.00
4 Mar $981.00
5
6 Apr $903.00
7 May $625.00
8 Jun $825.00
9
10 Jul $930.00
11 Aug $983.00
12 Sep $745.00
13
14 Oct $768.00
15 Nov $950.00
16 Dec $824.00
17 Sum =SUM(B2:B16)
18 SUM(number1, [number2], ...)
Drag up

Using AutoSum with Different Ranges

Sometimes the data you want to calculate may be in different parts of your worksheet or even on different sheets in the workbook. With AutoSum, you can have arguments for individual values, cell references, ranges, or a mix of all three. To calculate different ranges, you add different ranges to the AutoSum calculation.

To sum values in different ranges, do the following:

1. Click the cell where you want the formula, and then click **AutoSum**.
2. If AutoSum does not select the first range for you, then select it by clicking the first cell and dragging to the last cell of the range.
3. Hold down the **Ctrl** key and select any additional ranges you want to add to the calculation.
4. Click **Enter**.

B4 | fx =SUM(D4:D13,B4:B13)

	A	B	C	D	E
1					
2					
3		Month 1		Month 2	
4	Hugo	$1,848.00		$1,190.00	
5	Felipe	$1,897.00		$1,642.00	
6	Wayne	$1,267.00		$1,639.00	
7	Mae	$1,149.00		$1,421.00	
8	Lee	$1,571.00		$1,061.00	
9	Oscar	$1,659.00		$1,791.00	
10	Fannie	$1,509.00		$1,043.00	
11	Terrance	$1,307.00		$1,680.00	
12	Sylvester	$1,589.00		$1,884.00	
13	Elijah	$1,426.00		$1,768.00	
14					
15	Total (all months)			=SUM(D4:D13,B4:B13)	
16				SUM(number1, [number2], ...)	

The sum of both ranges will now be entered. You can include up to 255 ranges as arguments in the SUM function.

Using AutoSum for Other Aggregate Functions

Despite its name, you can also use the AutoSum feature to calculate the **Average**, **Count**, **Max**, and **Min**. To select these other functions, click the drop-down arrow on the AutoSum command button and select an option on the menu.

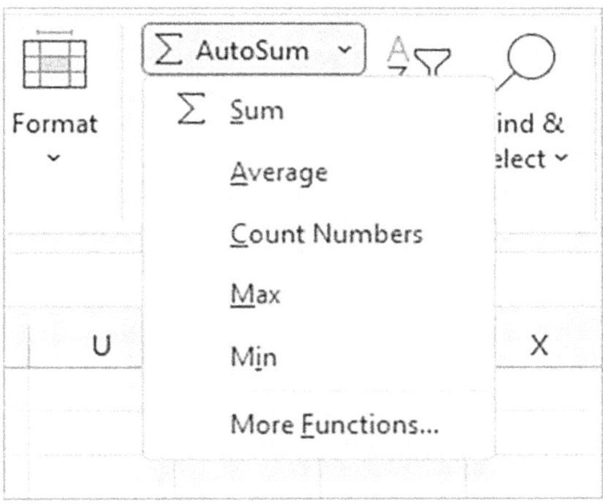

For example, to calculate the average of a row of numbers in cells B4 to G4, you would do the following:

1. Place the cell pointer in the cell where you want to display the average, which is H4 for this example (see image below).

2. On the **Home** tab, click **AutoSum** > **Average**.

   AutoSum will automatically select the cells with numbers next to the formula cell. In this example, AutoSum selects the range B4:G4.

3. Click **Enter** (or press the **Enter** key) to accept the selection.

   Excel calculates the average of the selection using the AVERAGE function in cell H4.

YEAR =AVERAGE(B4:G4)

	A	B	C	D	E	F	G	H	I	J
1	**Exam Marks**									
2										
3	**Students**	**Math**	**English**	**Physics**	**Chemistry**	**Biology**	**Computer Sci**	**Average**		
4	Barbara	44	69	25	83	78	35	=AVERAGE(B4:G4)		
5	Michelle	69	85	57	28	26	56	AVERAGE(**number1**, [number2], ...)		
6	Pamela	79	57	73	34	74	48			
7	Mildred	88	71	90	73	97	88			
8	Kathy	66	94	85	61	81	92			
9	Bruce	41	25	76	42	87	25			
10	Kathleen	90	77	31	43	61	63			
11	Joshua	92	84	64	78	82	56			
12	Andrew	91	73	42	87	90	88			
13	Todd	33	56	79	76	40	85			
14	Kathryn	55	33	30	33	69	43			
15	Irene	38	72	59	32	87	32			
16										

Quick Sum with the Status Bar

If you want to quickly see the sum of a range of cells, select the range and view the information on the Status Bar.

To select a range of cells, click the first cell in the range, hold down the **Shift** key, and click the last cell in the range.

Once you have selected the range, look at the lower right-hand side of the Excel **Status Bar**. You'll see the **Average**, **Count**, and **Sum** for the selected cells.

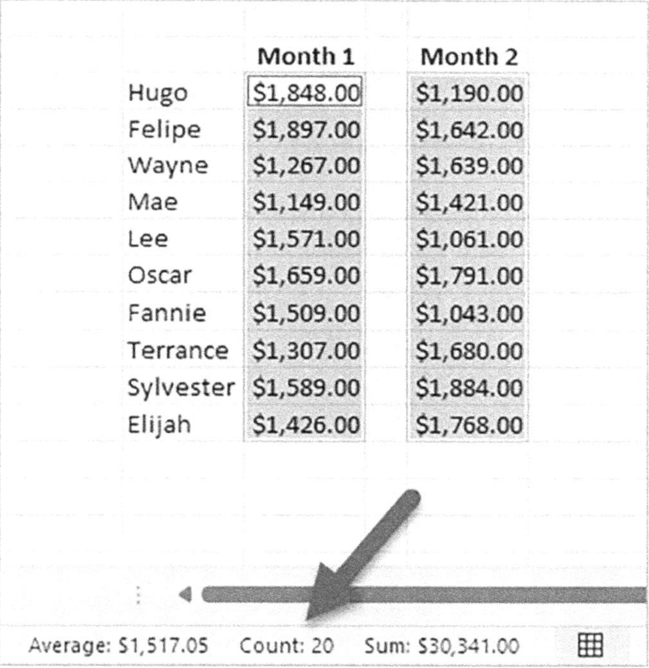

	Month 1	Month 2
Hugo	$1,848.00	$1,190.00
Felipe	$1,897.00	$1,642.00
Wayne	$1,267.00	$1,639.00
Mae	$1,149.00	$1,421.00
Lee	$1,571.00	$1,061.00
Oscar	$1,659.00	$1,791.00
Fannie	$1,509.00	$1,043.00
Terrance	$1,307.00	$1,680.00
Sylvester	$1,589.00	$1,884.00
Elijah	$1,426.00	$1,768.00

This feature provides a way of quickly viewing aggregate data for a range of values in a worksheet without entering a formula.

Calculating Date and Time

Native support for date and time calculations has vastly improved in Excel over previous editions. You can now perform many date and time calculations in the worksheet area using arithmetic operators where functions were previously needed. The trick is to apply the right data format to the cells to get the right results. This section will cover some of the common date and time calculations.

Adding Time

When you enter two numbers separated by a colon, for example, 8:45, Excel recognizes the value as time and will treat it as such when you perform calculations based on that cell.

In the following example, we calculate how many hours and minutes it took to complete two trips. The first trip took 8 hours and 45 minutes, and the second one took 6 hours and 30 minutes.

B4 | =SUM(B2:B3)

	A	B	C	D
1	Trip	Time		
2	Trip 1	08:45		
3	Trip 2	06:30		
4	Total	15:15		
5				

We enter **08:45** in B2 and **06:30** in B3.

The values are added in cell B4 with the formula **=SUM(B2:B3)**, and it returns an answer of **15:15** (15 hours and 15 minutes).

As you can see from the example above, when we sum the two values, Excel uses hours and minutes to perform the calculation rather than hundreds.

Note that Excel only recognizes time up to 24 hours by default. If you want to calculate time greater than 24 hours, you'll need to format the cell to accept time over 24 hours.

To format a cell to display values over 24 hours, do the following:

1. Click the dialog box launcher in the **Number** group on the Home tab.
2. In the **Format Cells** dialog box, click **Custom**.
3. In the **Type** box, enter **[h]:mm**. This custom format tells Excel to display values beyond 24 hours.

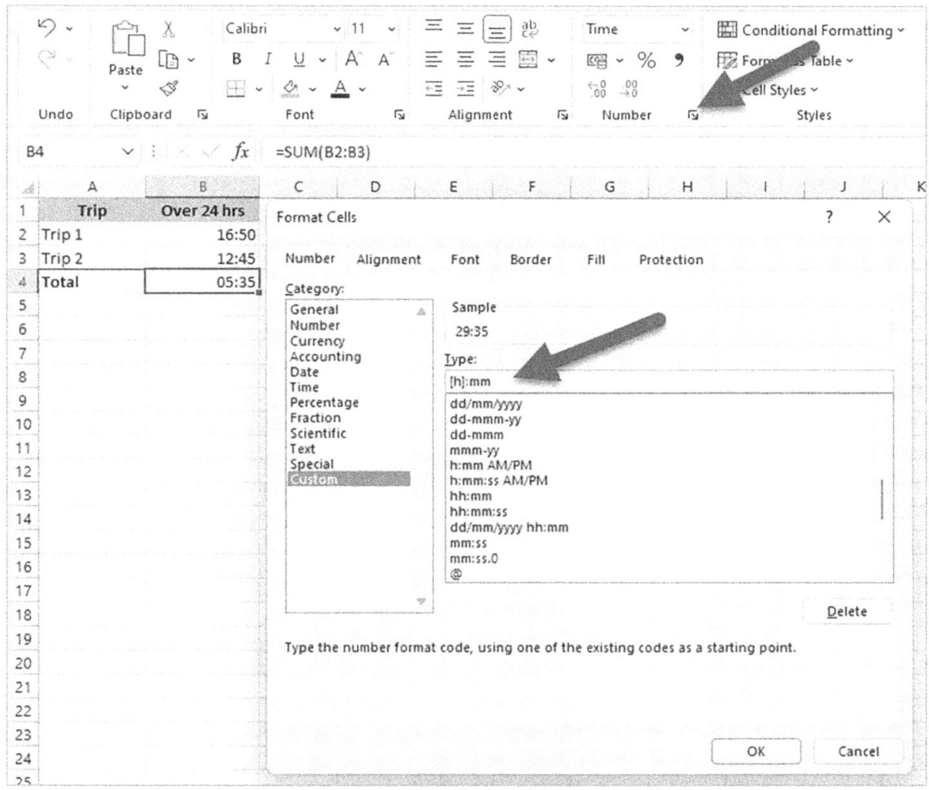

After this change to the cell format, when you add 16:50 + 12:45, you now get **29:35** instead of 05:35.

C4 =SUM(C2:C3)

	A	B	C	D
1		Less than 24 hrs	Over 24 hrs	
2	Trip 1	08:45	16:50	
3	Trip 2	06:30	12:45	
4	Total time	15:15	29:35	
5				

Subtracting Time

You can calculate the number of hours between two times by subtracting one from another, like in a work timesheet.

E4 =(D4-B4)-C4

	A	B	C	D	E	F
1	Timesheet					
2						
3		Start time	Break (hrs:min)	End time	Total (hrs:min)	
4	Mon	9:30 AM	1:00	7:30 PM	9:00	
5	Tue	9:00 AM	0:40	5:00 PM	7:20	
6	Wed	8:10 AM	0:50	4:30 PM	7:30	
7	Thu	7:50 AM	1:30	4:30 PM	7:10	
8	Fri	8:00 AM	0:30	4:30 PM	8:00	
9						

If you enter the time with a colon between the hours and minutes, a simple subtraction can be used to calculate the difference between two times.

In the example above, the simple formula we need to calculate the total time worked per day is:

=(D4-B4)-C4

This formula first subtracts the **Start time** (B4) from the **End time** (D4), then subtracts the **Break** (C4) from the difference to create the total time worked for the day.

Just a few years back, you would need a series of nested IF functions to create the same solution we have achieved above. You would have to perform all the calculations in hundredths and then use logical tests to derive the minutes. So, Excel (and spreadsheet technology in general) has come a long way since then!

Note To ensure the elapsed time is displayed correctly, format the cells showing hours and minutes rather than AM/PM (in this case, C4:C8 and E4:E8) with a custom time format **[h]:mm**. On the other hand, the cells showing AM/PM time (in this case, B4:B8 and D4:D8) have been given the custom format **h:mm AM/PM**.

Calculating Time Across Days

You can use the same method above to calculate the time elapsed across days.

In the following example, we have two times:

Time1: *11/24/22 12:30*

Time2: *11/25/22 14:40*

If **Time1** is in cell **A2** and **Time2** is in cell **B2**, the formula **=B2-A2** will produce the result **26:10** (26 hours and 10 minutes).

Note that the cell containing the result has to be formatted as **[h]:mm** to display the result accurately.

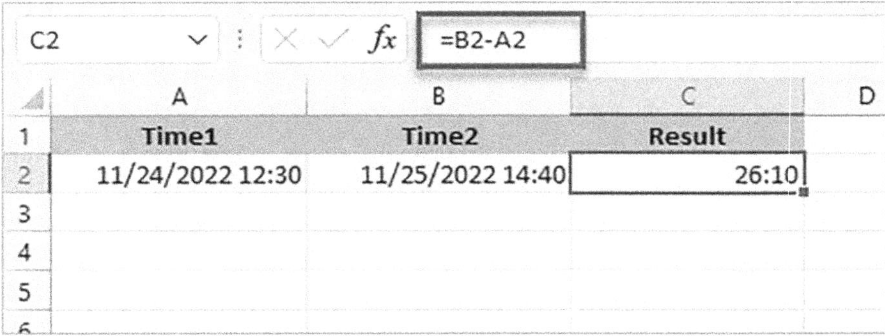

Using the TIME Function

You can use the TIME function to properly convert values to hours, minutes, and seconds if directly entered in the formula bar.

Syntax:

=TIME(hour, minute, second)

The following example subtracts 1 hour 40 minutes from 8:20 AM. We want to subtract the value in the formula bar rather than enter it in a cell. If the time is in cell A4, we could use the following formula to subtract 1 hour 40 minutes from it:

=A4 - TIME(1,40,0)

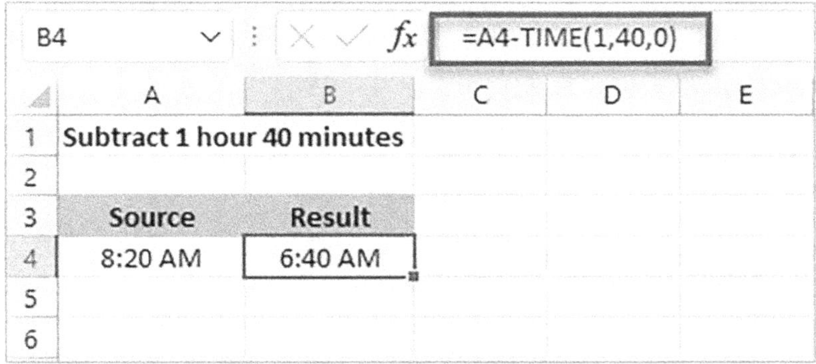

For more on date functions, see chapter 9 - Working with Functions.

Adding and Subtracting Dates

Excel now has improved native functionality for handling dates. For example, in the past, if you wanted to add several days to a date, you would need to use a specific function to make the calculation. You can now just use basic addition and subtraction, and Excel handles all the complexity behind the scenes.

Example 1

Add 40 days to 12/17/2023

1. Enter *12/17/2023* in cell A2 and *40* in cell B2.
2. Enter the formula *=A2+B2* in cell C2
3. Click Enter.

The result will be *01/26/2024*.

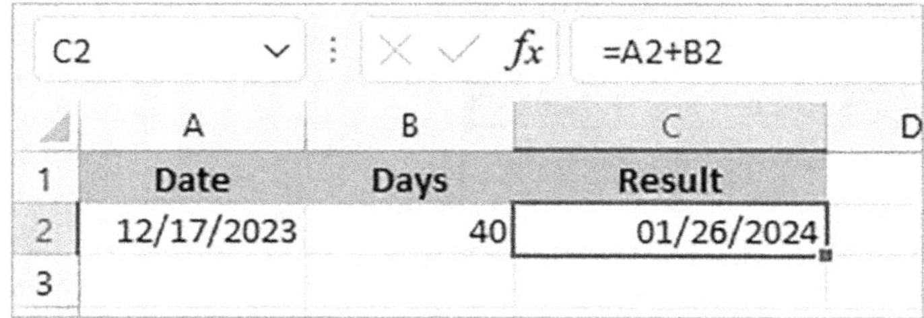

Example 2

Subtract 30 days from 12/14/2022

1. Enter *12/14/2022* in cell A2 and *30* in cell B2.
2. Enter the formula *=A2-B2* in cell C2
3. Click Enter.

The result will be *11/14/2022*.

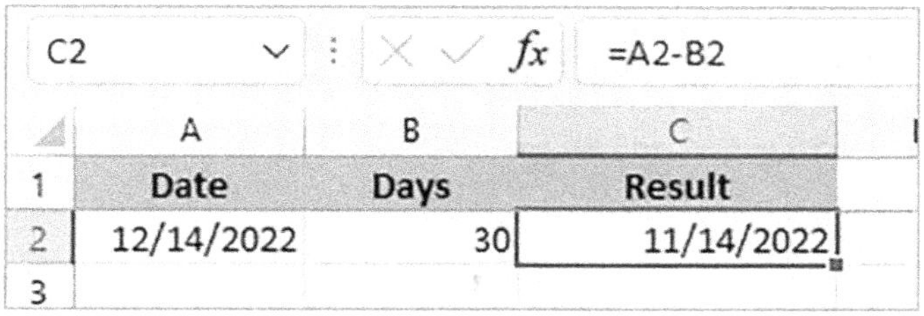

C2 =A2-B2

	A	B	C
1	Date	Days	Result
2	12/14/2022	30	11/14/2022
3			

For more on calculating dates, see chapter 9 - **Working with Functions**.

Relative and Absolute Cell Reference

Relative Cell Reference

By default, a cell reference in Excel is relative. When you refer to cell **B2** from cell **E3**, you are pointing to a cell that is three columns to the left (E minus B) and one row above (3-2). A formula with a relative cell reference changes as you copy it from one cell to another.

For example, if you copy the formula **=C2+D2** from cell E2 to E3, the formula changes to **=C3+D3**. The relative positions of the cells in the formula remain on the same columns but are one row down. When copying a formula with relative cell references, you need to be aware that the formula will change.

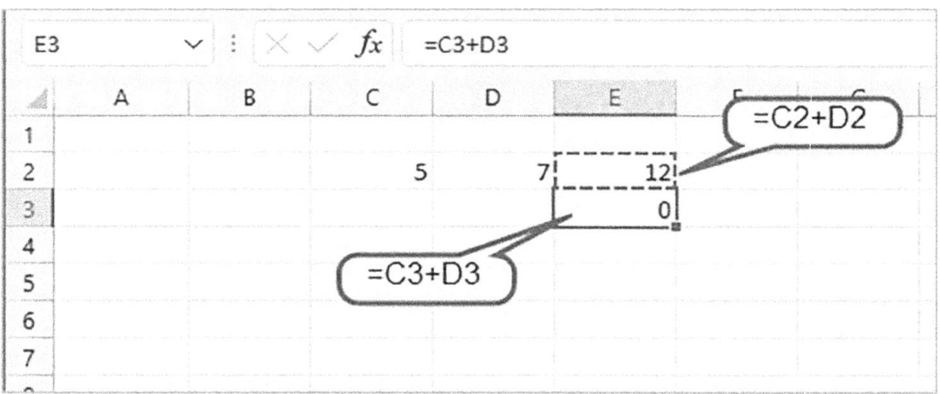

Examples of relative references:

=D2+E2

=A3*B3

Absolute Cell Reference

Suppose you want to maintain the original cell reference when copying a formula. In that case, you need to make the cell reference *absolute* by inserting a dollar sign (**$**) before the column letter and row number, for example, **=$C$2 + $D$2**. The dollar sign before the column and row tells Excel that the cell reference does not change when the formula is copied to other cells. When you copy the formula **=$C$2 + $D$2** from E2 to E3, the formula stays the same.

To convert a cell reference to an absolute reference, select the reference in the formula bar (or place the cursor between the column letter and row number) and press the **F4** key.

For example, if you have =C2 + D2 in the formula bar and want to make C2 an absolute reference, select C2 in the formula bar and press F4. Excel converts it to **$C$2**.

If you keep pressing F4, Excel cycles through the different types of cell references available as listed below:

- **Relative reference** (default): Relative columns and rows. For example, **A2**.
- **Absolute reference**: Absolute columns and rows. For example, **$A$2**.
- **Mixed reference**: Relative columns and absolute rows. For example, **A$2**.
- **Mixed reference**: Absolute columns and relative rows. For example, **$A2**.

Example

In the example below, we calculate the Sales Tax on various items. The Tax Rate of **20%** has been entered in cell B3. The cell format of B3 is **Percentage**.

The formula in cell C6 is **=B6*$B$3**.

As you can see, cell B3 in the formula has been set to an absolute reference. Thus, when we copy the formula (using autofill) to the rest of the cells under Tax (column C), the reference to cell B3 remains the same.

If the Tax Rate were to change in the future, we would only change the value in cell B3. The Tax for all the items will automatically be updated.

C6 | fx | =B6*$B$3

	A	B	C
1	**Sales Tax Calculation**		
2			
3	**Tax Rate:**	20%	
4			
5	**Product**	**Price (excl. tax)**	**Tax**
6	Item 1	$40.00	$8.00
7	Item 2	$58.00	$11.60
8	Item 3	$85.00	$17.00
9	Item 4	$47.00	$9.40
10	Item 5	$56.00	$11.20
11	Item 6	$28.00	$5.60
12	Item 7	$31.00	$6.20
13	Item 8	$65.00	$13.00
14	Item 9	$25.90	$5.18
15	Item 10	$78.30	$15.66
16	Item 11	$69.30	$13.86
17	Item 12	$56.80	$11.36
18			

Mixed Cell Reference

In some cases, you may want to use a "mixed" cell reference. You prefix either the column letter or row number with a dollar sign to lock it as an absolute reference, but allow the other to be a relative reference.

For example, **=$B2 + $C2**

This formula says the columns in cell references (B and C) are locked down as absolute, but row (2) is left free to be relative.

When this formula is copied from E4 to F5 (one column to the right and one row down), it will change to **=$B3 + $C3**. The columns remain the same, but the row changed because the formula moved down one row. You can also lock down the row and leave the column as relative, for example, **=B$2**.

Examples of mixed references:

=$D2+$E2

=A$3*$B3

Using Data from Other Worksheets

On some occasions, you may be working on one worksheet, and you want to access data on another worksheet in your formula. Or perhaps you may decide to separate your summary reports from your data using different worksheets. For example, you may want to have the raw data on **Sheet2** and the summary calculations on **Sheet1**.

Example 1

The following example has a formula in cell **A6** on **Sheet1** and grabs a value from cell **A1** on **Sheet2**.

1. Place the cell pointer in A6 on Sheet1.
2. Enter *=Sheet2!A1* in the formula bar.
3. Click **Enter**.

Excel will now reference cell A1 from Sheet2 as part of your formula in A6 on Sheet1.

Another way to reference a cell on another sheet in your formula is to select it with your mouse. Follow the steps below to reference a cell on another sheet:

1. Select **A6** on **Sheet1**.
2. Type the equal sign (=) in the formula bar.
3. Click the **Sheet2** tab (at the bottom of the window).
4. Select cell **A1** on **Sheet2**.
5. Click **Enter**.

Excel enters the reference **Sheet2!A1** automatically in cell A6 in Sheet1.

The same method applies when your reference is a range. Sometimes you may want your data on one sheet, and your summary calculations on another sheet.

If you want to reference more than one cell, like a range, click Sheet2 and select the range of cells. For example, A1:A10. The reference **Sheet2!A1:A10** will now be added to the formula bar in Sheet1. If you have a named range, you can use the range's name in place of the cell reference, for example, **Sheet2!MyRange**.

Example 2

In the following example, we have our raw data on Sheet2, and we're calculating the totals for each Quarter on Sheet1.

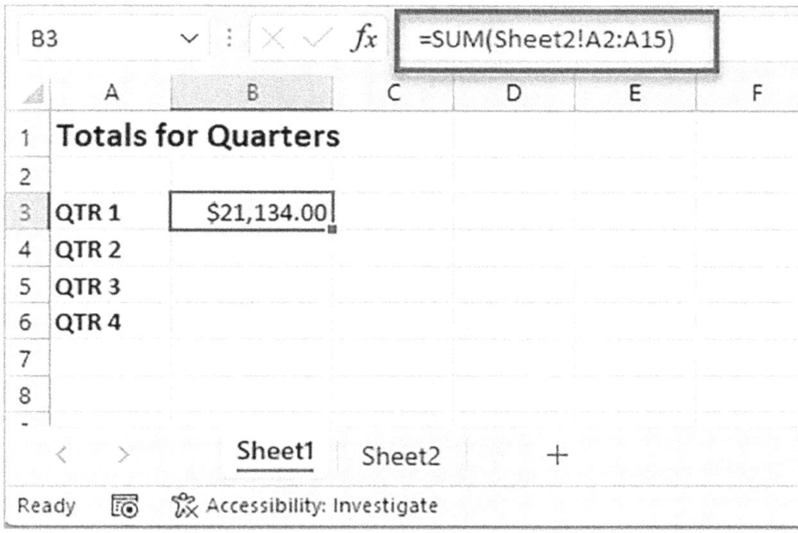

1. On **Sheet1**, select B3, and in the formula bar, enter ***=SUM(***
2. Click the **Sheet2** tab at the bottom of the window.
3. On Sheet 2, select cells **A2:A15** by selecting A2 and dragging down to A15.

   Excel adds **Sheet2!A2:A15** in the formula bar. Your syntax should now look like this **=SUM(Sheet2!A2:A15**.
4. Click in the formula bar and enter the closing bracket. Your formula should now look like this **=SUM(Sheet2!A2:A15)**.
5. Click **Enter** to confirm the entry.

The sum of the figures from A2 to B15 on Sheet2 will now be shown in sheet1.

Chapter 7

Drop-down Lists and Validation Rules

A drop-down list enables you to restrict the values users can enter in a cell to a subset of predefined values. Having a predefined list of values can help streamline workflow and minimize errors. A validation rule allows you to restrict the type of data, or the range of values users can enter into a cell. You can insert validation rules in cells to ensure the entered data meets a certain set of criteria.

In this chapter, we will cover:

- Entering data with a drop-down list.
- Creating data validation rules for cells.

Entering Data with a Drop-down List

There are occasions when you can make your worksheet more efficient by using drop-down lists in cells. Drop-down lists enable users to select an item from a list you create instead of entering their own values. On occasions where you have a defined set of values from a lookup list or column, being able to select the value directly from the source data saves time and reduces errors.

You can use a comma-delimited list or a range in your worksheet for the data source of your drop-down list.

Using a Comma-Delimited List as the Source

In the following example, we'll use a comma-delimited list for a drop-down list used to populate the grades for students. The grades we'll use as our source are - Merit, Credit, Pass, and Fail.

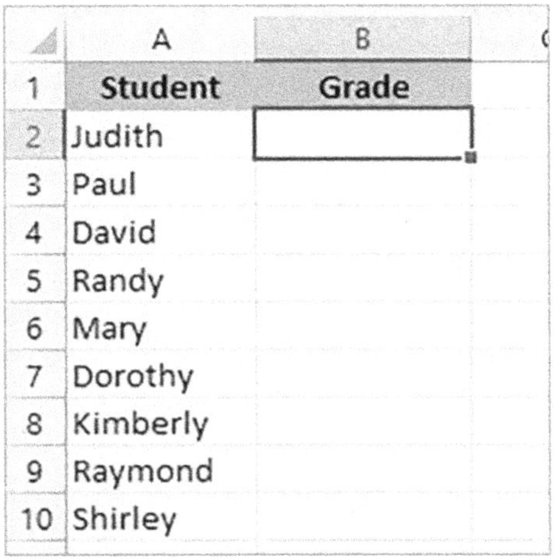

	A	B
1	**Student**	**Grade**
2	Judith	
3	Paul	
4	David	
5	Randy	
6	Mary	
7	Dorothy	
8	Kimberly	
9	Raymond	
10	Shirley	

Follow the steps below to create a drop-down list with comma-delimited values:

1. Select all the cells for which you want to add a drop-down list. For our example, we'll select B2:B10.

2. On the Ribbon, click the **Data** tab. Then click the **Data Validation** command.

3. In the Data Validation dialog box, set **Allow** to **List**.

4. Click in the **Source** box and enter your values separated by commas.

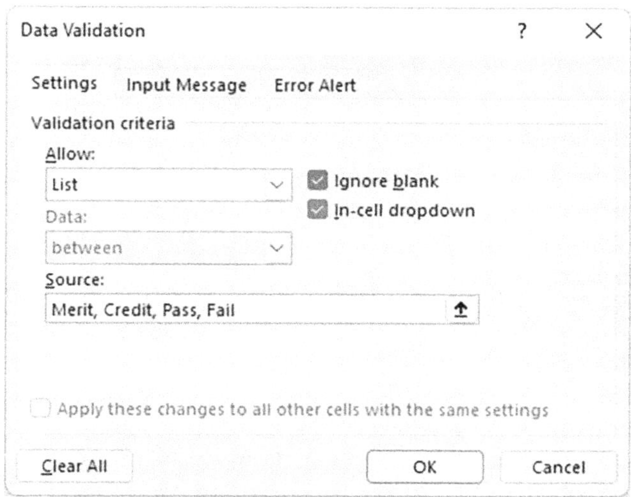

5. Click **OK**.

The selected cells now have a drop-down list.

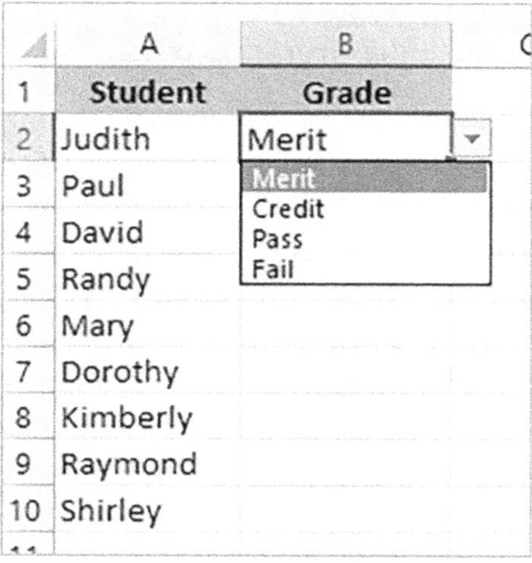

Using a Range as the Source

In the following example, the source for our drop-down list will be from a worksheet named **SalesData** in a different worksheet in the same workbook. Our drop-down list will be pulling data from the Product column (C4:C51).

	A	B	C
1	Sales		
2			
3	Date	Salesperson	Product
4	4/25/2022	Anne Hellung-Larsen	Cora Fabric Chair
5	4/26/2022	Jan Kotas	Lukah Leather Chair
6	4/27/2022	Mariya Sergienko	Habitat Oken Console Table
7	4/28/2022	Michael Neipper	Hygena Fabric Chair
8	4/29/2022	Anne Hellung-Larsen	Harley Fabric Cuddle Chair
9	4/30/2022	Jan Kotas	Windsor 2 Seater Cuddle Chair
10	5/1/2022	Mariya Sergienko	Fabric Tub Chair
11	5/2/2022	Laura Giussani	Verona 1 Shelf Telephone Table
12	5/3/2022	Anne Hellung-Larsen	Floral Fabric Tub Chair
13	5/4/2022	Jan Kotas	Fabric Chair in a Box
14	5/5/2022	Mariya Sergienko	Slimline Console Table
15	5/6/2022	Nancy Freehafer	Martha Fabric Wingback Chair
16	5/7/2022	Nancy Freehafer	Slimline Console Table
17	5/8/2022	Nancy Freehafer	Fabric Wingback Chair
18	5/9/2022	Nancy Freehafer	Fabric Chair in a Box

Follow the steps below to create the drop-down list:

1. On a blank worksheet, select the cell where you want to create the drop-down list. For example, cell B3 in a blank worksheet.
2. On the **Data** tab, in the **Data Tools** group, click the **Data Validation** command. Excel opens the **Data Validation** dialog box.
3. On the **Settings** tab, in the **Allow** box, select **List**.
4. Click in the **Source** box, then select the data range you want to display in your list.

For our example, we're selecting range C4:C51 on the SalesData worksheet. Excel will automatically enter the selected range in the Source box.

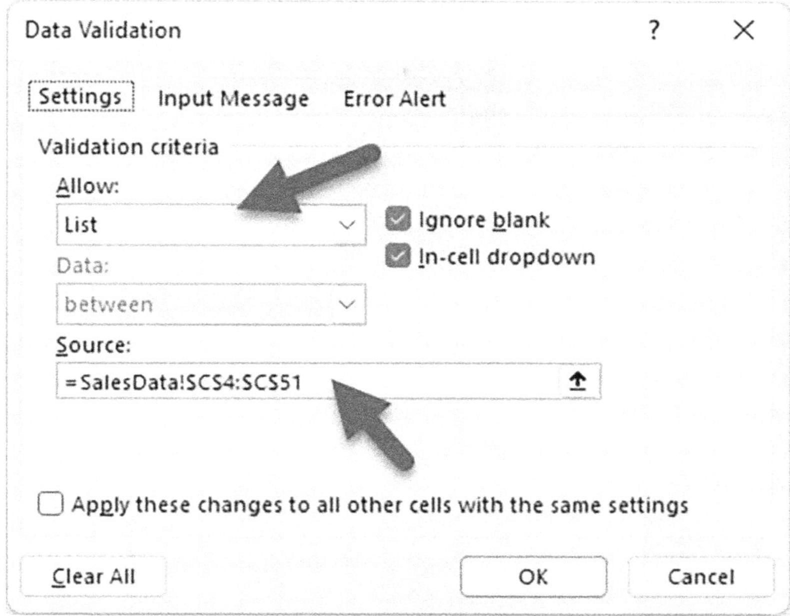

5. Click **OK** to finish creating the drop-down list.

When done, the drop-down list will display a list of values from the selected source when you click the drop-down arrow.

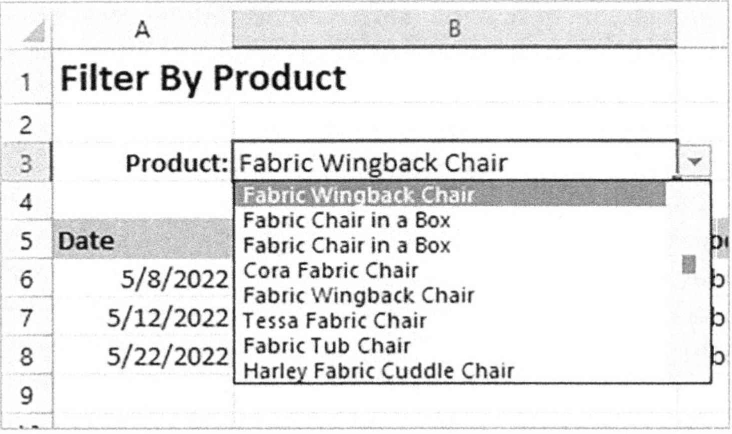
Filter By Product
Product:
Fabric Wingback Chair
Fabric Wingback Chair
Fabric Chair in a Box
Fabric Chair in a Box
Cora Fabric Chair
Fabric Wingback Chair
Tessa Fabric Chair
Fabric Tub Chair
Harley Fabric Cuddle Chair
Date
5/8/2022
5/12/2022
5/22/2022

Creating Data Validation Rules

In the following example, let's say we have a product list that is updated by different staff members, and we want to ensure data entry is consistent. The list has the following columns: **Product Code**, **Product Name**, and **Price**. We want to insert a validation rule to ensure that the **Product Code** (column A) can only be between 5 and 10 characters.

Below is an example of the list.

	A	B	C
1	**Product Code**	**Product Name**	**Price**
2	NWTB-1	Chai	18
3	NWTCO-3	Syrup	10
4	NWTCO-4	Cajun Seasoning	22
5	NWTO-5	Olive Oil	21.35
6	NWTJP-6	Boysenberry Spread	25
7	NWTDFN-7	Dried Pears	30
8	NWTS-8	Curry Sauce	40
9	NWTDFN-14	Walnuts	23.25
10	NWTCFV-17	Fruit Cocktail	39
11	NWTBGM-19	Chocolate Biscuits Mix	9.2
12	NWTJP-6	Marmalade	81
13	NWTBGM-21	Scones	10

To add a validation rule for the Product Code, do the following:

1. Select the cells for which you want to apply the rule. For our example, we select column A.

2. On the **Data** tab, in the **Data Tools** group, click the **Data Validation** command.

   Excel opens the Data Validation dialog box.

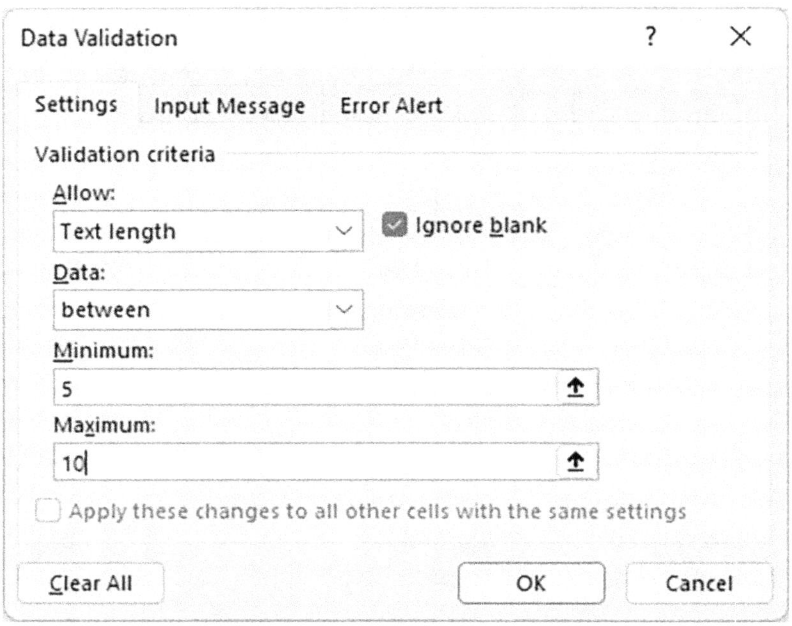

3. On the **Settings** tab, enter the following settings:
   - **Allow:** Text length
   - **Data:** between
   - **Minimum:** 5
   - **Maximum:** 10

4. On the **Input Message** tab, add a **Title** and the **Input message**.

   Excel displays this message as a small pop-up when the user clicks on a cell with the validation rule.

For this example, we can add a message like:

"The Product Code can be alphanumeric, and it should be between 5 and 10 characters."

5. On the **Error Alert** tab, we define the message to display when an entry fails the validation rule.

    - Set **Style** to **Stop**.

      The Stop icon is ideal for this scenario because a value that does not meet the validation rule cannot be entered.

    - In the **Title** box, enter: "*Invalid Entry.*"

    - In the **Error Message** box, enter**:** "*Invalid entry. Please enter a value between 5 and 10 characters in length.*"

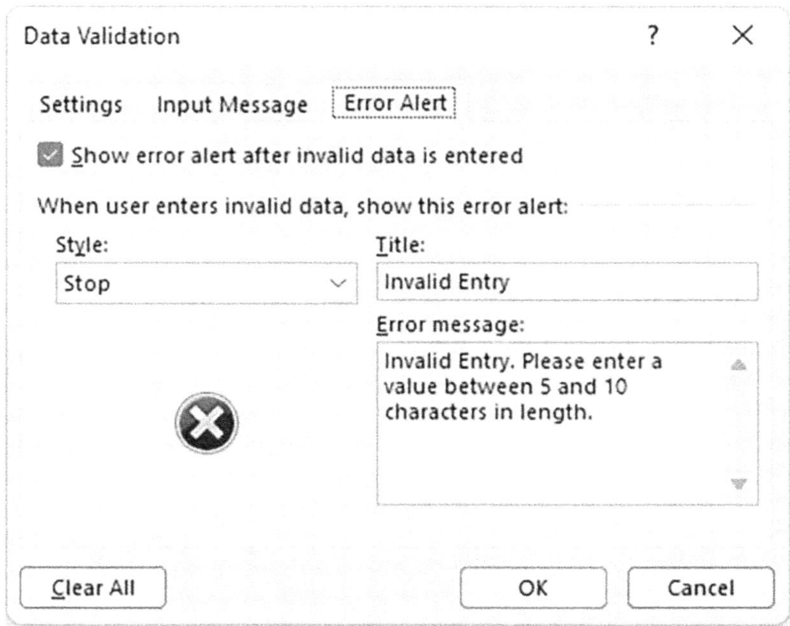

6. Once you have completed all the tabs, click **OK.**

Data validation will now be applied to the selected cells.

Editing or Removing Data Validation Rules

Occasionally you may want to change or remove data validation. To remove data validation, do the following:

1. Select the cells where data validation has been applied.
2. On the **Data** tab, in the **Data Tools** group, click the **Data Validation** command to open the Data Validation dialog box.
3. To change the validation rule, simply edit the various entries and click OK when done.
4. To remove the validation rule, click **Clear All**.
5. Click **OK**.

Chapter 8

Named Ranges

When working with a lot of data, it is sometimes useful to identify your data as a group with one name to make it easier to reference in your formulas. A named range is a group of cells in Excel selected and given one name. After you specify a name for the selection, the range can now be referenced as one unit using that name in Excel formulas and functions. A named range is similar to a table with a name but different from Excel tables.

This chapter will cover:

- Defining a named range.
- Editing and renaming a named range.
- Removing a named range.
- How to use named ranges in your formulas.

Creating a Named Range

In the following example, we have a list of contacts we would like to use in formulas. We could either use A1:G17 to identify the range of data, or we could name the range "Contacts" and then use that name to reference the data throughout our worksheet.

One of the benefits of using a named range is that Excel makes it an absolute reference by default. When you create a formula with that name, you can copy and paste the formula anywhere in your workbook, including different worksheets in the workbook, and the name will always point to the same group of cells.

There are two ways you can create a named range:

Method 1

1. Select the cells you want to include in the named range.
2. Click in the **Name** box (the box on the left side of the window, just above the worksheet area) and enter the name for your named range.
3. Press **Enter** on your keyboard to save the name.

The example below has A1:G17 defined as a named range called "Contacts" in the Name box. You can now use Contacts in place of A1:G17 in all formulas and functions in the workbook. When you create a named range using this method, the name will be available across all worksheets in your workbook.

	A	B	C	D	E	F	G
1	Company	Last Name	First Name	Job Title	Address	City	State/Province
2	Company A	Bedecs	Anna	Owner	123 1st Street	Seattle	WA
3	Company B	Gratacos Solsona	Antonio	Owner	123 2nd Street	Boston	MA
4	Company C	Axen	Thomas	Purchasing Representative	123 3rd Street	Los Angelas	CA
5	Company D	Lee	Christina	Purchasing Manager	123 4th Street	New York	NY
6	Company E	O'Donnell	Martin	Owner	123 5th Street	Minneapolis	MN
7	Company F	Pérez-Olaeta	Francisco	Purchasing Manager	123 6th Street	Milwaukee	WI
8	Company G	Xie	Ming-Yang	Owner	123 7th Street	Boise	ID
9	Company H	Andersen	Elizabeth	Purchasing Representative	123 8th Street	Portland	OR
10	Company I	Mortensen	Sven	Purchasing Manager	123 9th Street	Salt Lake City	UT
11	Company J	Wacker	Roland	Purchasing Manager	123 10th Street	Chicago	IL
12	Company K	Krschne	Peter	Purchasing Manager	123 11th Street	Miami	FL
13	Company L	Edwards	John	Purchasing Manager	123 12th Street	Las Vegas	NV
14	Company M	Ludick	Andre	Purchasing Representative	456 13th Street	Memphis	TN
15	Company N	Grilo	Carlos	Purchasing Representative	456 14th Street	Denver	CO
16	Company O	Kupkova	Helena	Purchasing Manager	456 15th Street	Honolulu	HI
17	Company P	Goldschmidt	Daniel	Purchasing Representative	456 16th Street	San Francisco	CA

Method 2

This method enables you to specify more settings as you create the named range:

1. Select the cells you want to include in the named range.

2. On the Ribbon, click the **Formulas** tab, and in the **Defined Names** group, click **Define Name**.

   Excel displays the **New Name** dialog box.

3. In the **New Name** dialog box, specify the following settings:

   - In the **Name** box, enter the name of your range.
   - Leave the **Scope** box as **Workbook** (the default) unless you want to restrict the name to the current worksheet.
   - In the **Refers to** box, check the reference that it matches your selection. You can use the up-arrow on the box to reselect the range if necessary.

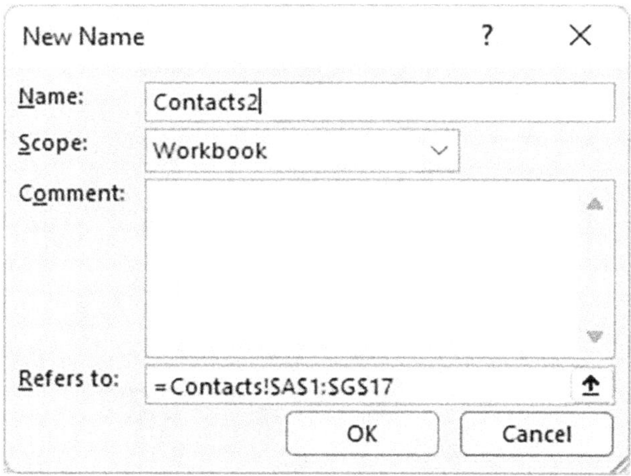

4. Click **OK** when done.

Note If you set the scope of a named range to **Workbook**, the name will be available in all worksheets in the workbook. You can't create another named range using the same name in that workbook. If the scope is set to a particular sheet, then the name can be used within the sheet only. Also, you'll be able to use that name for named ranges within the scope of other sheets.

Note Excel creates a named range that is an absolute reference by default. If you want a relative named range, remove the $ sign from the reference in the **Refers to** box. See chapter 6 for more on relative and absolute references.

Editing a Named Range

Follow the steps below to edit a named range:

1. On the **Formulas** tab, in the **Defined Names** group, click **Name Manager**.

   Excel displays the Name Manager dialog box with a list of all the named ranges and tables in the workbook.

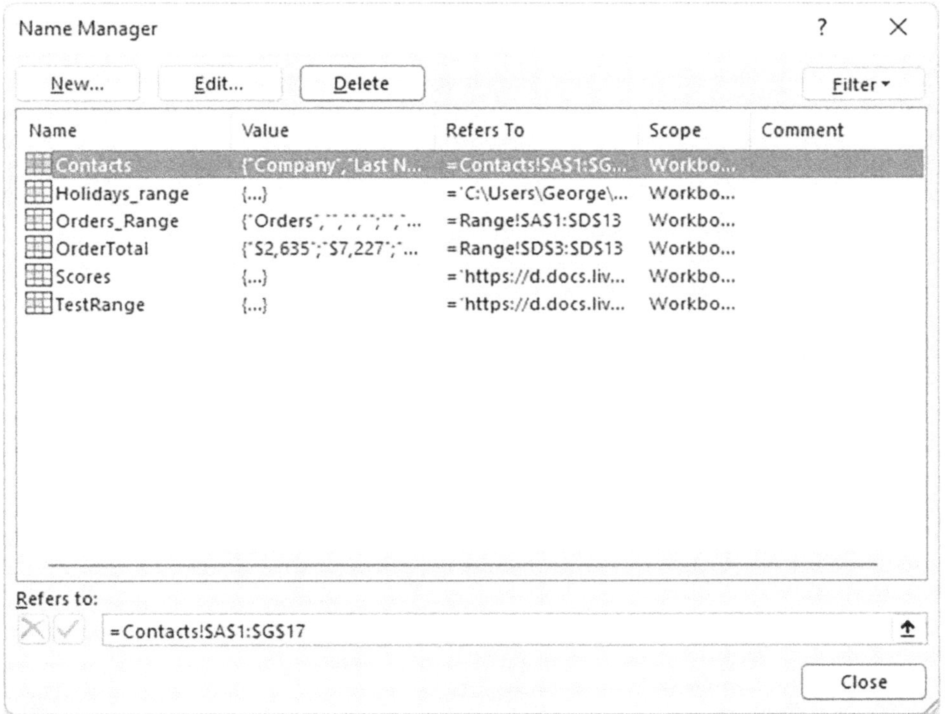

2. In the Name Manager dialog box, select the name you want to edit and click the **Edit** button.

3. In the Edit Name dialog box, enter the name in the **Name** box.

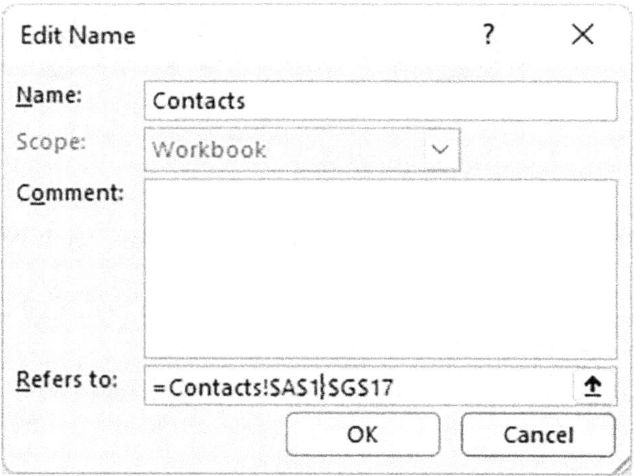

4. To change the reference, click in the **Refers to** box.

   Excel selects the current range on the worksheet, allowing you to resize it if necessary. You can adjust the current selection by holding down the **Shift** key and resizing it with your mouse.

5. Click **OK** on the Edit Name box.

6. Click **Close**.

Using a Named Range

To select a named range, click the drop-down arrow on the Name box and select the name from the drop-down list. Excel will display the worksheet with the range (if you're on a different worksheet) and select all the rows and columns in the range.

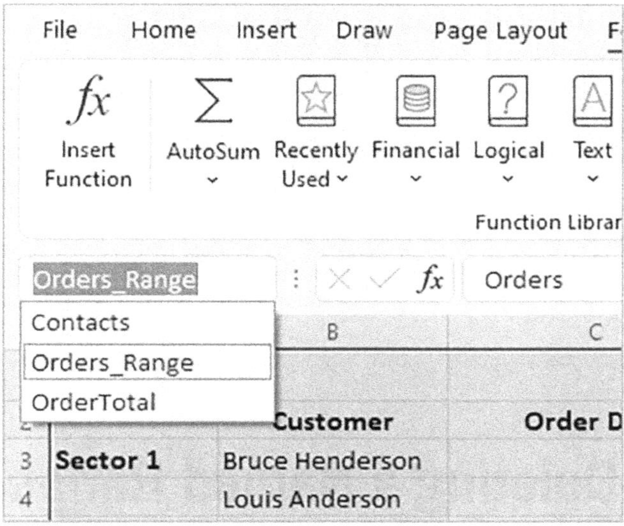

Example

The following example shows the use of two named ranges, *Orders_Range and OrderTotal,* in place of the cell references, A1:D13 and D3:D13. The formulas below use the named ranges as arguments in place of cell references.

=COUNT(Orders_Range)

=COUNTBLANK(Orders_Range)

=SUM(OrderTotal)

Orders_Range | fx Orders

	A	B	C	D	E
1	Orders				Orders_Range
2		Customer	Order Date	Order Total	
3	Sector 1	Bruce Henderson	1/15/2022	$2,635	
4		Louis Anderson	2/2/2022	$7,227	
5		Earl Foster	3/3/2022	$4,426	
6		Sean Hill	4/4/2022	$8,774	
7					OrderTotal
8	Sector 2	Benjamin Martinez	4/12/2022	$9,829	
9		Joe Perez	4/15/2022	$2,194	
10		Shawn Johnson	4/17/2022	$2,459	
11		Kenneth Roberts	5/8/2022	$3,920	
12		Cynthia Martin	5/19/2022	$2,566	
13		Susan Mitchell	6/10/2022	$7,034	
14					
15			Numeric values	20	=COUNT(Orders_Range)
16			Blank cells	16	=COUNTBLANK(Orders_Range)
17			Order Total	$51,064	=SUM(OrderTotal)
18					

Deleting a Named Range

You may need to delete names as you tidy up your workbook on some occasions. Also, a name can only be used once in a workbook, so deleting a name frees that name for reuse. Deleting a name does not delete the data. It simply removes that name as a reference from the worksheet.

Follow the steps below to delete a named range:

1. On the **Formulas** tab, click **Name Manager**.
2. Select the named range you want to delete from the list.
3. Click the **Delete** button.
4. Click **Close** when done.

Chapter 9

Working with Functions

The Excel function library is vast, ranging from basic aggregate functions to more specialized functions for statisticians, mathematicians, and engineers. This book will cover some of the most useful functions for everyday Excel tasks at home or work.

The more specialized and dedicated functions are outside the scope of this book. However, information is provided at the end of the chapter on how to access other functions in Excel.

This chapter will cover:

- Carrying out calculations with aggregate functions like SUM, AVERAGE, MIN, MAX, and COUNT.
- Creating conditional formulas with the IF function.
- Finding and returning information from a range using XLOOKUP and VLOOKUP.
- Performing date calculations using various date functions.
- Manipulating and rearranging strings with text functions.

How to Enter a Function

You enter a function in the same way you enter a formula. All functions have an opening and closing bracket, and most functions have arguments enclosed in the brackets.

A **function argument** is a piece of data that a function needs to run. Most functions need at least one argument, but a select few, like the TODAY and NOW functions, do not have arguments.

To insert a function:

1. Click in the cell where you want to display the result.
2. Click in the formula bar.
3. Enter an equal sign (=) and start typing the function name. At this point, you'll get a drop-down list with all the Excel functions related to your entry.

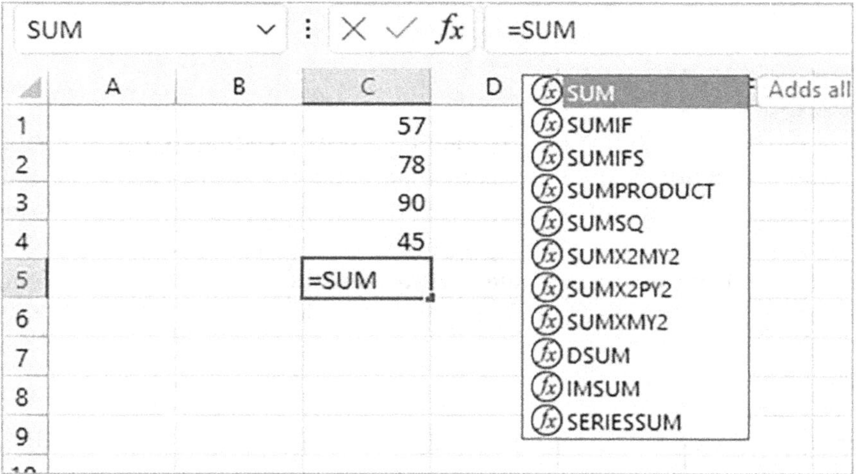

4. Use your up/down arrow keys to highlight the function you want on the list, and press the **Tab** key once to select it. Excel enters the function and the opening bracket in the formula bar, enabling you to enter the argument(s).
5. Enter the argument(s) and the closing bracket, for example, =SUM(C1:C4).

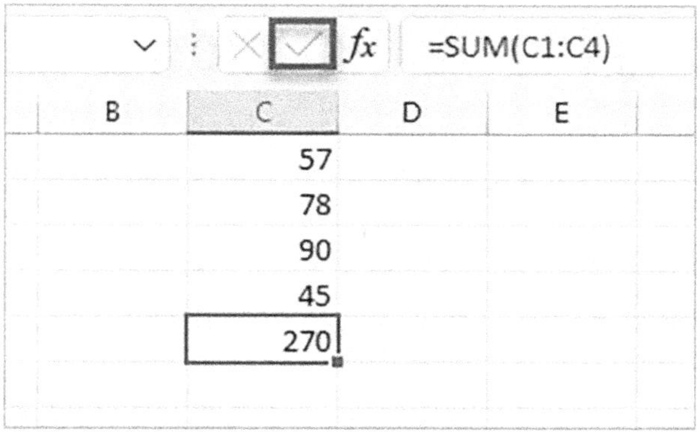

6. Click **Enter** or press the **Enter** key to confirm your entry.

Tip

As much as possible, avoid typing cell references directly into the formula bar as it could introduce errors. Instead, enter the name of the formula and the open bracket. For example, enter **=SUM(**. Then select the cells you want for your argument in the worksheet before entering the closing bracket.

Using the Insert Function Dialog Box

A second way you can enter a function is by using the **Insert Function** dialog box:

1. Click in the formula bar and click the **Insert Function** command on the **Formulas** tab or the Insert Function button next to the formula bar.

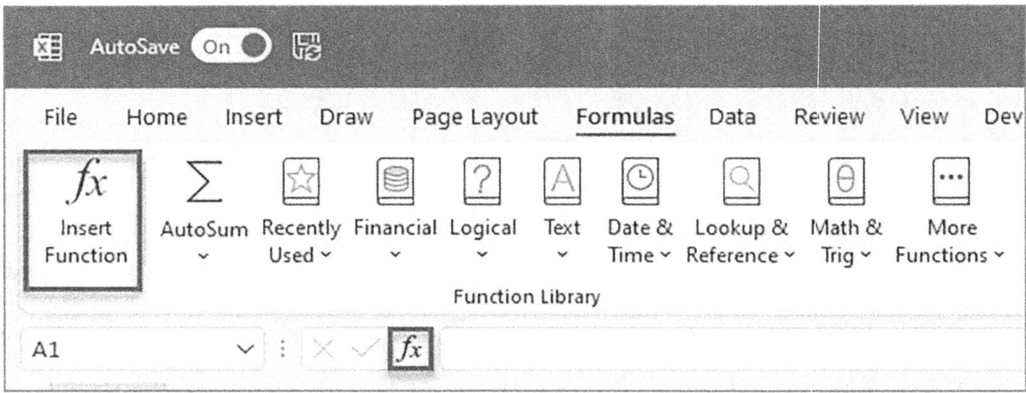

Excel displays the **Insert Function** dialog box. This dialog box provides the option to search for the function or select it from a category.

2. To search for the function, enter the function's name in the **Search for a function** box.

For example, if you're searching for the IF function, enter IF in the search box and click **Go**. The **Select a function** list will display all functions related to your search term.

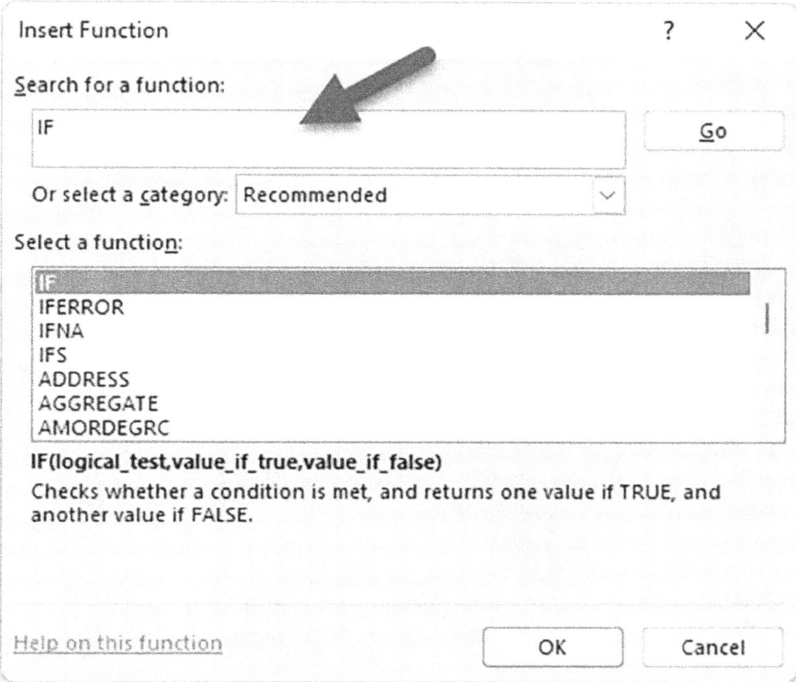

You can also use the **category** drop-down list to narrow down the functions in the list below when looking for a function in a specific category. For example, you can find the IF function in the **Logical** category.

If you have used a function recently, it'll be listed in the **Most Recently Used** category.

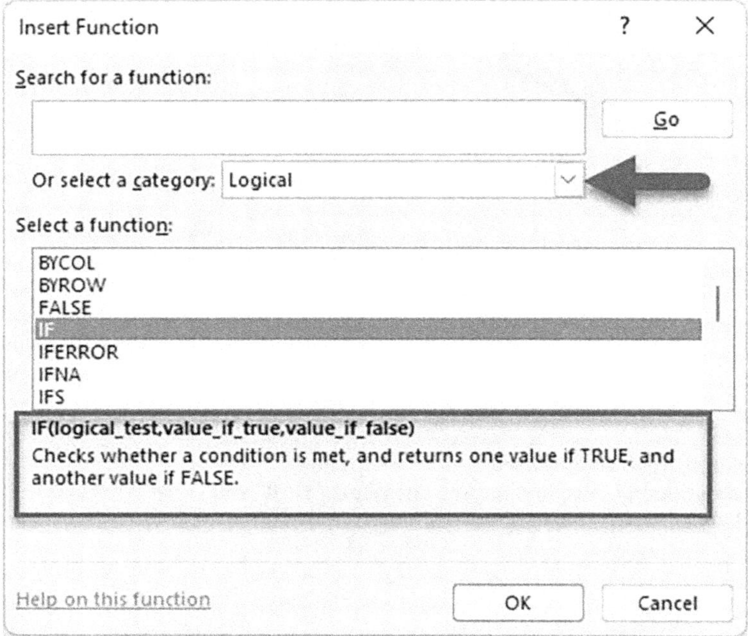

3. Select a function on the list to see the syntax and description of the function in the box below.

4. Click OK.

   Excel opens the **Function Arguments** dialog box.

5. Enter your arguments in the Function Arguments dialog box.

   The Function Arguments dialog box is particularly useful if you are unfamiliar with a particular function. It describes each argument, the results of any logical tests, and the result returned by the function.

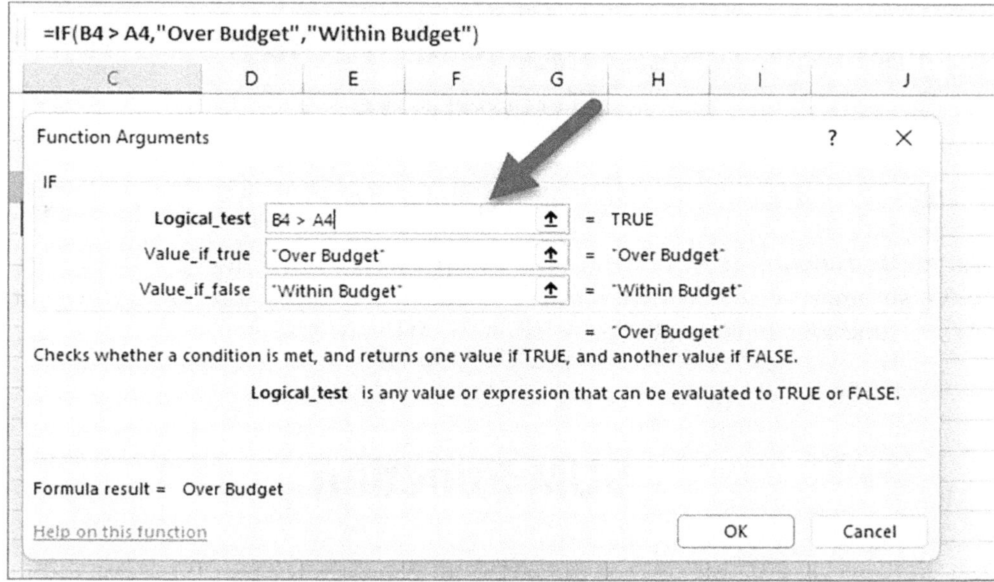

6. Click **OK** after entering the arguments.

   Excel inserts the formula in the formula bar.

Perform Aggregate Calculations with Functions

An aggregate function is a function that groups values from multiple rows into a single value. A summary can add meaning to the data depending on what you're analyzing. Aggregate functions include SUM, AVERAGE, MIN, MAX, etc.

SUM Function

The SUM function enables you to sum values in your spreadsheet. You can add individual values, cell references, ranges, or a mix of all three. You can sum up adjacent cells or non-adjacent cells.

Syntax

=SUM(number1,[number2],...)

Arguments

Argument	Description
Number1	Required. The first cell reference, range, or number for which you want to calculate the sum. The argument can be a number like 4, a cell reference like A10, or a range like A2:A10.
Number2, ...	Optional. Additional cell references, ranges, or numbers for which you want to calculate the sum, up to a maximum of 255.

Example 1 - Summing contiguous data:

This example has values in cells B2 to B13 that we want to sum up. We could either use the AutoSum command on the Ribbon or enter the formula in the formula bar:

=SUM(B2:B13)

Entering the formula manually:

1. Select the cell you want to use for the sum. In this case, it is B14.
2. Click in the formula bar and enter **=SUM(**.
3. Select B2 and drag down to B13.
4. Type **)** in the formula bar to close the function.

   The contents of the formula bar should now look like this **=SUM(B2:B13)**.
5. Click the **Enter** button or press **Enter** on your keyboard.

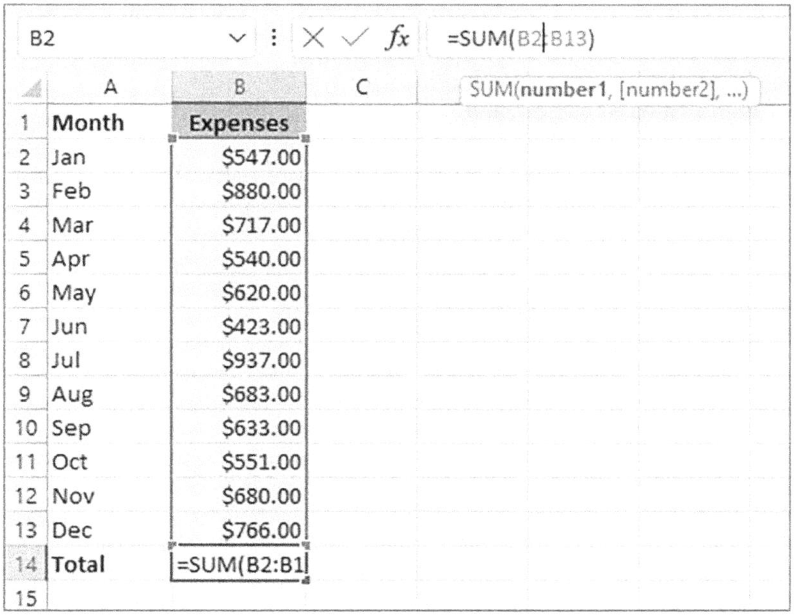

B2 =SUM(B2:B13)

SUM(number1, [number2], ...)

	A	B	C
1	**Month**	**Expenses**	
2	Jan	$547.00	
3	Feb	$880.00	
4	Mar	$717.00	
5	Apr	$540.00	
6	May	$620.00	
7	Jun	$423.00	
8	Jul	$937.00	
9	Aug	$683.00	
10	Sep	$633.00	
11	Oct	$551.00	
12	Nov	$680.00	
13	Dec	$766.00	
14	**Total**	=SUM(B2:B1	
15			

Example 2: Summing non-contiguous data:

To sum up data in different ranges, i.e., non-contiguous data, you can enter the ranges as different arguments in the SUM function.

For example:

=SUM(B2:B13,D2:D13,F2:F13,H2:H13)

Entering the formula:

1. Select the cell where you want to place the formula.
2. Click in the formula bar and type the function name with the opening bracket. For example ***=SUM(***
3. Select the first range.
4. Type in a comma i.e. ***=SUM(B2:B13,***.
5. Select the next range and type in a comma.
6. Select any additional ranges, making sure you type a comma after each range.
7. Enter the closing bracket. You should now have something like this,

   =SUM(B2:B13,D2:D13,F2:F13,H2:H13).
8. Click **Enter** to confirm your entry.

SUM | =SUM(B2:B13,D2:D13,F2:F13,H2:H13)

SUM(number1, [number2], **[number3]**, [number4

	A	B	C	D	E	F	G	H
1		**Store1**		**Store2**		**Store3**		**Store4**
2	Jan	$547.00		$934.00		$412.00		$447.00
3	Feb	$880.00		$590.00		$961.00		$605.00
4	Mar	$717.00		$961.00		$460.00		$652.00
5	Apr	$540.00		$542.00		$574.00		$754.00
6	May	$620.00		$497.00		$531.00		$462.00
7	Jun	$423.00		$874.00		$799.00		$699.00
8	Jul	$937.00		$755.00		$877.00		$446.00
9	Aug	$683.00		$715.00		$792.00		$742.00
10	Sep	$633.00		$421.00		$877.00		$576.00
11	Oct	$551.00		$941.00		$675.00		$598.00
12	Nov	$680.00		$520.00		$867.00		$916.00
13	Dec	$766.00		$524.00		$401.00		$707.00
14								
15	**Total**							F2:F13,H2:
16								

AVERAGE Function

The AVERAGE function is one of the widely used aggregate functions in Excel. It returns the average of the arguments. The average is the arithmetic mean of a series of numbers and is calculated by adding up the numbers and then dividing by the count of those numbers.

Syntax

=AVERAGE(number1, [number2], ...)

Arguments

Argument	Description
Number1	Required. The first cell reference, range, or number for which you want to calculate an average.
Number2, ...	Optional. Additional cell references, ranges, or numbers for which you want to calculate an average, up to a maximum of 255.

Notes

- Arguments can be numbers, named ranges, or cell references that contain numbers.
- AVERAGE returns an error if any of the cells referenced in the arguments contain an error value.
- Text, logical values, and empty cells are ignored, but cells with the value zero (0) are included.

Example

In the example below, we use the AVERAGE function to calculate the average of the scores in the range B2:C16.

Formula: =AVERAGE(B2:C16)

F1 fx =AVERAGE(B2:C16)

	A	B	C	D	E	F
1	**Student**	**Subject 1**	**Subject 2**		**Average score**	53.3
2	Bruce	0	55			
3	Louis	57	61			
4	Earl	51	47			
5	Sean	74	74			
6	Benjamin	50	50			
7	Joe	30	52			
8	Shawn	95	N/A			
9	Kenneth	8	70			
10	Cynthia	30	45			
11	Susan	57	40			
12	John	67	76			
13	Bruce	81	60			
14	Louis	50	61			
15	Earl	30	47			
16	Kenneth	79	50			
17						

Notice that one of the cells has N/A. That cell will be ignored and not counted as part of the average.

MAX, MIN, MEDIAN Functions

The MAX, MIN, and MEDIAN functions are some of the most used functions in Excel and are very similar in their arguments and how they're used. MAX returns the largest number in a specified set of values. MIN returns the smallest number in a set of values. MEDIAN returns the median, which is the number in the middle of a set of numbers.

Syntax

=MAX(number1, [number2], ...)

=MIN(number1, [number2], ...)

=MEDIAN(number1, [number2], ...)

Arguments (similar for all three functions)

Argument	Description
Number1	Required. The first argument is required and can be a number, range, array, or reference that contains numbers.
number2, ...	Optional. You can have additional numbers, cell references, or ranges up to a maximum of 255 arguments that you want to evaluate.

Remarks

- If the arguments contain no numbers, these functions return 0 (zero).
- If an argument is a reference or an array, only numbers in that reference or array are used. Logical values, text values, and empty cells in the reference or array are ignored.
- If arguments contain error values or text that cannot be translated into numbers, the functions will return an error.
- Text representations of numbers and logical values that you directly type into the arguments list are counted.

- The MEDIAN function will calculate the average of the two middle numbers if there is an even number of numeric arguments.

Example

In the example below, we want to show the maximum, minimum, and median values for the Sales column (D2:D12) in our table.

The following formulas return the desired results:

- =MAX(D2:D12)
- =MIN(D2:D12)
- =MEDIAN(D2:D12)

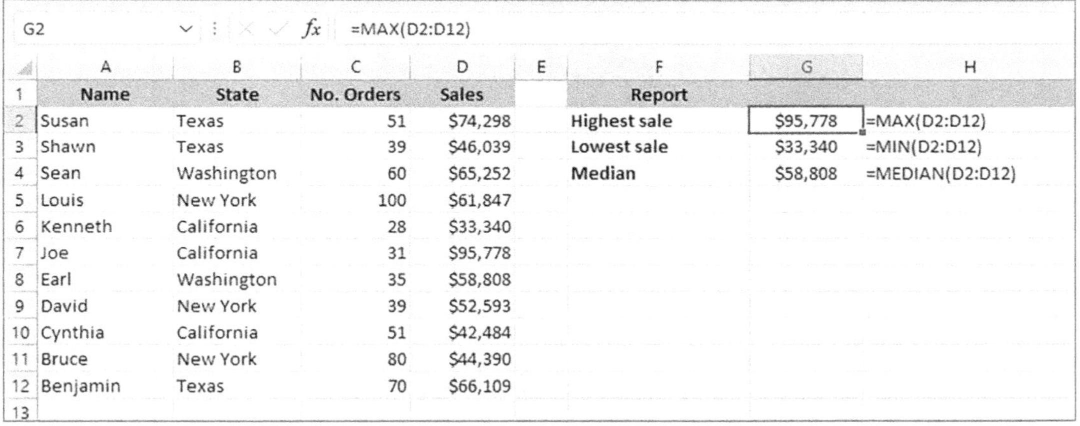

	A	B	C	D	E	F	G	H
1	Name	State	No. Orders	Sales		Report		
2	Susan	Texas	51	$74,298		Highest sale	$95,778	=MAX(D2:D12)
3	Shawn	Texas	39	$46,039		Lowest sale	$33,340	=MIN(D2:D12)
4	Sean	Washington	60	$65,252		Median	$58,808	=MEDIAN(D2:D12)
5	Louis	New York	100	$61,847				
6	Kenneth	California	28	$33,340				
7	Joe	California	31	$95,778				
8	Earl	Washington	35	$58,808				
9	David	New York	39	$52,593				
10	Cynthia	California	51	$42,484				
11	Bruce	New York	80	$44,390				
12	Benjamin	Texas	70	$66,109				
13								

To add more cell references or ranges to the list of arguments, separate them with a comma, for example, MAX(C1:C5, G1:G5).

COUNT Function

The COUNT function will count the number of cells that contain numbers in a range or a list of numbers provided as arguments. The COUNT function only counts populated cells. For example, if you have a range with 20 cells, and only 5 of the cells have numbers, the count function will return 5.

Syntax

=COUNT(value1, [value2], ...)

Arguments

Argument	Description
Value1	Required. The first range in which you want to count numbers.
Value2	Optional. Additional cell references or ranges in which you want to count numbers. You can have a maximum of 255 arguments for this function.

Remarks

- Each argument could be a number, a cell reference, or a range.
- The COUNT function counts numbers, dates, or text representations of numbers (i.e., a number enclosed in quotation marks, like "1").
- Cells with error values or text that can't be translated into numbers are not counted.
- Use the COUNTIF or COUNTIFS function when only counting numbers that meet a certain condition.

Example

In this example, we use the COUNT function to count the values in two ranges.

The formula is:

=COUNT(A3:D20,F3:I20)

Here, we have a simple formula with two arguments to represent the two ranges we want to count: A3:D20 and F3:I20. Note that the blank cells are not counted.

L2 fx =COUNT(A3:D20,F3:I20)

	A	B	C	D	E	F	G	H	I	J	K	L
1		2021					2022					
2	QTR1	QTR2	QTR3	QTR4		QTR1	QTR2	QTR3	QTR4		Count	131
3	70	83	16	37		26	56	47	17			
4	73	71	88	52		87	57	36	87			
5	38	65		19		38	50	51	68			
6	87	56	91	55		62	40	26	77			
7	18	97	39	82			98	98	25			
8	86	15		85		47	59	60	61			
9	28		98	86		41	19	10	11			
10	45	80	43	73			92	95	59			
11	60	92	98	34		51	38	13	91			
12	51	64	25	50		81	84		60			
13	79	29	69	27		62	69	17	65			
14	65	54	95	22		73	53	40	67			
15	91		10	91		66		83	74			
16	88	97	91	89		48	58	78	25			
17	40	88		15		66	12	55	85			
18	12	54	22	87		59	10	66	20			
19	42	17	51	33			67		26			
20	78			32		52	32	62	61			
21												

Creating Conditional Formulas

A conditional function requires a test before carrying out one of two calculations. If the test evaluates to TRUE, it executes one statement, and if the test is FALSE, it executes a different statement. The statements can be calculations, text, or even other functions.

A conditional formula requires:

- The logical test to carry out.
- What to return if the test evaluates to TRUE.
- What to return if the test evaluates to FALSE.

Conditional functions can also be nested if we have more than one test to perform.

IF Function

The IF function is the most popular conditional function in Excel. The IF function allows you to perform a logical test with an expression using comparison operators. The function returns one value if the expression is TRUE and another if FALSE.

Syntax:

=IF(logical_test, value_if_true, [value_if_false])

Arguments

Argument	Description
logical_test	Required. A value or expression that can be TRUE or FALSE.
value_if_true	Required. The value returned if the logical test is true.
value_if_false	Optional. The value returned if the logical test is false. If the logical test is FALSE and this argument is omitted, nothing happens.

In its simplest form, this is what the function says:

IF (something is TRUE, then do A, otherwise do B)

Therefore, the IF function will return a different result for TRUE and FALSE.

Entering IF with Insert Function

If you're new to the IF function, you could use the **Insert Function** dialog box to enter the function. This process provides a wizard that guides you through entering the function arguments, enabling you to see if your logical test produces the expected result.

The **Function Arguments** dialog box lets you debug your logical tests and fix errors before inserting the function.

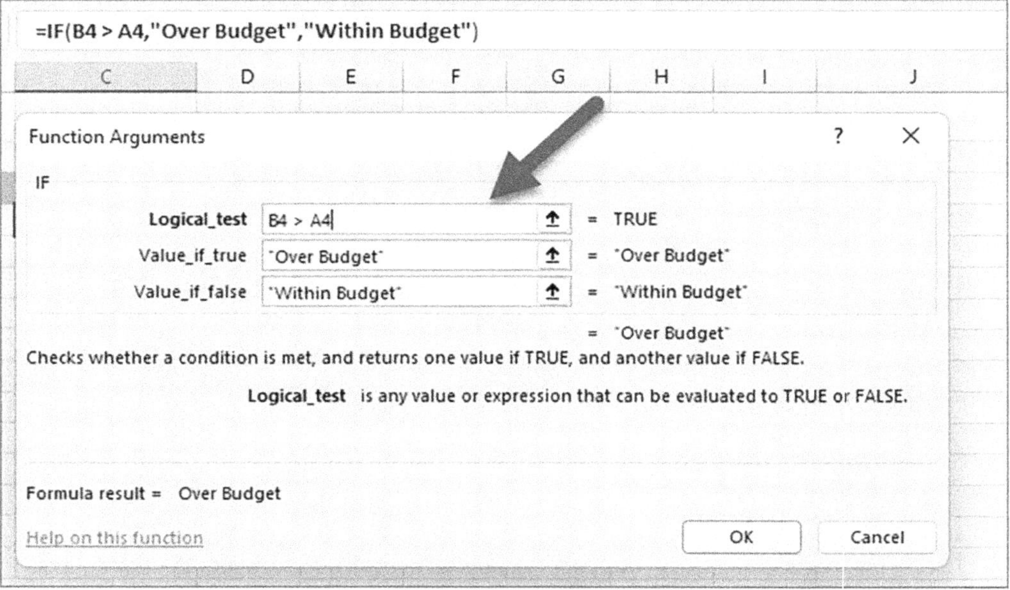

See the section, **How to Enter a Function** earlier in this chapter for how to use the Insert Function feature.

Example 1

A common way the IF function is used is to determine if a calculated cell has any value or not. If the result is false, then it returns a blank cell.

In the example below, the formula for the total for **Jan** was entered in cell **I2.** We then autofill the formula for the other cells in the column covering Feb to Dec. Without the IF function, Excel would display $0 for the unpopulated months. We want the totals for the unpopulated months to be blank instead of $0, even with the formula in place.

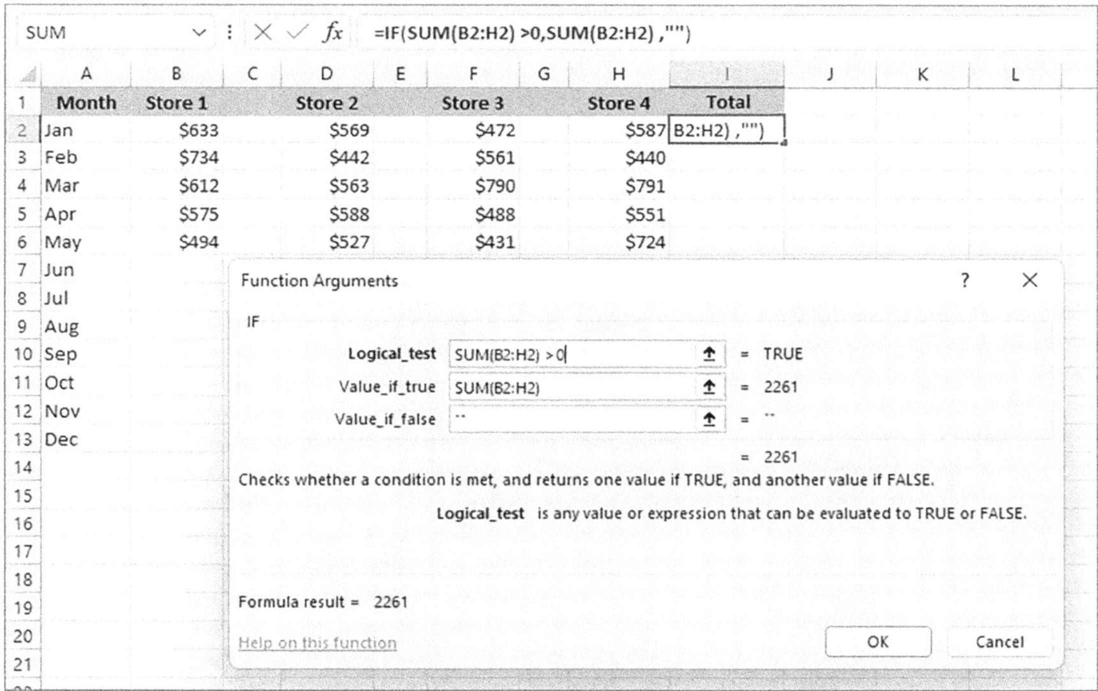

Thus, the formula for Jan in cell **I2** is:

=IF(SUM(B2:H2) >0,SUM(B2:H2) ,"")

The IF function in this example checks to see if the sum of Jan is greater than zero. If true, it returns the sum. If it is false, then it returns a blank string.

When we populate the other fields with the formula, we get the following.

I2 | =IF(SUM(B2:H2) >0,SUM(B2:H2),"")

	Month	Store 1	Store 2	Store 3	Store 4	Total
2	Jan	$633	$569	$472	$587	$2,261
3	Feb	$734	$442	$561	$440	$2,177
4	Mar	$612	$563	$790	$791	$2,756
5	Apr	$575	$588	$488	$551	$2,202
6	May	$494	$527	$431	$724	$2,176
7	Jun					
8	Jul					
9	Aug					
10	Sep					
11	Oct					
12	Nov					
13	Dec					

Example 2

In another example, we could use the results of an evaluation to return different values in our worksheet. The following budget report has a **Status** column that reports whether a project is within or over budget.

We can use an IF statement to test whether the actual figure is greater than the budgeted figure. If **Actual** is greater than **Budgeted**, the formula returns **Over Budget**. Otherwise, it returns **Within Budget**.

C4 =IF(B4 > A4,"Over Budget","Within Budget")

	A	B	C	D	E	F
1	**Expenses**					
2						
3	**Budgeted**	**Actual**	**Status**			
4	$138,000	$140,050	Over Budget			
5	$132,000	$132,000	Within Budget			
6	$157,000	$160,040	Over Budget			
7	$193,000	$193,574	Over Budget			
8	$360,000	$360,854	Over Budget			
9	$332,000	$332,717	Over Budget			
10	$229,000	$229,010	Over Budget			
11	$230,000	$220,244	Within Budget			
12	$263,000	$253,409	Within Budget			
13	$215,000	$245,183	Over Budget			
14	$373,000	$343,749	Within Budget			
15	$173,000	$183,769	Over Budget			
16	$361,000	$311,880	Within Budget			
17						

=IF(B2 > A2,"Over Budget", "Within Budget")

The IF function checks whether the value in B2 is greater than the value in A2. If true, the formula returns **Over Budget.** Otherwise, the formula returns **Within Budget**.

Example 3

In another example, we have products for sale, and when **ten or more** of a product is purchased, we apply a **10%** promotional discount.

The logical test checks if C4 is greater than or equal to 10.

If true, the formula returns the subtotal minus 10%.

If false, the formula returns the subtotal.

=IF(C4>=10,D4 - (D4 * 0.1),D4)

When we populate the other cells with the AutoFill handle (a + sign that appears when you place the mouse pointer on the lower-right corner of the active cell), we get the following result (shown in the image below).

E4 | fx | =IF(C4>=10,D4 - (D4 * 0.1),D4)

	A	B	C	D	E	F
1	**Sales**					
2						
3	**Product**	**Cost**	**Qty**	**Sub total**	**Total (with discount)**	**Formulatext**
4	Beer	$1.50	15	$22.50	$20.25	=IF(C4>=10,D4 - (D4 * 0.1),D4)
5	Brownie Mix	$4.20	10	$42.00	$37.80	=IF(C5>=10,D5 - (D5 * 0.1),D5)
6	Cake Mix	$4.80	10	$48.00	$43.20	=IF(C6>=10,D6 - (D6 * 0.1),D6)
7	Chai	$1.80	10	$18.00	$16.20	=IF(C7>=10,D7 - (D7 * 0.1),D7)
8	Chocolate Biscuits Mix	$5.20	5	$26.00	$26.00	=IF(C8>=10,D8 - (D8 * 0.1),D8)
9	Coffee	$2.00	25	$50.00	$45.00	=IF(C9>=10,D9 - (D9 * 0.1),D9)
10	Green Tea	$2.00	50	$100.00	$90.00	=IF(C10>=10,D10 - (D10 * 0.1),D10)
11	Scones	$4.90	5	$24.50	$24.50	=IF(C11>=10,D11 - (D11 * 0.1),D11)
12	Tea	$1.30	20	$26.00	$23.40	=IF(C12>=10,D12 - (D12 * 0.1),D12)
13						
14						
15	***Apply a 10% discount if the quantity sold per item is 10 or more.**					
16						

Nested IF Functions

You can use an IF function as an argument inside another IF function. This kind of formula is called a nested IF statement.

If you need to carry out more than one logical test in your function, you might require a nested IF statement. In the example below, we use a nested IF statement to test for three possible values and return a different result for each one.

Let's say we have a spreadsheet to record the score of exams, and we want to mark everything under 40 as FAIL, between 40 and 69 as CREDIT, and 70 or more as MERIT.

The formula would look like this:

=IF(B2 < 40, "FAIL",IF(B2 < 70,"CREDIT","MERIT"))

C2 =IF(B2 < 40, "FAIL",IF(B2 < 70,"CREDIT","MERIT"))

	A	B	C
1	Student	Mark	Grade
2	Judith	67	CREDIT
3	Paul	57	CREDIT
4	David	51	CREDIT
5	Randy	74	MERIT
6	Mary	50	CREDIT
7	Dorothy	30	FAIL
8	Kimberly	95	MERIT
9	Raymond	8	FAIL
10	Shirley	30	FAIL
11	Gary	57	CREDIT
12	Lori	67	CREDIT
13	Fred	81	MERIT
14	Virginia	50	CREDIT
15	Cheryl	30	FAIL
16	Ruth	79	MERIT

Formula explanation:

The first IF function checks if B2 is less than 40. If it is true, it returns FAIL. If it is false, it executes the second IF function.

The second IF function checks if B2 is less than 70. If true, it returns CREDIT, and if false, it returns MERIT.

Advanced IF Functions

Excel also includes several other conditional functions you could use in place of the standard IF function. These functions are a combination of a logical function and an aggregate function. These are known as advanced IF functions, hence outside the scope of this book regarding in-depth coverage.

To learn more about advanced If functions, enter the function name in the Search box on Excel's title bar, and select *Get Help on [function name]* from the pop-up menu.

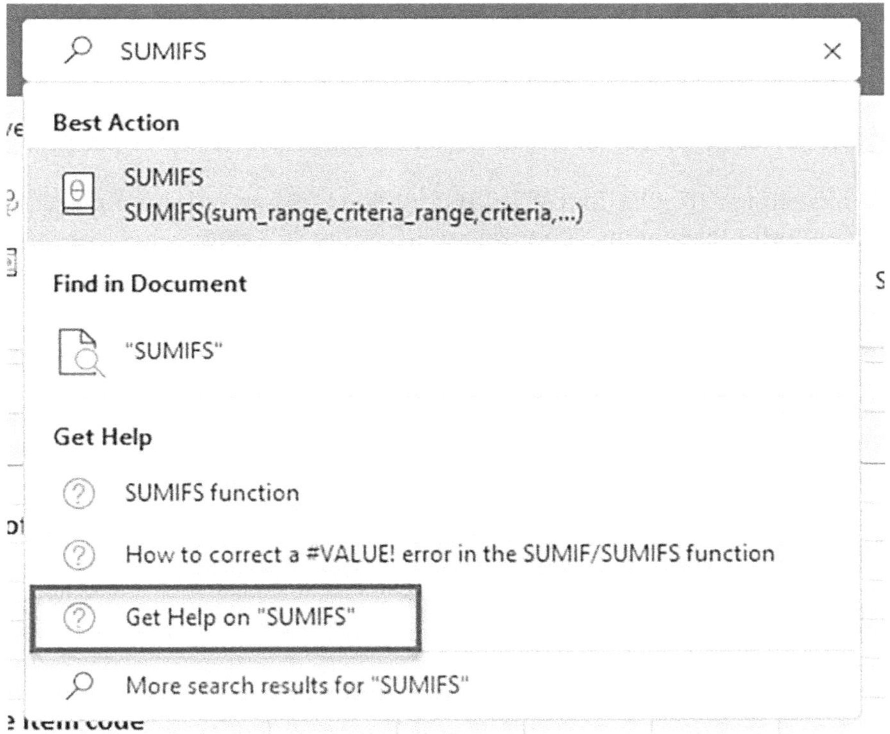

AVERAGEIF

Syntax:

=AVERAGEIF(range, criteria, [average_range])

This function returns the average (arithmetic mean) of data that meets the value you've entered as your criteria. The optional *average_range* argument allows you to specify another range for the values if it is separate from the one with the criteria.

Example:

=AVERAGEIF(A2:A20,"<2000")

This formula returns the average of all the values in cells A2 to A20 over 2000.

AVERAGEIFS

Syntax:

=AVERAGEIFS(average_range, criteria_range1, criteria1, [criteria_range2, criteria2], ...)

This function is similar to AVERAGEIF, but it allows you to specify multiple ranges and multiple criteria in the arguments. You can specify up to 127 ranges and criteria.

COUNTIF

This function returns the count of the values in a range that meets the specified criteria.

Syntax:

=COUNTIF(range, criteria)

In its simplest form, this function says:

=COUNTIF(Where do you want to look?, What do you want to look for?)

Example:

=COUNTIF(A2:A10, "New York")

This formula will return the count of the number of cells in A2:A10 with the value "New York."

COUNTIFS

COUNTIFS(criteria_range1, criteria1, [criteria_range2, criteria2]…)

This function is like the COUNTIF function in that it returns a count based on a condition you specify. However, you can specify multiple ranges and criteria. You can specify up to 127 range/criteria pairs.

SUMIF

This function returns the sum of values in a range based on the specified criteria.

Example:

=SUMIF(A2:A10, ">10")

This formula returns the sum of all the values in cells A2 to A10 greater than 10.

SUMIFS

Syntax:

SUMIFS(sum_range, criteria_range1, criteria1, [criteria_range2, criteria2], ...)

This function returns the sum of values that meet multiple criteria. You can specify up to 127 range/criteria pairs.

Calculate Dates with Functions

Date functions enable you to calculate and manipulate dates and times. In this section, we will be covering the most common date functions for general use.

Note that you can now perform some date calculations in Excel without using functions. Some date calculations that previously required a function can now be done in Excel using arithmetic operators. See chapter 6 on Calculating Date and Time for more. The date convention used in the following examples is **m/d/yyyy**.

Note Excel sometimes automatically detects a date entry and formats the cell accordingly. However, if you copied and pasted a date from another source, you may need to manually set the cell to a date format to display the date properly.

Add and Subtract Dates Using the DATE Function

The DATE function enables you to combine different values into a single date.

Syntax

=DATE (year, month, day)

Arguments

Argument	Description
Year	Required. This argument can have one to four digits. Excel uses the Date & time settings on your computer to interpret the year argument.
Month	Required. The month argument should be a positive or negative integer between 1 to 12, representing January to December.
Day	Required. This argument can be a positive or negative integer from 1 to 31, representing the day of the month.

Notes:

- If the month argument is a negative number (-*n*), the function returns a date that is *n* months back from the last month of the previous year. For example, =DATE(2024,-4,2) will return the serial number representing August 2, 2023.
- If the month argument is greater than 12, the function adds that number of months to the last month of the specified year. If Day is greater than the number of days in the specified month, the function adds that number of days to the first day of the next month of the specified date.

Tip To prevent unwanted results, always use four digits for the year argument. For example, "04" could mean "1904" or "2004." Using four-digit years prevents any confusion.

Example 1

In this example, we want to combine values from different cells for the month, day, and year into a date value recognized in Excel.

- Month: 4
- Day: 14
- Year: 1980

When we use the DATE function to combine the values into a single date, we get the following:

=DATE(C2,A2,B2)

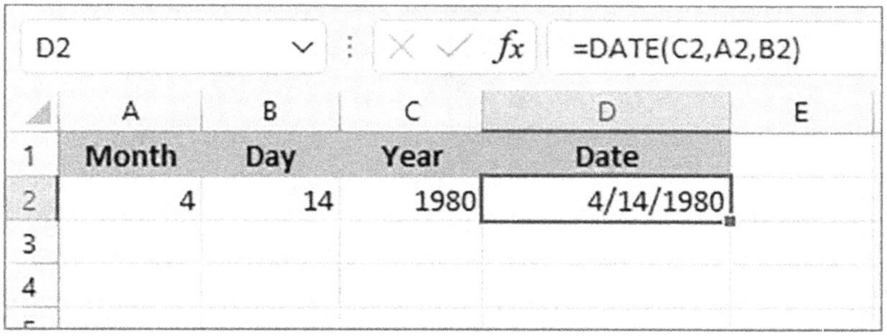

D2 =DATE(C2,A2,B2)

	A	B	C	D	E
1	Month	Day	Year	Date	
2	4	14	1980	4/14/1980	
3					
4					

Example 2

The following example calculates contract dates for different durations. We can combine the YEAR, MONTH, and DAY functions
with the DATE function to perform these calculations.

Function	Description
YEAR(serial_number)	Returns the year corresponding to a date entered as its argument.
MONTH (serial_number)	Returns the month corresponding to a date entered as its argument.
DAY (serial_number)	Returns the day corresponding to a date entered as its argument.

When we combine these functions with the DATE function, we can perform the following date calculations:

- Add 5 years to 12/15/2022.
- Add 15 months to 12/15/2022.
- Add 60 days to 12/15/2022.

The image below shows the formulas used to perform these calculations.

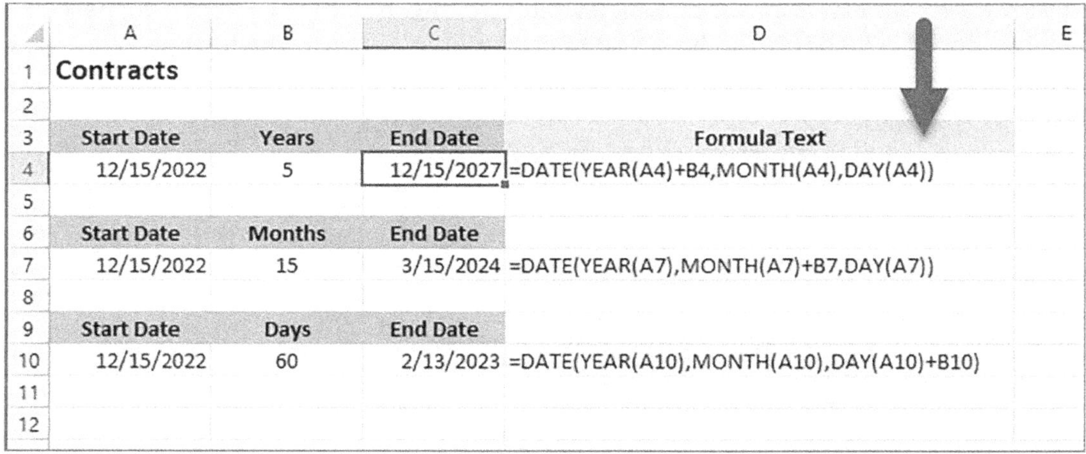

	A	B	C	D	E
1	Contracts				
2					
3	Start Date	Years	End Date	Formula Text	
4	12/15/2022	5	12/15/2027	=DATE(YEAR(A4)+B4,MONTH(A4),DAY(A4))	
5					
6	Start Date	Months	End Date		
7	12/15/2022	15	3/15/2024	=DATE(YEAR(A7),MONTH(A7)+B7,DAY(A7))	
8					
9	Start Date	Days	End Date		
10	12/15/2022	60	2/13/2023	=DATE(YEAR(A10),MONTH(A10),DAY(A10)+B10)	
11					
12					

Formula Explanation

Add 5 years to 12/15/2022

=DATE(YEAR(A4)+B4,MONTH(A4),DAY(A4))

The **year** argument of the DATE function has **YEAR(A4)+B4** (i.e., 2022 + 5, which returns 2027). The other nested functions return the month and day respectively in the **month** and **day** arguments. To subtract years, use the minus sign (**–**) in place of the plus sign (**+**) in the formula.

Add 15 Months to 12/15/2022

=DATE(YEAR(A7),MONTH(A7)+B7,DAY(A7))

In this formula, **MONTH(A7)+B7** adds 15 months to the start date. The other nested functions return the year and day respectively in the year and day arguments of the DATE function. To subtract months, use the – sign in place of the + sign in the formula.

Add 60 days to 12/15/2022

=DATE(YEAR(A10),MONTH(A10),DAY(A10)+B10)

In this formula, **DAY(A10)+B10** adds 60 days to the start date. The other nested functions return the year and month respectively in the year and month arguments of the DATE function. To subtract days, use the – sign in place of the + sign in the formula.

Calculate the Difference Between Two Dates Using DATEDIF

The DATEDIF function calculates the difference between two dates. This function provides one of the easiest ways in Excel to calculate the difference between two dates. It can return the number of days, months, or years between two dates.

DATEDIF is a "hidden" function in Excel because you'll not find it on the list of date functions or when you search for it using the Insert Function dialog box. You must enter it manually any time you want to use it. It is a legacy function from Lotus 1-2-3 but operational on all versions of Excel.

Syntax

=DATEDIF(start_date, end_date, unit)

Arguments

Argument	Description
start_date	Required. This argument represents the start date of the period.
end_date	Required. This argument represents the end date of the period.
unit	Required. This argument represents the unit of measurement you want to return - days, months, or years. It should be entered as a string. It can be one of Y, M, D, YM, or YD. "Y" = Calculates the number of years in the period. "M" = Calculates the number of months in the period. "D" = Calculates the number of days in the period. "YM" = Calculates the difference between the months in start_date and end_date. The days and years of the dates are ignored. "YD"= Calculates the difference between the days of start_date and end_date. The years of the dates are ignored.

Note An "MD" argument also calculates the number of days while ignoring the month and years. However, Microsoft no longer recommends using the MD argument in this function because, under some conditions, it could return a negative number.

Example 1

In the example below, we want to calculate the age of someone born on December 26, 1980. Combining the DATEDIF function with the TODAY function gets the desired result.

Formula:

=DATEDIF(A2,TODAY(),"Y")

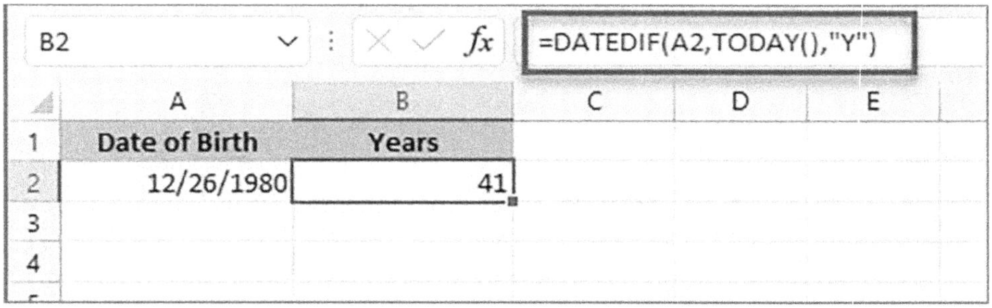

B2 | fx =DATEDIF(A2,TODAY(),"Y")

	A	B	C	D	E
1	Date of Birth	Years			
2	12/26/1980	41			
3					
4					

The TODAY function returns today's date, so this formula will always use the current date to calculate the age. Using "Y" for the unit argument returns the difference in years.

Example 2

To calculate the number of months between two dates, enter "M" in the unit argument of the function.

=DATEDIF(A2,B2,"M")

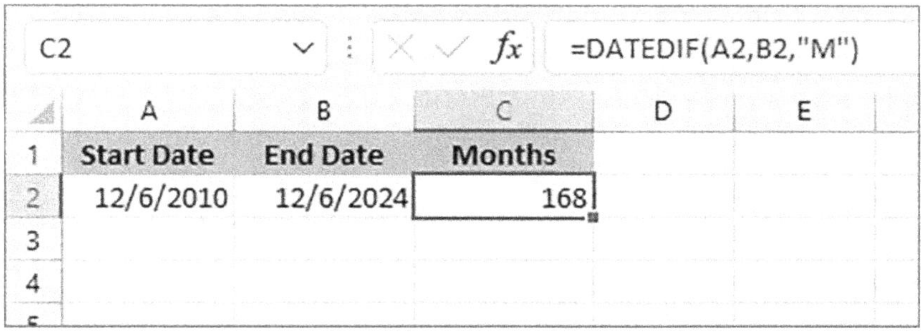

C2 =DATEDIF(A2,B2,"M")

	A	B	C	D	E
1	Start Date	End Date	Months		
2	12/6/2010	12/6/2024	168		
3					
4					

Calculate the Days Between Two Dates Using the DAYS Function

The DAYS function returns the number of days between two dates.

Syntax

=DAYS (end_date, start_date)

Arguments

Argument	Description
start_date	Required. This argument represents the start date of the period.
end_date	Required. This argument represents the end date of the period.

Example

In this example, we want to calculate the number of days between two dates, December 6, 2023, and December 5, 2024.

Formula:

=DAYS(B2, A2)

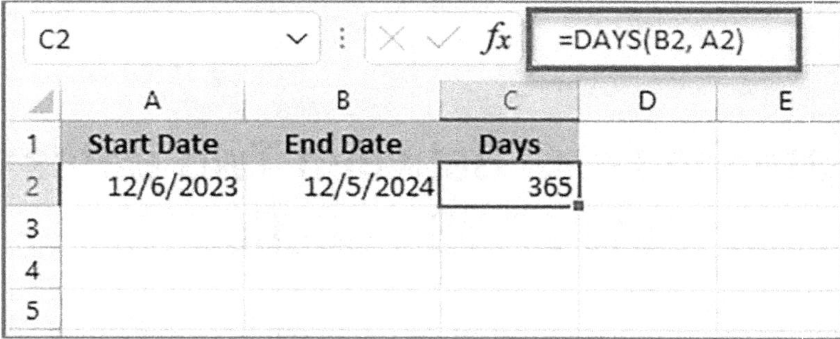

If you're entering the dates directly into the formula bar, you must enclose them in quotation marks.

For example:

=DAYS("11/30/2024","12/01/2023") will return 365 days.

Lookup and Reference Functions

Find Data with XLOOKUP

XLOOKUP is a fairly new function introduced as a replacement for the VLOOKUP function. Like its predecessor, XLOOKUP searches a range or an array and returns a value corresponding to the first match it finds on the same row in another range.

For instance, you can look up the **Price** of a product in a data list using the **Product ID** or **Name**. Similarly, you can return an employee's name using their employee ID. If XLOOKUP does not find a match, you can tell it to return the closest (approximate) match.

Unlike VLOOKUP, which only allows you to return values from a column to the right of the lookup range, XLOOKUP can return values from columns to the left or the right of the lookup range. XLOOKUP also returns exact matches by default, making it easier and more convenient than its predecessor.

Note The XLOOKUP function was introduced in 2020 and is available in Excel for Microsoft 365 and Excel 2021. If you're using an older perpetual license version of Excel, XLOOKUP will not be available.

Syntax:

=XLOOKUP(lookup_value, lookup_array, return_array, [if_not_found], [match_mode], [search_mode])

Arguments and Descriptions

Argument	Description
lookup_value	Required. What value are you searching for? Excel will look for a match for this value in the *lookup_array*. You can provide a value here or a cell reference containing the value you want to find.
lookup_array	Required. Where do you want to search? This value is the lookup range containing the columns you want to include in your search, for example, A2:D10.
return_array	Required. Which range contains the values you want to return? This value is the return range. The return range can have one or more columns as XLOOKUP is about to return more than one value.
[if_not_found]	Optional. This optional argument enables you to enter a piece of text to return if a valid match is not found. If this argument is omitted and a valid match is not found, XLOOKUP will return the #N/A error.
[match_mode]	Optional. This optional argument enables you to specify a match mode from four options: 0 (or omitted) = Exact match. If no match is found, Excel returns an error (#N/A), the default if you omit this argument. -1 - Exact match or the next smallest item if an exact match is not found. 1 - Exact match or the next largest item if an exact match is not found. 2 - Performs a wildcard match where you can use the characters *, ?, and ~ for wildcard searches.
[search_mode]	Optional. This optional argument enables you to specify the order in which you want to perform the search: 1 (or omitted) - Search first to last. This setting is the default if this argument is omitted.

	-1 - Perform the search in reverse order - last to first. 2 - Perform a binary search for data sorted in ascending order. If lookup_array is not sorted in ascending order, invalid results will be returned. -2 - Perform a binary search for data sorted in descending order. If lookup_array is not sorted in descending order, invalid results will be returned.

Tip

Regarding the **search_mode** argument, in earlier versions of Excel, performing binary searches on sorted lists produced quicker results, but in Microsoft 365, non-binary searches are equally fast. Hence, it is no longer beneficial to use binary search options for sorted lists. Using 1 or -1 for the search_mode argument is easier because you don't require a sorted table.

Vertical Lookup

In this example, we are using XLOOKUP to return the Reorder Level of the product entered in cell F1. The formula is in cell F2.

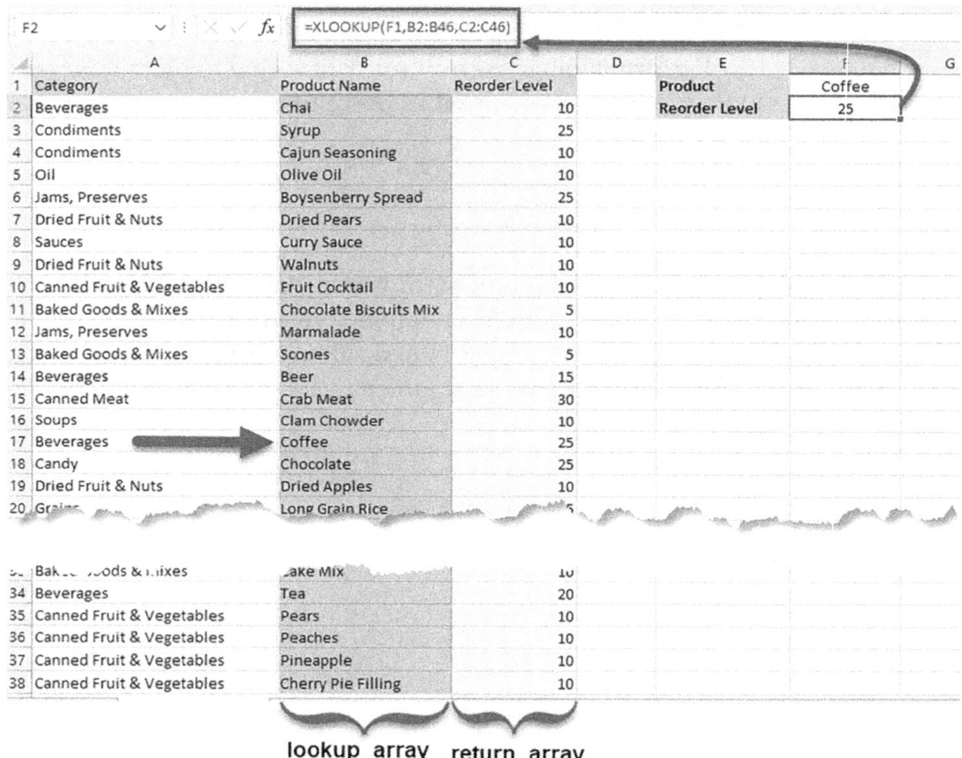

	A	B	C	D	E	F
1	Category	Product Name	Reorder Level		Product	Coffee
2	Beverages	Chai	10		Reorder Level	25
3	Condiments	Syrup	25			
4	Condiments	Cajun Seasoning	10			
5	Oil	Olive Oil	10			
6	Jams, Preserves	Boysenberry Spread	25			
7	Dried Fruit & Nuts	Dried Pears	10			
8	Sauces	Curry Sauce	10			
9	Dried Fruit & Nuts	Walnuts	10			
10	Canned Fruit & Vegetables	Fruit Cocktail	10			
11	Baked Goods & Mixes	Chocolate Biscuits Mix	5			
12	Jams, Preserves	Marmalade	10			
13	Baked Goods & Mixes	Scones	5			
14	Beverages	Beer	15			
15	Canned Meat	Crab Meat	30			
16	Soups	Clam Chowder	10			
17	Beverages	Coffee	25			
18	Candy	Chocolate	25			
19	Dried Fruit & Nuts	Dried Apples	10			
20	[illegible]	Long Grain Rice	[illegible]			
[illegible]	[illegible]	[illegible]	[illegible]			
34	Beverages	Tea	20			
35	Canned Fruit & Vegetables	Pears	10			
36	Canned Fruit & Vegetables	Peaches	10			
37	Canned Fruit & Vegetables	Pineapple	10			
38	Canned Fruit & Vegetables	Cherry Pie Filling	10			

Formula explanation:

=XLOOKUP(F1,B2:B46,C2:C46)

The formula says, in range B2:B46, find the value in cell F1 (which in this case is "Coffee") and return the value on the same row in range C2:C46.

The *if_not_found* argument has not been provided here, so if a match is not found, it will return an error which is the default behavior.

The VLOOKUP equivalent of this formula would look like this:

=VLOOKUP(F1,B2:C46,2,0)

One benefit of using the XLOOKUP equivalent over this formula is that if we decide at some point to insert a column between columns B and C, it will not break the formula.

The lookup_array does not need to be sorted because XLOOKUP will return an exact match by default.

Horizontal Lookup

XLOOKUP can perform both vertical and horizontal lookups. So, you can also use it in place of the HLOOKUP function.

In the example below, we can retrieve the value associated with a month using the month.

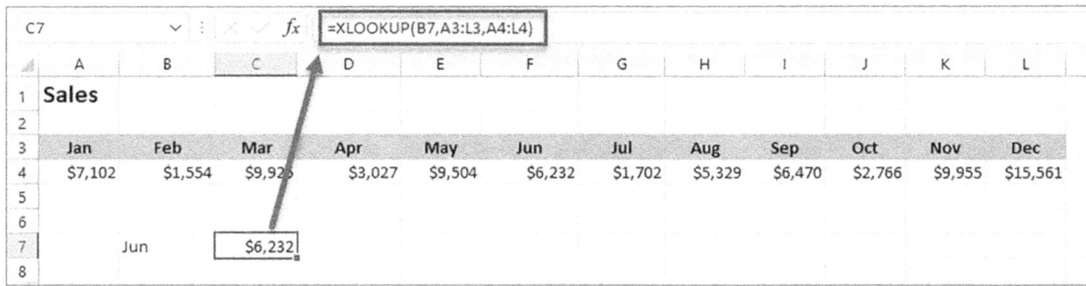

C7
=XLOOKUP(B7,A3:L3,A4:L4)
Sales
Jan Feb Mar Apr May Jun Jul Aug Sep Oct Nov Dec
$7,102 $1,554 $9,92 $3,027 $9,504 $6,232 $1,702 $5,329 $6,470 $2,766 $9,955 $15,561
Jun
$6,232

=XLOOKUP(B7,A3:L3,A4:L4)

The formula uses only the first three arguments of the XLOOKUP function. B7 is the lookup_value, A3:L3 is the lookup_array, and A4:L4 is the return_array.

Note that a horizontal lookup_array must contain the same number of columns as the return_array.

Simultaneous Vertical and Horizontal Lookup

This example will use two XLOOKUP functions to perform both a vertical and horizontal match. Here, the formula will first look for a "Mark" in range A4:A15, then look for "Q3" in the top row of the table (range B3:E3) and return the value at the intersection of the two. Previously, you would need to use the INDEX/MATCH/MATCH combination to achieve the same result.

I4 | fx | =XLOOKUP(G4,A4:A15,XLOOKUP(H4,B3:E3,B4:E15))

	A	B	C	D	E	F	G	H	I
1	**Sales data**								
2									
3	Salesperson	Q1	Q2	Q3	Q4				
4	Penny	17,526	23,972	61,066	22,596		Mark	Q3	19,062
5	Leslie	49,405	36,646	21,899	62,629				
6	Sally	78,658	16,529	14,976	68,184				
7	Shaun	80,176	84,918	66,561	65,326				
8	Julie	86,988	29,692	30,197	80,960				
9	Velma	94,514	13,333	78,000	59,718				
10	Ian	23,183	21,547	40,408	57,767				
11	Cassandra	70,597	19,615	54,664	68,175				
12	Mark	16,832	91,907	19,062	[illegible]				
13	Kathy	45,446	14,638	52,312	92,069				
14	Renee	34,583	78,213	21,295	26,964				
15	Judith	18,689	91,081	66,795	96,860				

Formula explanation:

=XLOOKUP(G4,A4:A15,XLOOKUP(H4,B3:E3,B4:E15))

The first XLOOKUP function has the following arguments:

- lookup_value = G4
- lookup_array = A4:A15
- return_array = XLOOKUP(H4,B3:E3,B4:E15)

The second XLOOKUP, executed first, performs a horizontal search on B3:E3, using the value in cell H4 ("Q3") as the lookup_value, then returns the range **D4:D15**. Notice that the second XLOOKUP returns a range rather than a value. This range is used as the return_array argument for the first XLOOKUP.

So, after the second XLOOKUP has been executed, the first XLOOKUP will look like this:

=XLOOKUP(G4,A4:A15,D4:D15)

Examining the Formula with the Evaluate Formula Command

To examine how the formula performs the task, you can use the **Evaluate Formula** command to see how each formula part is evaluated.

Follow the steps below to open the Evaluate Formula dialog box:

1. Select the cell with the formula you want to evaluate. In this case, it is cell **I4**.
2. On the Formulas tab, in the **Formula Auditing** group, click the **Evaluate Formula** command button.
3. In the Evaluate Formula dialog box, click the **Evaluate** button until the nested XLOOKUP function has been evaluated and its result displayed in the formula.

   For this example, we need to click the Evaluate button three times.

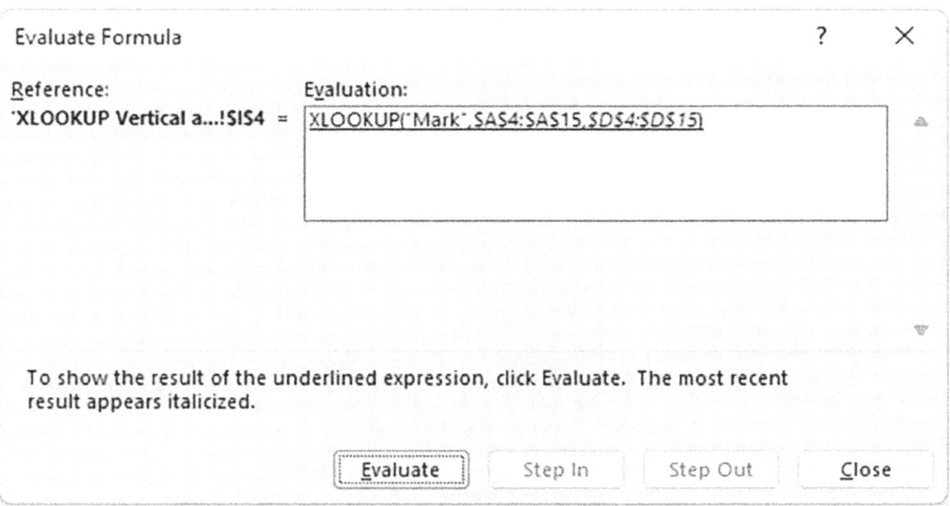

You will notice that the second XLOOKUP performs a search using the lookup_value, "Q3", and then returns the range **D4:D15** (displayed as an absolute reference **$D$4:D15**). We can use XLOOKUP here as the *return_array* argument of the first XLOOKUP function because XLOOKUP can return a range and value.

Next, the main XLOOKUP performs a lookup using the value in cell G4, "Mark" as the lookup_value, cells A4:A15 as the lookup_array, and cells D4:D15 as the return_array to return the final result.

Return Multiple Values with Horizontal Spill

In this example, we want to be able to enter the name of a sales rep and return the number of orders and sales associated with them. Hence, the function will return more than one value. XLOOKUP is also an array function in that it can return an array of values from the return_array.

In the formula below, the lookup_value is in cell G2, the *lookup_array* argument is range A2:A12, and the *return_array* argument is range C2:D12.

H2 =XLOOKUP(G2,A2:A12,C2:D12)

	A	B	C	D	E	F	G	H	I
1	Name	State	# Orders	Sales			Name	# Orders	Sales
2	Bruce	New York	51	$74,298			Bruce	51	$74,298
3	Louis	New York	39	$46,039					
4	Earl	Washington	60	$65,252					
5	Sean	Washington	100	$61,847					
6	Benjamin	Texas	28	$33,340					
7	Joe	California	31	$95,778					
8	Shawn	Texas	35	$58,808					
9	Kenneth	California	39	$52,593					
10	Cynthia	California	51	$42,484					
11	Susan	Texas	80	$44,390					
12	David	New York	70	$66,109					

Horizontal spill

Formula explanation:

=XLOOKUP(G2,A2:A12,C2:D12)

As you can see from the formula, the return_array contains columns C and D. When we enter the name "Bruce" in cell G2, XLOOKUP returns the values in columns C and D from the same row. As the function returns more than one value, the result spills into cell I2.

The range containing the spilled result has a blue border around it, which is how you can tell that the result has spilled into other cells.

Return Multiple Values with Vertical Spill

To get the formula to spill vertically, we can use another example where we need to return the sales for more than one person on our list.

In this example, we first use the FILTER function to generate a filtered list of names based in **New York**. The function returns an array of names that spill vertically in the range G2:G4.

G2 =FILTER(A2:A12,B2:B12="New York")

	A	B	C	D	E	F	G	H
1	Name	State	# Orders	Sales			Name	Sales
2	Bruce	New York	51	$74,298			Bruce	
3	Louis	New York	39	$46,039			Louis	
4	Earl	Washington	60	$65,252			David	
5	Sean	Washington	100	$61,847				
6	Benjamin	Texas	28	$33,340				
7	Joe	California	31	$95,778				
8	Shawn	Texas	35	$58,808				
9	Kenneth	California	39	$52,593				
10	Cynthia	California	51	$42,484				
11	Susan	Texas	80	$44,390				
12	David	New York	70	$66,109				
13								

Next, we want to get the **Sales** associated with the names on our filtered list and insert them in column H. To do this, we use XLOOKUP in cell H2 and select cells G2:G4 for our lookup_value argument.

When you select the *lookup_value* (G2:G4), XLOOKUP will recognize the range as a dynamic array and denote that with a hash (#) in the formula.

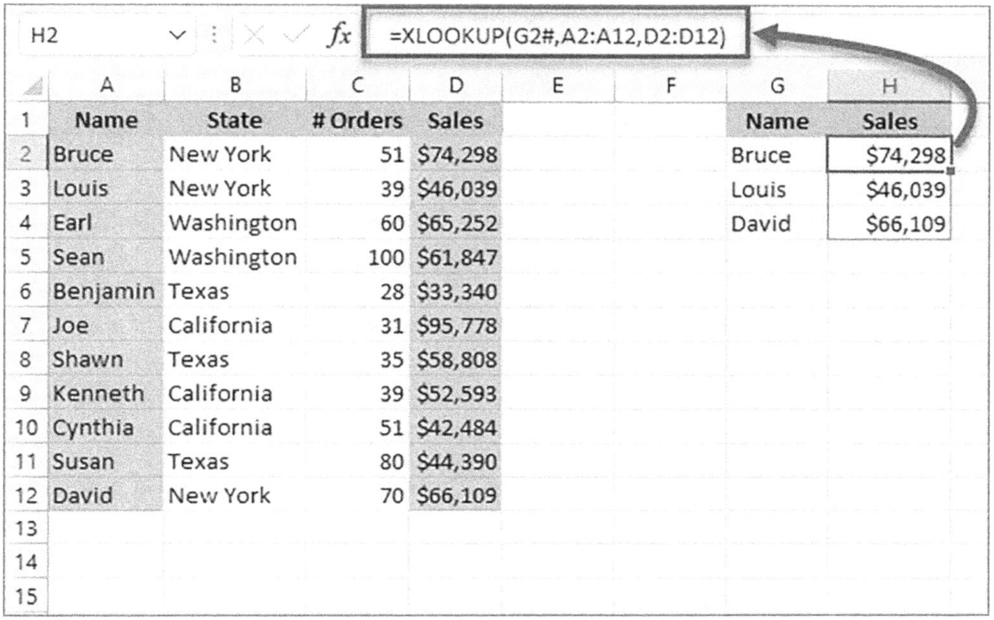

H2 =XLOOKUP(G2#,A2:A12,D2:D12)

	A	B	C	D	E	F	G	H
1	Name	State	# Orders	Sales			Name	Sales
2	Bruce	New York	51	$74,298			Bruce	$74,298
3	Louis	New York	39	$46,039			Louis	$46,039
4	Earl	Washington	60	$65,252			David	$66,109
5	Sean	Washington	100	$61,847				
6	Benjamin	Texas	28	$33,340				
7	Joe	California	31	$95,778				
8	Shawn	Texas	35	$58,808				
9	Kenneth	California	39	$52,593				
10	Cynthia	California	51	$42,484				
11	Susan	Texas	80	$44,390				
12	David	New York	70	$66,109				
13								
14								
15								

Formula explanation:

=XLOOKUP(G2#,A2:A12,D2:D12)

The lookup_value argument in the formula is G2#.

G2# (note the hash) designates the entire range of the spill data. It tells us that G2 is the starting point of the array of values returned from a dynamic array formula.

The lookup_array is the Name column (A2:A12), and the return_array is the Sales column (D2:D12).

When you type in the formula in cell H2 and press Enter, XLOOKUP will return all the sales related to the names in the dynamic array in column G. As we have more than one value, it will spill down vertically in column H2.

One benefit of using XLOOKUP is that the formula will adjust to the dynamic array in column G. If we change the filter and add more names to column G, the formula in cell H2 would still work in finding the values corresponding to the new names. We don't have to worry about copying the formula down to additional cells.

Common XLOOKUP Errors and Solutions

#N/A error

If an exact match is not found, and the **if_not_found** and **match_mode** arguments are omitted, XLOOKUP will return an #N/A error.

There may be scenarios where you will not know if your formula will generate this error, for example, when a formula is copied to multiple cells in a column. If you want to catch and replace this error with a meaningful message, specify it in the **if_not_found** argument.

For example:
=XLOOKUP(F2,B2:B12,D2:D12,"Item not found")

#VALUE! error

This error is often generated because the lookup and return arrays are not the same length. When you get this error, check that these ranges are the same length. If you are carrying out a vertical lookup, they should have the same number of rows. If the lookup is horizontal, they should have the same number of columns.

#NAME? in cell

This error usually means that there is an issue with a cell reference. A typo in the cell reference or omitting the colon can generate this error. When you get this error, check your cell references. To help avoid errors and typos in cell references, select them on the worksheet with your mouse rather than typing them in the formula.

#REF! error

If XLOOKUP is referencing another workbook that is closed, you will get a #REF! error. Ensure all workbooks referenced in your formula are open to avoid this error.

#SPILL! Error

When returning multiple values, if there is already data in the spill range, Excel returns the #SPILL! error. To avoid this error, ensure there is no data in the range that will contain the returned results.

Find Data with VLOOKUP

VLOOKUP is still one of the most popular lookup functions in Excel despite the introduction of XLOOKUP. If you intend to share your workbook with people using older versions of Excel without XLOOKUP, you might want to use VLOOKUP for looking up data. VLOOKUP enables you to find one piece of information in a workbook based on another piece of information. For example, if you have a product list, you can find and return a **Product Code** by providing the corresponding **Product Name** to the VLOOKUP function.

Syntax

=VLOOKUP (lookup_value, table_array, col_index_num, [range_lookup])

Arguments

Argument	Description
lookup_value	Required. What value are you searching for? This argument is the lookup value. Excel will look for a match for this value in the leftmost column of your chosen range. You can provide a value here or a cell reference.
table_array	Required. What columns do you want to search? This argument is the range you want to include in your search, e.g., A2:D10.
col_index_num	Required. Which column contains the search result? Count from the first column to determine what this number should be, starting from 1.
range_lookup	Optional. For an exact match, enter FALSE/0. For an approximate match, enter TRUE/1. For TRUE, ensure the leftmost column is sorted in ascending order for correct results. This argument defaults to TRUE if omitted.

Example

In the example below, we use VLOOKUP to find the *Price* and Reorder Level of a product by entering the **Product Name** in cell G2. The formula is in cell G3, and as you can see from the image below, it searches the table for **Pears** and returns the price from the next column.

G3 fx =VLOOKUP(G2,B2:D46,2,FALSE)

	A	B	C	D	E	F	G
1	Product Code	Product Name	Price	Reorder Level	Category		
2	NWTB-1	Chai	$18.00	10	Beverages	Protuct name:	Pears
3	NWTB-34	Beer	$14.00	15	Beverages	Price:	$1.30
4	NWTB-43	Coffee	$46.00	25	Beverages	Reorder Level:	10
5	NWTB-81	Green Tea	$2.99	100	Beverages		
6	NWTB-87	Tea	$4.00	20	Beverages		
7	NWTBGM-19	Chocolate Biscuits Mix	$9.20	5	Baked Goods & Mixes		
8	NWTBGM-21	Scones	$10.00	5	Baked Goods & Mixes		
9	NWTBGM-85	Brownie Mix	$12.49	10	Baked Goods & Mixes		
10	NWTBGM-86	Cake Mix	$15.99	10	Baked Goods & Mixes		
11	NWTC-82	Granola	$4.00	20	Cereal		
12	NWTC-82	Hot Cereal	$5.00	50	Cereal		
13	NWTCA-48	Chocolate	$12.75	25	Candy		
14	NWTCFV-17	Fruit Cocktail	$39.00	10	Canned Fruit & Vegetables		
15	[illegible]	Pears	$1.30	10	Canned Fruit & Vegetables		
16	NWTCFV-89	Peaches	$1.50	10	Canned Fruit & Vegetables		
17	NWTCFV-90	Pineapple	$1.80	10	Canned Fruit & Vegetables		

Formula Explanation

To look up the **Price** for **Pears**, the formula is:

=VLOOKUP(G2, B2:D46, 2, FALSE)

The function uses a lookup_value from cell **G2** to search a table_array which is **B2:D46.**

The col_index_num is **2,** so it returns a value from the second column in the search range (table_array), the **Price** column.

The range_lookup is **FALSE**, meaning we want an exact match.

To look up the **Reorder Level** for Pears, we use the same formula and just change the column containing the search result (col_index_num) to 3 to return a value from the third row of the table array.

=VLOOKUP(G2, B2:D46, **3**, FALSE)

In this case, the VLOOKUP search for Pears returns a Reorder Level of **10**.

Best Practices for VLOOKUP

- **Use absolute references for the table array**.

  Using absolute references allows you to fill down a formula without changing the cell references. An absolute reference ensures VLOOKUP always looks at the same table array when the formula is copied to other cells.

- **Do not store a number or date as a text value.**

  When searching for numbers or dates, ensure the data in the first column of the table array is not stored as text. Otherwise, the formula might return an incorrect or unexpected value. Number and date values are right-aligned, while text values are left-aligned by default. Therefore, if your numbers or dates are left-aligned in the cell, you must check that they are using the right cell format.

- **Sort the first column.**

  If you want VLOOKUP to find the next best match when the **range_lookup** argument is TRUE, make sure the first column in **table_array** is sorted.

- **Use wildcard characters.**

  You can use a wildcard in **lookup_value** if **range_lookup** is FALSE and lookup_value is text. A question mark (?) matches any single character, and an asterisk (*) matches any sequence of characters. If you want to find an actual question mark or asterisk as part of the search criteria, type a tilde (~) in front of the character.

  For example, =VLOOKUP("Dried*",B2:D46,2,FALSE) will find the first item starting with "Dried" in the first column of table_array.

- **Make sure your data does not contain erroneous characters.**

  If you are searching for text values in the first column of the table array, ensure the data in the first column does not have leading or trailing spaces, non-printable characters, and inconsistent use of straight and curly quotation marks. In cases like these, the formula might return an unexpected value.

  To clean up your data, you can use the TRIM function to remove any extra spaces or use the CLEAN function to remove all nonprintable characters.

Common VLOOKUP Errors and Solutions

- **Wrong value returned**

  If you omit the **range_lookup** argument or set it to TRUE (for an approximate match), you need to sort the first column of **table_array** in alphanumeric order. If the first column is not sorted, Excel may return an unexpected value. Use FALSE for an exact match or sort the first column of the table array for an approximate match.

- **#N/A error in cell**

  If the range_lookup argument is FALSE, and an exact match is not found, you will get an #N/A error. You will also get an #N/A error if **range_lookup** is TRUE and the **lookup_value** is smaller than the smallest value in the first column of **table_array**.

- **#REF! in cell**

  You will get the #REF error if the col_index_num argument is greater than the number of columns in the table array.

- **#VALUE! in cell**

  You will encounter a #VALUE! error if the **lookup_value** argument is over 255 characters. Use wildcards for partial matches if the values in the lookup range are over 255 characters.

Excel will also generate the #VALUE! error if the **col_index_num** argument contains text or is less than 1. Ensure **col_index_num** is not less than 1.

- **#NAME? in cell**

  This error usually means that the formula is missing quotes. If you enter a text value directly in your formula (instead of a cell reference), ensure you enclose the value in quotes. For example, =VLOOKUP("Dried Pears", B2:D46, 2, FALSE). You will also get this error if you make a mistake when typing in the cell reference. Select cell references on the worksheet with your mouse rather than typing them in the formula to avoid cell reference typos.

Manipulating Text with Functions

If you work with Excel extensively, there will be occasions when you would need to use functions to manipulate text, especially when you work with data imported from other programs. For example, you may want to strip off part of a text value or rearrange text.

Tip The **Flash Fill** command on the **Home** tab enables you to perform many text manipulation tasks for which you would previously use functions. For example, the quickest way to split text into several columns is to use Flash Fill as described in Chapter 2.

Extracting Text Portions with LEN and MID

The LEN function returns the number of characters in a text string. This function is mostly used with other Excel functions like MID, where you use LEN to return the length of a string for one of the arguments in MID.

The MID function lets you extract a portion of a text string based on the starting position you specify and the number of characters you want to extract.

Syntax

=LEN(text)

Argument	Description
Text	Required. This argument is a text string or a cell reference containing the text for which you want to find the length. Spaces are counted as characters.

=MID(text, start_num, num_chars)

Argument	Description
text	Required. A text string or a cell reference containing the characters you want to extract.
start_num	Required. The position of the first character you want to extract in *text*. The first character position in *text* 1, the second is 2, and so on.
num_chars	Required. This argument is a number that specifies the number of characters you want to extract from *text*.

Remarks:

- If the start_num argument is larger than the length of the string in our text argument, MID will return an empty text ("").
- MID will return the #VALUE! error if start_num is less than 1.
- MID returns the #VALUE! error if num_chars is a negative value.

Example 1

In the following example, we use the LEN function to count the number of characters in an item code. The example also demonstrates how the LEN function can be combined with the MID function to return part of a string.

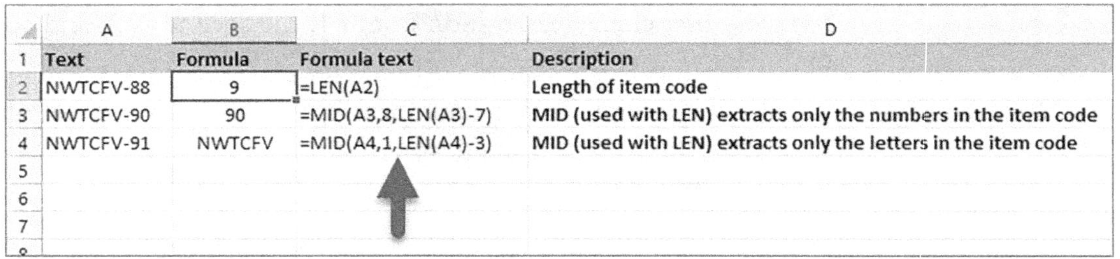

	A	B	C	D
1	Text	Formula	Formula text	Description
2	NWTCFV-88	9	=LEN(A2)	Length of item code
3	NWTCFV-90	90	=MID(A3,8,LEN(A3)-7)	MID (used with LEN) extracts only the numbers in the item code
4	NWTCFV-91	NWTCFV	=MID(A4,1,LEN(A4)-3)	MID (used with LEN) extracts only the letters in the item code
5				
6				
7				

Column C shows the formulas in column B

=LEN(A2)

This formula simply returns the length of a text value in its argument.

=MID(A3,8,LEN(A3)-7)

LEN returns the length of the string, and we subtract 7 character from it for the num_chars argument of MID. MID is used here with LEN to extract only the numbers in the item code.

=MID(A4,1,LEN(A4)-3)

MID is used here with LEN to extract a portion of the string minus the last 3 characters.

Example 2

The examples below use the MID function to extract characters from several text values.

B2 =MID(A2,4,3)

	A	B	C	D
1	**Product Number**	**Extracted**	**Formula Text**	
2	01-345-4000	345	=MID(A2,4,3)	**Extract the 3 characters in the middle of the serial number**
3	01-378-7890	378	=MID(A3,4,3)	
4	01-375-7891	375	=MID(A4,4,3)	
5	01-376-7892	376	=MID(A5,4,3)	
6				
7	NWTCFV-88	88	=MID(A7,8,2)	**Extract only the number portion of the item code**
8	NWTCFV-89	89	=MID(A8,8,2)	
9	NWTCFV-90	90	=MID(A9,8,2)	
10	NWTCFV-91	91	=MID(A10,8,2)	

Column C shows the formulas in column B

Formula description

=MID(A2,4,3)

For this formula, A2 is the cell containing the string from which we want to extract text - "01-345-4000". The first character we want to extract is 3, which starts at position four, so we have 4 as our **start_num** argument. We want to return three characters, so we have 3 as the **num_chars** argument.

=MID(A7,8,2)

This formula has A7 as the **text** argument and 8 as **start_num** because we want to start with the 8th character in the string. The **num_chars** argument is 2 as this is the number of characters we want to return.

The benefit of using formulas like these is that you create them once and use the fill handle of the first cell to copy the formula to the other cells.

Joining Text Values with TEXTJOIN

The TEXTJOIN function lets you combine text values from multiple text strings into one string. The difference between the TEXTJOIN and the CONCAT function is that TEXTJOIN has extra arguments that allow you to specify a delimiter as a separator. It also has an argument you can set to ignore empty cells. If you enter an empty text string in the delimiter, this function will concatenate the values.

Syntax

=TEXTJOIN(delimiter, ignore_empty, text1, [text2], ...)

Arguments

Argument	Description
delimiter	Required. This argument is the delimiter you want to use as a separator for text items in your string. The delimiter can be a string, one or more characters enclosed in double quotes, or a cell reference containing a text string. If this argument is a number, it will be treated as text.
ignore_empty	Required. This argument should be either TRUE or FALSE. If TRUE, it ignores empty cells.
text1	Required. This argument is the first text item to be joined. It can be a string, a cell reference, or a range with several cells.
[text2, ...]	Optional. Additional optional text items to be joined. You can have up to 252 arguments for the text items, including text1. Each can be a string, a cell reference, or a range with several cells.

TEXTJOIN will return the #VALUE! error if the resulting string exceeds 32767 characters, which is the cell limit.

Example

In the following example, we use TEXTJOIN in column C to combine the First name and Last name values from A2:A7 and B2:B7. The flexibility of TEXTJOIN enables us to swap the order of the names in some of the formulas.

C2 fx =TEXTJOIN(", ", TRUE,B2,A2)

	A	B	C	D
1	**First name**	**Last name**	**Combined**	**Formula**
2	Bruce	Henderson	Henderson, Bruce	=TEXTJOIN(", ", TRUE,B2,A2)
3	Louis	Anderson	Anderson, Louis	=TEXTJOIN(", ", TRUE,B3,A3)
4	Earl	Foster	Foster, Earl	=TEXTJOIN(", ", TRUE,B4,A4)
5	Sean	Hill	Sean Hill	=TEXTJOIN(" ", TRUE,A5,B5)
6	Benjamin	Martinez	Benjamin Martinez	=TEXTJOIN(" ", TRUE,A6,B6)
7	Joe	Perez	Joe Perez	=TEXTJOIN(" ", TRUE,A7,B7)
8				
9	**Name**			
10	Bruce Henderson			
11	Louis Anderson			
12	Earl Foster			
13	Sean Hill			
14				
15	**Combined**			
16	Bruce Henderson, Louis Anderson, Earl Foster, Sean Hill			=TEXTJOIN(", ",TRUE,A10:A13)
17				

Explanation of formula

=TEXTJOIN(", ", TRUE,B2,A2)

The **delimiter** argument in the formula above is a comma enclosed in quotes. The **ignore_empty** argument is set to TRUE to ignore empty cells. The **text1** and **text2** arguments are the cell references for the text values we want to combine.

=TEXTJOIN(" ", TRUE,A5,B5)

The delimiter in the formula above is a blank space in quotes to separate the first name and the last name.

=TEXTJOIN(", ",TRUE,A10:A13)

The above formula uses the TEXTJOIN function to concatenate names in a range of cells (A10:A13) into a single string with a comma used as a separator.

Accessing More Functions in Excel

To access the full function library in Excel, click the **Formulas** tab on the Ribbon. You will see a list of command buttons for several categories of functions.

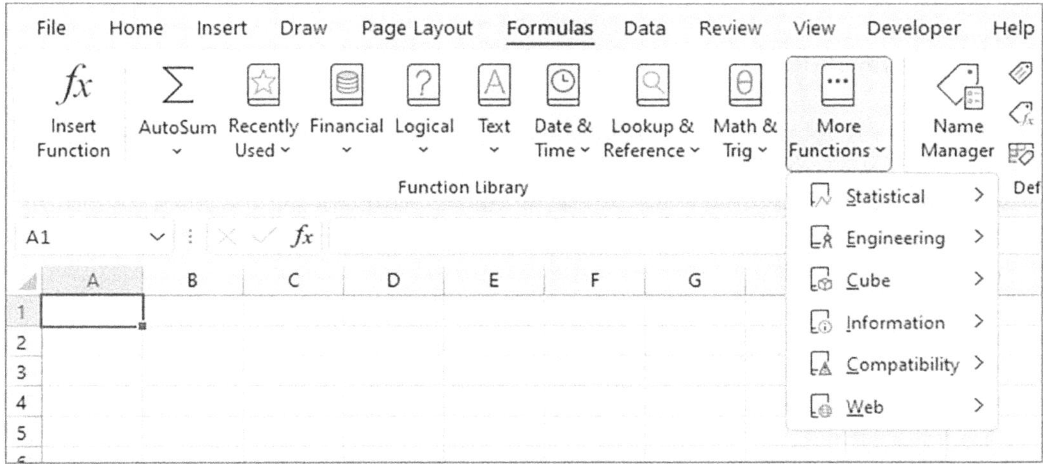

The functions are grouped under the following categories:

- Recently Used
- Financial
- Logical
- Text
- Date & Time
- Lookup & Reference
- Math & Trig
- Statistical
- Engineering
- Cube
- Information
- Compatibility
- Web

You can explore the various functions by clicking on the drop-down button for each one of the command buttons, and you'll get a dropdown list of the functions related to each button.

Many of these functions are for specialist tasks and professions, so don't let them overwhelm you, as you'll never get to use most of them. For example, the **Financial** functions will mostly be used by accountants, and engineers mostly use the **Engineering** functions, etc.

The most used functions will be listed under the **Recently Used** list for easy access.

To get more details about each function, hover over a function name on the list, and a small pop-up message will appear, giving you more details of the function and what arguments it takes. For example, if you hover over the **IF** function, you will see the function description and the arguments it takes.

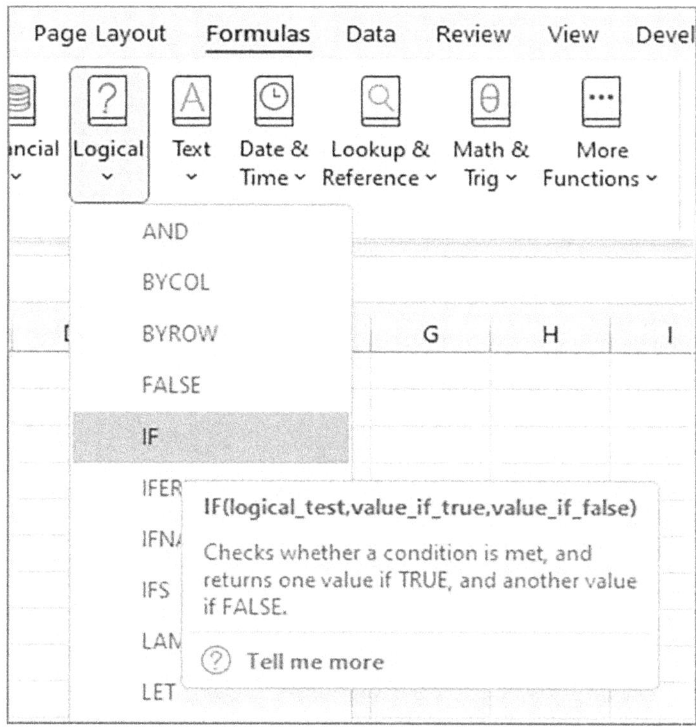

Getting More Help with Functions

To get more information on using any function in Excel, press **F1** to display the Help panel. Then type "Excel functions" in the search bar. Excel will give you a list of all the functions in Excel by category. You can locate the one you want and click it to see more details on its use.

Chapter 10

Working with Tables

You can turn your Excel data into a table. Creating a table in Excel makes managing and analyzing your data easier. You also get built-in sorting, filtering, Banded Rows, and you can add a Total Row.

In this chapter, we will cover how to:

- Convert a range to an Excel table.
- Apply different styles to a table.
- Sort and filter data in a table.
- Add a totals row to a table.
- Remove table attributes (if you want to convert your list back to a range).
- Use a table name in a formula.

Preparing Your Data

Before creating a table, ensure there are no empty columns or rows in the data.

In the next example, we will convert the following range of data into a table.

	A	B	C	D	E
1	Last Name	First Name	Company	Job Title	Address
2	Bedecs	Anna	Company A	Owner	123 1st Street
3	Gratacos Solsona	Antonio	Company B	Owner	123 2nd Stree
4	Axen	Thomas	Company C	Purchasing Represen	123 3rd Street
5	Lee	Christina	Company D	Purchasing Manager	123 4th Street
6	O'Donnell	Martin	Company E	Owner	123 5th Street
7	Pérez-Olaeta	Francisco	Company F	Purchasing Manager	123 6th Street
8	Xie	Ming-Yang	Company G	Owner	123 7th Street
9	Andersen	Elizabeth	Company H	Purchasing Represen	123 8th Street
10	Mortensen	Sven	Company I	Purchasing Manager	123 9th Street
11	Wacker	Roland	Company J	Purchasing Manager	123 10th Street
12	Krschne	Peter	Company K	Purchasing Manager	123 11th Stree
13	Edwards	John	Company L	Purchasing Manager	123 12th Stre
14	Ludick	Andre	Company M	Purchasing Represen	456 13th Stree
15	Grilo	Carlos	Company N	Purchasing Represen	456 14th Street
16	Kupkova	Helena	Company O	Purchasing Manager	456 15th Stre

First, check that there are no empty columns or rows in your data:

1. Select any cell within the data and press **Ctrl** + **A**.
2. Then press **Ctrl** + **.** (period) a few times to move around the data.

Note **Ctrl** + **A** selects the data range in question. **Ctrl** + **.** moves around the four edges of the data so you can see where the data starts and ends.

Create an Excel Table

To convert a range to a table, do the following:

1. Select any cell within the data.
2. Click the **Insert** tab, and in the **Tables** group, click **Table**.
3. Excel displays a dialog box showing you the range for the table. You can adjust the range here if necessary.
4. Select **My table has headers** to ensure that the first row of your table is used as the header.

Tip If your table has no column headers, create a new row on top and add column headers. Row headers make it easier to work with tables in Excel.

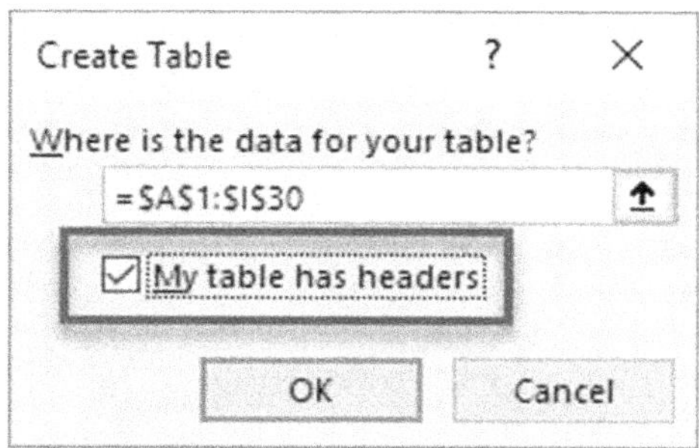

5. Click **OK**.

Excel creates the table with the first row used as column headers.

	A	B	C	D	E
1	Last Name	First Name	Company	Job Title	Address
2	Bedecs	Anna	Company A	Owner	123 1st Street
3	Gratacos Solsona	Antonio	Company B	Owner	123 2nd Street
4	Axen	Thomas	Company C	Purchasing Represen	123 3rd Street
5	Lee	Christina	Company D	Purchasing Manager	123 4th Street
6	O'Donnell	Martin	Company E	Owner	123 5th Street
7	Pérez-Olaeta	Francisco	Company F	Purchasing Manager	123 6th Street
8	Xie	Ming-Yang	Company G	Owner	123 7th Street
9	Andersen	Elizabeth	Company H	Purchasing Represen	123 8th Street
10	Mortensen	Sven	Company I	Purchasing Manager	123 9th Street
11	Wacker	Roland	Company J	Purchasing Manager	123 10th Street
12	Krschne	Peter	Company K	Purchasing Manager	123 11th Street
13	Edwards	John	Company L	Purchasing Manager	123 12th Street
14	Ludick	Andre	Company M	Purchasing Represen	456 13th Street
15	Grilo	Carlos	Company N	Purchasing Represen	456 14th Street
16	Kupkova	Helena	Company O	Purchasing Manager	456 15th Street

Tip Other ways to quickly create a table:

- Select the cells in the range, and on the Ribbon, click **Home** > **Format as Table.**
- Select any cell within the range, and press **Ctrl+T**.

Choosing a Table Style

When you convert a range to a table, Excel applies a style with alternating row colors to the table. You can change this style by selecting a new style from many options provided by Excel if you want.

When you select any cell in the table, Excel displays the **Table Design** contextual tab on the Ribbon. This tab includes the groups, **Table Style Options**, and **Table Styles**. Table Styles provides several predefined styles you can apply to your table, while Table Style Options provides further options to style your table.

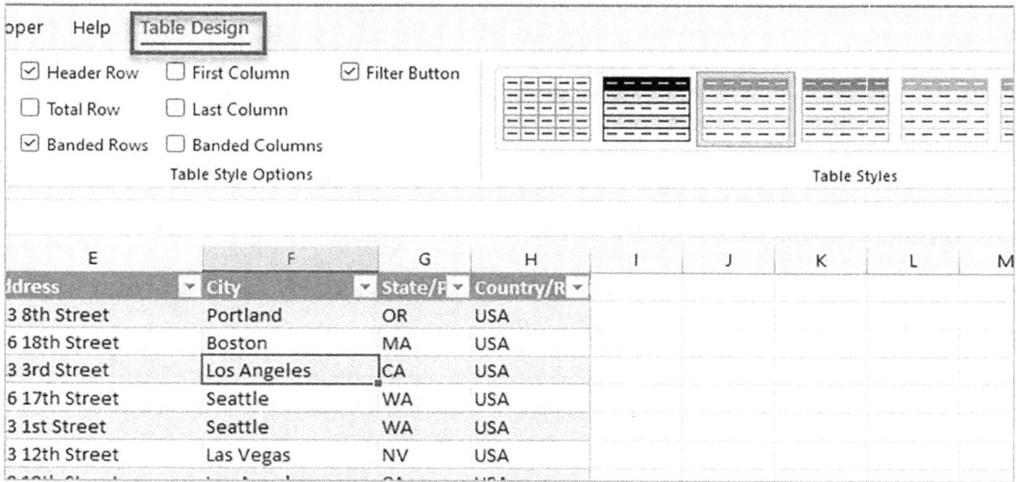

Applying a Table Style

To apply a predefined style to your table, do the following:

1. Select a cell within the table.
2. On the **Table Design** tab, locate the **Table Styles** group and click the drop-down button for the styles. A drop-down menu will show you more styles.
3. Hover over each style to preview how applying it would look on your worksheet.
4. When you find a style you want, click it to apply it to your table.

Applying Table Style Options

Here you have several options for configuring the style of your table.

For example, you can change your table from **Banded Rows** to **Banded Columns**. Banded rows are the alternating colors applied to your table rows. The Banded Rows setting is the default, but if you want banded columns instead, uncheck **Banded Rows** and check **Banded Columns** to have your columns alternate in color instead of your rows.

Note that if a new column or row is added to the table, it will inherit the current table style automatically. When you add a new row, any formulas applied to your table will also be copied to the new row.

Sorting Data in a Table

Before sorting data, ensure there are no blank rows and blank columns. Also, ensure your table header is a single row. If the header is more than one row, change it to a single row to make things easier.

Tip To check for blank rows or columns, select a cell within the data and press **Ctrl** + **A**. Then press **Ctrl** + **.** (period) a few times. This keystroke moves the cell pointer around the four corners of the range so that you can see the whole area.

Sort by One Column

To quickly sort your table using one column, do the following:

1. Select a cell in the column you want to use for the sorting. For example, **Last Name**.
2. On the **Data** tab, in the **Sort & Filter** group, click **AZ** (to sort the table in ascending order) or **ZA** (to sort the table in descending order).

That's it. Excel sorts your table in the order you've chosen.

Sort by Multiple Columns

There are often occasions when you want to sort a table using more than one column. A **Custom Sort** is required to sort a table by multiple columns.

To sort your data using several columns, follow these steps:

1. Select any cell within the data.
2. On the **Home** tab, in the **Editing** group, click **Sort & Filter**.
3. Select **Custom Sort** from the drop-down menu.

   Excel displays the **Sort** dialog box.

Tip: Another way to open the Custom Sort dialog box is to click **Data** > **Sort** (in the **Sort & Filter** group).

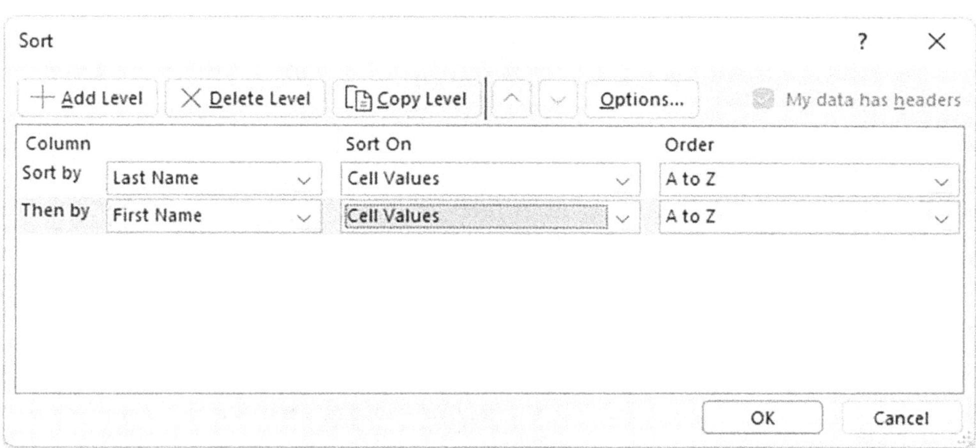

4. Click **Add Level**.

5. Under **Column**, select the column you want to **Sort by** from the drop-down list. Select the second column you want to include in the sort in the **Then by** field. For example, Sort by Last Name and First Name.

6. Under **Sort On**, select **Cell Values**.

7. Under **Order**, select the order you want to sort on, **A to Z** for ascending order, and **Z to A** for descending order.

8. Click **OK**.

You can add additional columns to your sort. Excel allows you to have up to 64 sort levels. For each additional column you want to sort by, repeat steps 4-7 above.

Filtering Table Data

Excel provides an array of options to filter your data so that you can view only the data you want to see. Filters provide a quick way to work with a subset of data in a range or table. When you apply the filter, you temporarily hide some of the data so that you can focus on the data you need to view.

Follow the steps below to filter data in an Excel table:

1. Select any cell in the table that you want to filter.
2. Click **Home** > **Sort & Filter** > **Filter** (or click **Data** > **Filter**).
3. You will get filter arrows at the top of each column.
4. Click the arrow in the column header. For example, **Price**. This arrow is also known as the AutoFilter.
5. Uncheck **Select All** and check the values you want to use for the filter.
6. Click **OK**.

	A	B	C	D	E
1	Product Code	Product Name	Price	Reorder Level	Category
16	NWTSO-41	Clam Chowder	$9.6[illegible]	10	Soups
17	NWTB-43	Coffee	$46.00	25	Beverages
18	NWTCA-48	Chocolate	$12.75	25	Candy
19	NWTDFN-51	Dried Apples	$53.00	10	Dried Fruit & Nuts
20	NWTG-52	Long Grain Rice	$7.00	25	Grains
21	NWTP-56	Gnocchi	$38.00	30	Pasta
22	NWTP-57	Ravioli	$19.50	20	Pasta
23	NWTS-65	Hot Pepper Sauce	$21.05	10	Sauces
24	NWTS-66	Tomato Sauce	$17.00	20	Sauces
25	NWTD-72	Mozzarella	$34.80	10	Dairy Products
26	NWTDFN-74	Almonds	$10.00	5	Dried Fruit & Nuts
27	NWTCO-77	Mustard	$13.00	15	Condiments
28	NWTDFN-80	Dried Plums	$3.50	50	Dried Fruit & Nuts
29	NWTB-81	Green Tea	$2.99	100	Beverages
30	NWTC-82	Granola	$4.00	20	Cereal

The AutoFilter changes to a funnel icon to indicate that the column is filtered. If you look at the row heading numbers, you'll see that they're now blue, indicating which rows are included in the filtered data.

To remove the filter, on the **Data** tab, in the **Sort & Filter** group, click **Clear**. The filter will be removed, and all data will be displayed.

Applying a Custom Filter

A custom filter allows you to manually define your criteria for filtering the data.

To apply a custom filter to an Excel table, do the following:

1. Click the arrow (AutoFilter) on the column you want to filter.
2. Depending on the format of the column being filtered, you'll get one of the following options:
    - **Text Filters:** Available when the column has text values or has a mixture of text and numbers.
    - **Number Filters:** Available when the column contains only numbers
    - **Date Filters:** Available when the column contains only dates.
    - **Clear Filter from [Column name]**: Available when a filter has already been applied to the column. Select this option to clear the filter.

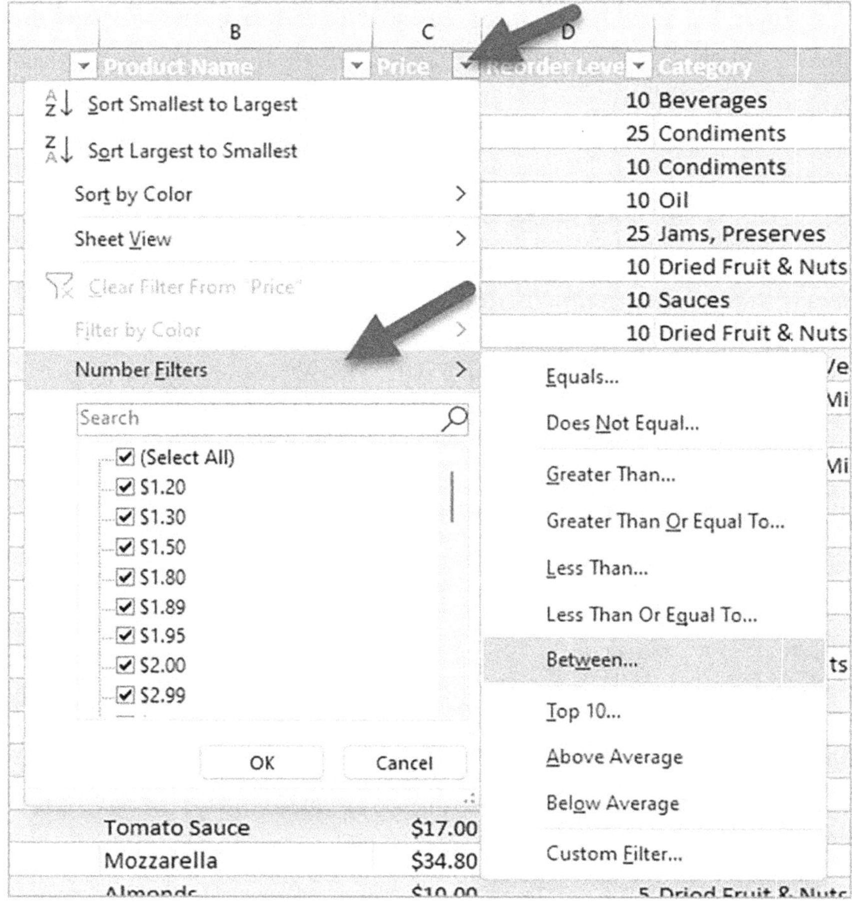

3. Select one of the first three options (Text Filters, Number Filters, or Date Filters) and then select a comparison. For this example, we've selected **Between**.

   Excel opens the **Custom AutoFilter** dialog box.

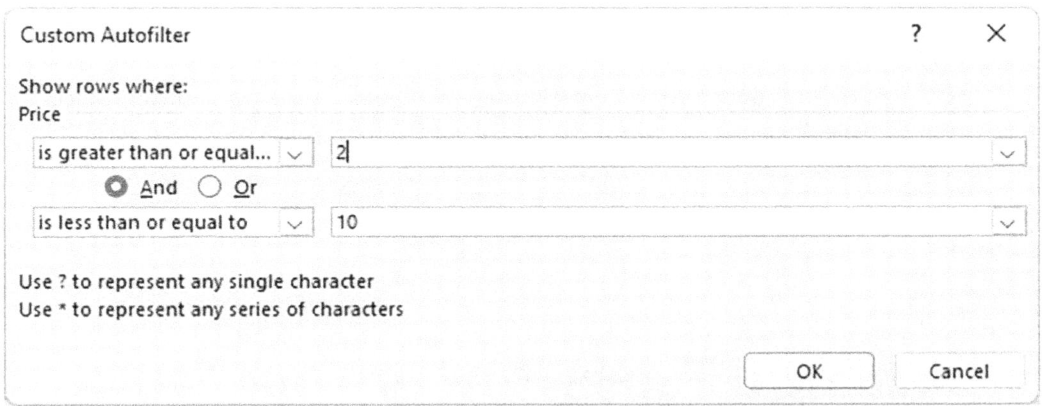

4. Enter the filter criteria.

   For the logical operator, select **And** if both conditions must be true, or select **Or** if only one of the conditions needs to be true.

   Our example filters the **Price** column so that only rows between $2 and $10 are displayed in the table.

5. Click **OK**.

   The AutoFilter changes to a Filter icon. You can click this icon to change or clear the filter.

	A	B	C		E
1	Product Code	Product Name	Price	Reorder Level	Category
3	NWTCO-3	Syrup	$10.00	25	Condiments
11	NWTBGM-19	Chocolate Biscuits Mix	$9.20	5	Baked Goods & Mixes
13	NWTBGM-21	Scones	$10.00	5	Baked Goods & Mixes
16	NWTSO-41	Clam Chowder	$9.65	10	Soups
20	NWTG-52	Long Grain Rice	$7.00	25	Grains
26	NWTDFN-74	Almonds	$10.00	5	Dried Fruit & Nuts
28	NWTDFN-80	Dried Plums	$3.50	50	Dried Fruit & Nuts
29	NWTB-81	Green Tea	$2.99	100	Beverages
30	NWTC-82	Granola	$4.00	20	Cereal
34	NWTB-87	Tea	$4.00	20	Beverages
38	NWTCFV-91	Cherry Pie Filling	$2.00	10	Canned Fruit & Vegetables
42	NWTCM-95	Tuna Fish	$2.00	30	Canned Meat
43	NWTCM-96	Smoked Salmon	$4.00	30	Canned Meat
44	NWTC-82	Hot Cereal	$5.00	50	Cereal

Filtered results

Tip To change the order of the filtered results, click the filter icon and then select either **Sort Largest to Smallest** or **Sort Smallest to Largest**. For a text column, it would be **Sort A to Z** or **Sort Z to A.**

Adding a Totals Row to Your Table

You can add totals to a table by selecting the **Total Row** check box on the **Design** tab. Once added to your worksheet, the Total Row drop-down button allows you to add a function from a list of options.

To add totals to your table:

1. Select a cell in a table.
2. Select **Table Design** > **Total Row**. Excel adds a new row to the bottom of the table called the **Total Row**.
3. On the Total Row drop-down list, you have an array of functions you can select like **Average**, **Count**, **Count Numbers**, **Max**, **Min**, **Sum**, **StdDev**, **Var**, and more.

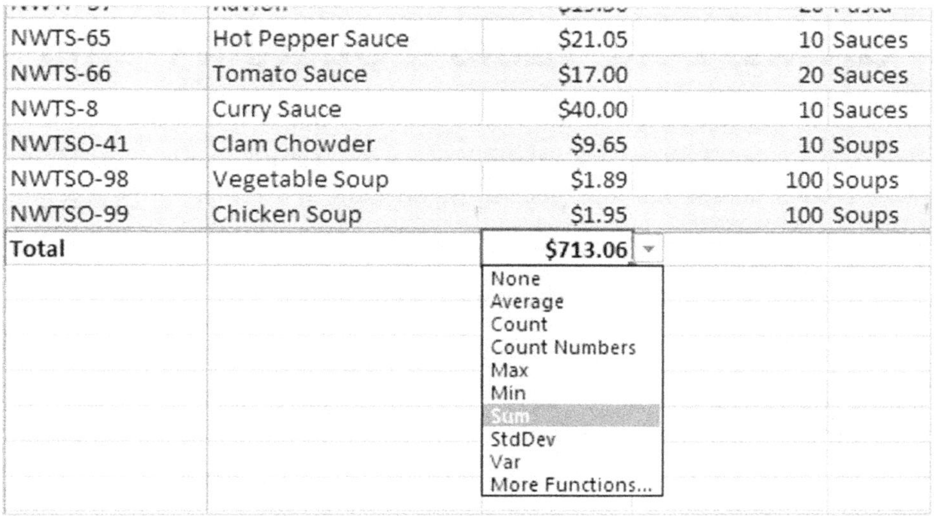

NWTS-65	Hot Pepper Sauce	$21.05	10	Sauces
NWTS-66	Tomato Sauce	$17.00	20	Sauces
NWTS-8	Curry Sauce	$40.00	10	Sauces
NWTSO-41	Clam Chowder	$9.65	10	Soups
NWTSO-98	Vegetable Soup	$1.89	100	Soups
NWTSO-99	Chicken Soup	$1.95	100	Soups
Total		$713.06		

None
Average
Count
Count Numbers
Max
Min
Sum
StdDev
Var
More Functions...

Tip If you need to add a new row of data to your table at any point, deselect **Total Row** on the **Table Design** tab, add the new row, and then reselect **Total Row**.

Giving Your Table a Custom Name

After creation, Excel gives your table a default name like Table1, Table2, etc. However, you can give your table a custom name, especially if you want to use that name to reference data in the table in formulas.

Follow the steps below to give your table a custom name:

1. On the Ribbon, click the **Table Design** tab.
2. In the **Properties** group, type in your table name in the **Table Name** field (overwriting the default name).
3. Press **Enter**.

   You can now use to table name in formulas to reference data in the table.

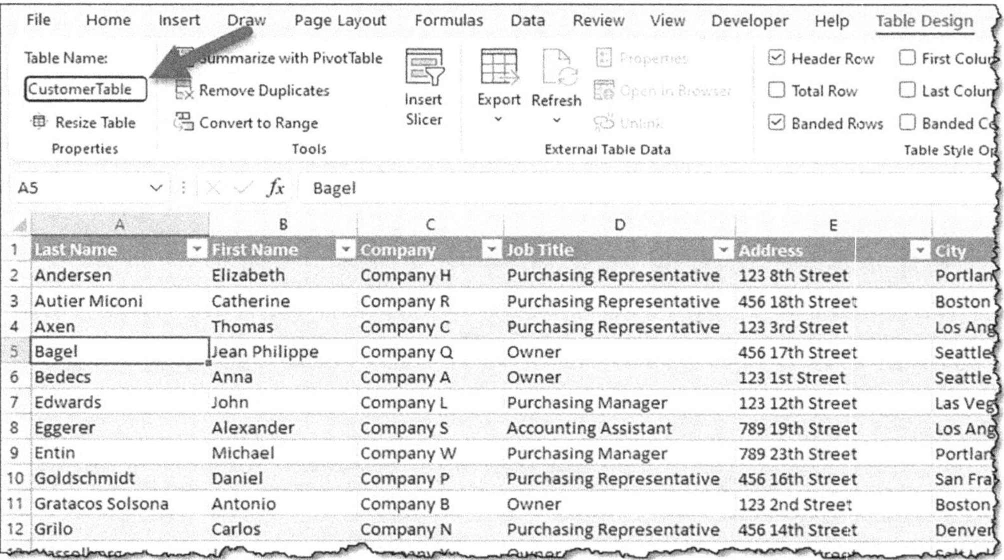

Using Table Names in Formulas

In the following example, instead of using the range **B2:B11**, the formulas use **Sales[Sales Amount]** to refer to that range. The table name is **Sales**, and the column name is **Sales Amount**.

This reference uses the combination of the table and column names to refer to the data range in the table. This type of reference is called a structured reference.

=SUM(Sales[Sales Amount])

=MAX(Sales[Sales Amount])

=AVERAGE(Sales[Sales Amount])

E2 fx =SUM(Sales[Sales Amount])

	A	B	C	D	E	F
1	Sales Person	Sales Amount				Formula Text
2	Hugo	$1,848.00		Total sales	$23,222.00	=SUM(Sales[Sales Amount])
3	Felipe	$3,897.00		Max sale	$5,509.00	=MAX(Sales[Sales Amount])
4	Wayne	$1,267.00		Average	$2,322.20	=AVERAGE(Sales[Sales Amount])
5	Mae	$1,149.00				
6	Lee	$2,571.00				
7	Oscar	$1,659.00				
8	Ming-Yang	$5,509.00				
9	Terrance	$2,307.00				
10	Sylvester	$1,589.00				
11	Elijah	$1,426.00				
12						

Structured references provide certain benefits, including the following:

- The name is an absolute reference, so you can copy the formula to any part of your workbook without the reference changing.
- You don't need to adjust the reference in your formulas when you add or remove rows from the table.
- You could find it easier to refer to ranges in your formulas. For example, it may be easier to enter the table and column name in your formula in a large workbook instead of identifying explicit cell references.

Removing Table Attributes

On some occasions, you may want to switch a table back to a normal range. Maybe you want to perform tasks where a table is unnecessary or transform the data before converting it to a table again.

You can convert an Excel table back to a range using one of the following methods.

Method 1

1. Click anywhere in the table so that the cell pointer is inside the table.
2. Click the **Table Design** tab, and in the Tools group, click **Convert to Range**.
3. Click **Yes** to confirm the action.

   The table will now be converted to a normal range of cells without Excel's table features.

Method 2

1. Right-click anywhere in the table.
2. On the pop-up menu, select **Table** > **Convert to Range**.
3. Click **Yes** at the confirmation prompt.

   Excel removes all table attributes and returns the data to a range.

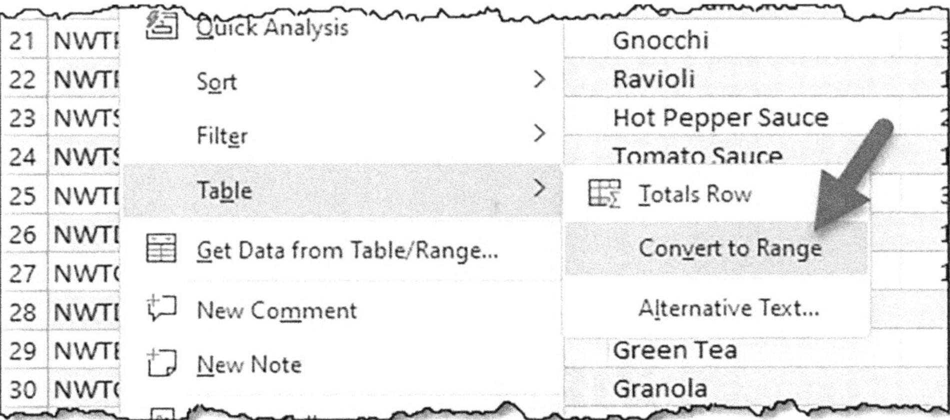

After converting a table back to a range, the range will still retain the style and formatting that was applied to the table, like banded rows, for example. However, the formatting does not affect the behavior of the range.

To clear all formatting, do the following:

1. Select the range.
2. Click the **Home** tab.
3. In the **Editing** group, click **Clear** > **Clear Formats**.

Chapter 11

Introduction to Pivot Tables

An Excel PivotTable is a powerful tool that dynamically calculates, summarizes, and analyzes data from different views. You can change the grouped columns or change the arrangement of the summarized data by switching between row and column headings. An Excel PivotTable allows you to group your data into summary information from different views without affecting the original data.

This chapter covers:

- How to create a pivot table manually.
- Formatting your pivot table.
- Filtering and sorting data in a pivot table.

Preparing Your Data

Some preparation is required to get a dataset ready for a PivotTable. The source data used for a PivotTable needs to be organized as a list or converted to an Excel table (recommended although not compulsory).

A few steps to prepare the source data for a PivotTable:

1. The data should have column headings in a single row on top.
2. Remove any temporary totals or summaries.
3. The data cannot have empty rows, so delete any empty rows.
4. Ensure you do not have any extraneous data surrounding the list.
5. Ideally, you may want to create an Excel table with the data (although it is not a pre-requisite).

	A	B	C	D	E	F	G	H
1	Employee	Product	Customer	Order Date	Ship City	Item Cost	No. of Items	Total Cost
2	Anne Hellung-Larsen	Cora Fabric Chair	Acme LTD	11/24/2016	Las Vegas	$475.00	20	$9,500.00
3	Jan Kotas	Lukah Leather Chair	Elgin Homes	05/13/2016	New York	$345.00	9	$3,105.00
4	Mariya Sergienko	Habitat Oken Console Table	Mecury Builders	04/28/2016	Las Vegas	$36.00	28	$1,008.00
5	Michael Neipper	Hygena Fabric Chair	Infinity Homes	11/06/2016	Portland	$407.00	23	$9,361.00
6	Anne Hellung-Larsen	Harley Fabric Cuddle Chair	Elgin Homes	07/16/2016	New York	$803.00	20	$16,060.00
7	Jan Kotas	Windsor 2 Seater Cuddle Chair	B&B Seaside	04/27/2017	Denver	$302.00	8	$2,416.00
8	Mariya Sergienko	Fabric Chair	B&B Seaside	06/26/2016	Los Angelas	$425.00	11	$4,675.00
9	Laura Giussani	Verona 1 Shelf Telephone Table	Home Designers	04/07/2016	Milwaukee	$282.00	8	$2,256.00
10	Anne Hellung-Larsen	Floral Fabric Tub Chair	Acorn USA	08/17/2016	Memphis	$158.00	2	$316.00
11	Jan Kotas	Fabric Chair in a Box	Infinity Homes	04/20/2017	Portland	$857.00	28	$23,996.00
12	Mariya Sergienko	Slimline Console Table	Apex Homes	11/01/2016	Chicago	$534.00	29	$15,486.00
13	Nancy Freehafer	Collection Martha Fabric Wingback Chair	Empire Homes	09/24/2017	Boise	$137.00	15	$2,055.00
14	Nancy Freehafer	Slimline Console Table	Apex Homes	04/15/2017	Chicago	$433.00	16	$6,928.00
15	Nancy Freehafer	Fabric Wingback Chair	Express Builders	09/03/2016	Miami	$210.00	2	$420.00
16	Nancy Freehafer	Fabric Chair in a Box - Denim Blue	Impressive Homes	04/23/2016	Seattle	$634.00	14	$8,876.00
17	Nancy Freehafer	Tessa Fabric Chair	Acorn USA	02/10/2017	Memphis	$252.00	23	$5,796.00
18	Robert Zare	Collection Bradley Riser Recline Fabric Chair	Northern Contractors	01/05/2016	Salt Lake City	$281.00	5	$1,405.00
19	Michael Neipper	Fabric Wingback Chair	Home Designers	05/15/2017	Milwaukee	$405.00	30	$12,150.00
20	Mariya Sergienko	Tessa Fabric Chair	Infinity Homes	05/11/2017	Portland	$472.00	5	$2,360.00
21	Anne Hellung-Larsen	Fabric Tub Chair	Orion Spaces	03/29/2017	Chicago	$206.00	9	$1,854.00
22	Anne Hellung-Larsen	Harley Fabric Cuddle Chair	Elgin Homes	08/15/2017	Miami	$247.00	18	$4,446.00
23	Nancy Freehafer	New Paolo Manual Recliner Chair	B&B Seaside	01/02/2016	Denver	$778.00	19	$14,782.00
24	Andrew Concini	Floral Fabric Tub Chair	Home Designers	06/22/2016	Milwaukee	$780.00	10	$7,800.00

Sales Sheet1 +

Once the data has been prepared, we can now create a PivotTable.

Creating a Pivot Table

To create a PivotTable:

1. Click any cell in your range or table.
2. On the Insert tab, click the PivotTable button.

The **Create PivotTable** dialog will be displayed.

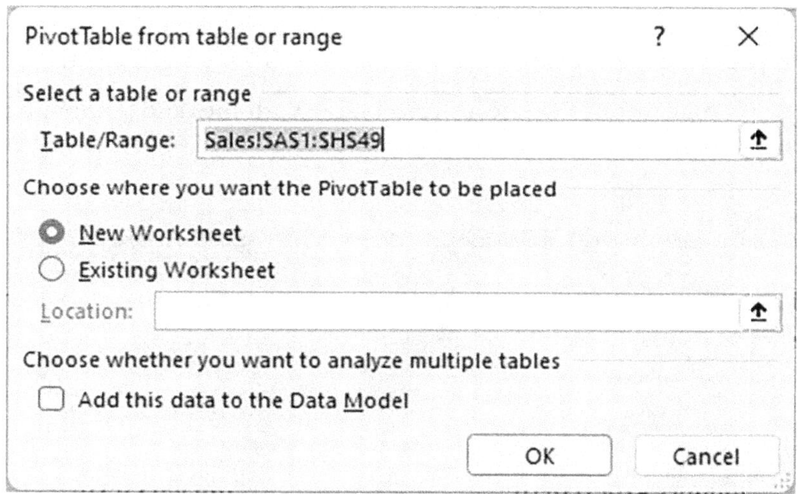

Excel will figure out the table or range you intend to use for your PivotTable and select it in the **Table/Range** field. If this is not accurate, you can manually select the range by clicking the up arrow (Expand Dialog) on the field.

The next option on the screen is where you want to place the PivotTable. The default location is a new worksheet. It is best to have your PivotTable on its own worksheet, separate from your source data, so you want to leave the default selected here.

3. Click **OK**.

A new worksheet will now be created with a PivotTable placeholder, and on the right side, you'll see a dialog box - **PivotTable Fields**.

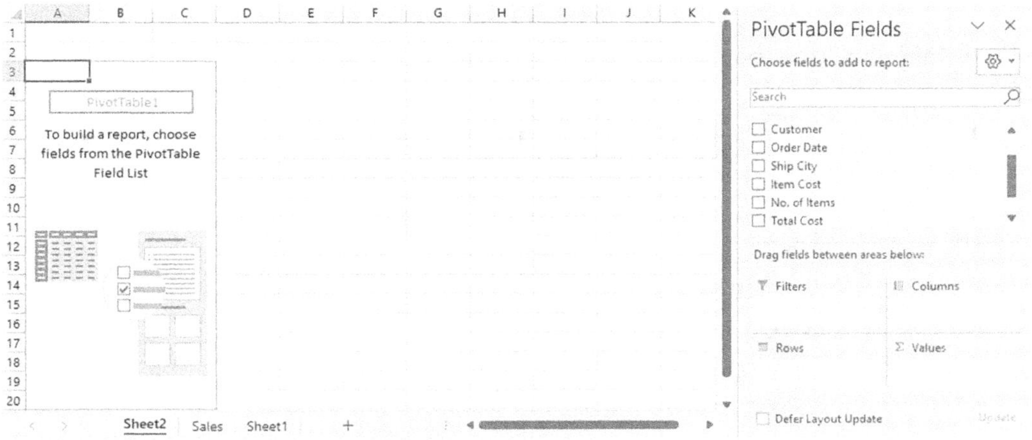

The bottom half of the PivotTable Fields pane has four areas where you can place fields:

Rows, **Columns**, **Values**, and **Filters**.

To add a field to your PivotTable, select the checkbox next to the field name in the PivotTables Fields pane. When you select fields, they are added to their default areas. Non-numeric fields are added to the **Rows** box. Date and time fields are added to the **Columns** box. Numeric fields are added to the **Values** box.

You can also drag fields from the list to one of the four areas you want to place it. To move one field to another, you can drag it there.

To remove a field from a box, click it and click **Remove Field** from the pop-up menu. You can also just uncheck it in the fields list or drag it away from the box and drop it back on the fields list.

Example

In this example, let's say we want a summary of our data that shows the total spent by each customer.

1. Select the **Customer** field on the list to add it to the Rows box.

   Excel updates the PivotTable with the list of customers as row headings.

2. Next, select the **Total Cost** field to add it to the **Values** box.

The PivotTable will now be updated with the **Sum of Total Cost** for each Customer.

3	Row Labels	Sum of Total Cost
4	Acme LTD	13226
5	Acorn USA	13292
6	Apex Homes	33082
7	B&B Seaside	48997
8	Elgin Homes	54504
9	Empire Homes	9355
10	Express Builders	11004
11	Home Designers	52322
12	Impressive Homes	14775
13	Infinity Homes	85612
14	Mecury Builders	17760
15	Northern Contractors	2001
16	Orion Spaces	4806
17	**Grand Total**	**360736**

We have been able to get a quick summary of our data, grouped by Customer, with just a few clicks. If you had hundreds of thousands of records, this task could have taken many hours to accomplish if done manually.

We can add more values to the table by dragging them to the Values box from the list.

For example, if we wanted to add the total number of items per customer, we'll select **No. of Items** on the list or drag it to the **Values** box.

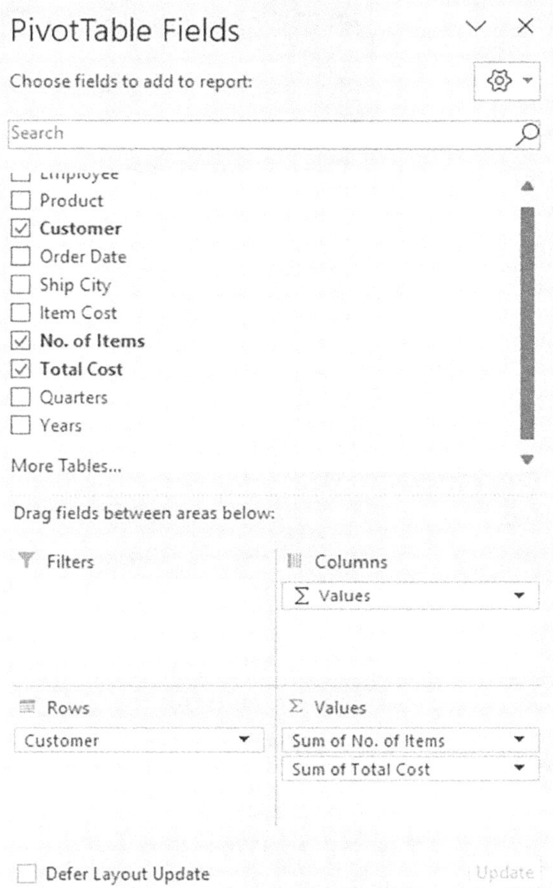

Excel adds the **Sum of No. of Items** for each customer to the PivotTable, as shown below.

Row Labels	Sum of No. of Items	Sum of Total Cost
Acme LTD	43	13226
Acorn USA	53	13292
Apex Homes	73	33082
B&B Seaside	88	48997
Elgin Homes	123	54504
Empire Homes	40	9355
Express Builders	14	11004
Home Designers	94	52322
Impressive Homes	31	14775
Infinity Homes	143	85612
Mecury Builders	52	17760
Northern Contractors	7	2001
Orion Spaces	33	4806
Grand Total	**794**	**360736**

To view the summary from the perspective of **Products**, that is, the total number of items sold and the total cost for each product, we would put the **Product** field in the Rows box and both **Total Cost** and **No. of Items** in the Values box.

To view the summary from the perspective of the **Employees** column, we would place the **Employee** field in the Rows box and **No. of Items** and **Total Cost** in the Values box.

Here we see the data summarized by Employee, i.e., how many items each employee sold, and the revenue generated.

Row Labels	Sum of No. of Items	Sum of Total Cost
Andrew Cencini	40	21418
Anne Hellung-Larsen	149	53969
Jan Kotas	110	70865
Laura Giussani	26	18690
Mariya Sergienko	176	78334
Michael Neipper	105	40203
Nancy Freehafer	181	75256
Robert Zare	7	2001
Grand Total	**794**	**360736**

If we wanted to see the number of items sold per city, we would place **Ship City** in the Rows box and **No. of Items** in the Values box.

3	**Row Labels**	**Sum of No. of Items**
4	Boise	40
5	Chicago	106
6	Denver	45
7	Las Vegas	95
8	Los Angelas	43
9	Memphis	53
10	Miami	44
11	Milwaukee	94
12	New York	93
13	Portland	143
14	Salt Lake City	7
15	Seattle	31
16	**Grand Total**	**794**

Summarizing Data by Date

To display the columns split into years, drag a date field into the Columns box, for example, Order Date. The PivotTable tool will automatically generate PivotTable fields for Quarters and Years. Once these fields have been generated, you should remove the Order Date field from the Columns box and place it in the Quarter or Year field, depending on which one you want to use for your summary.

To display the row headings by date, place **Order Date** (or your date field) in the Rows box.

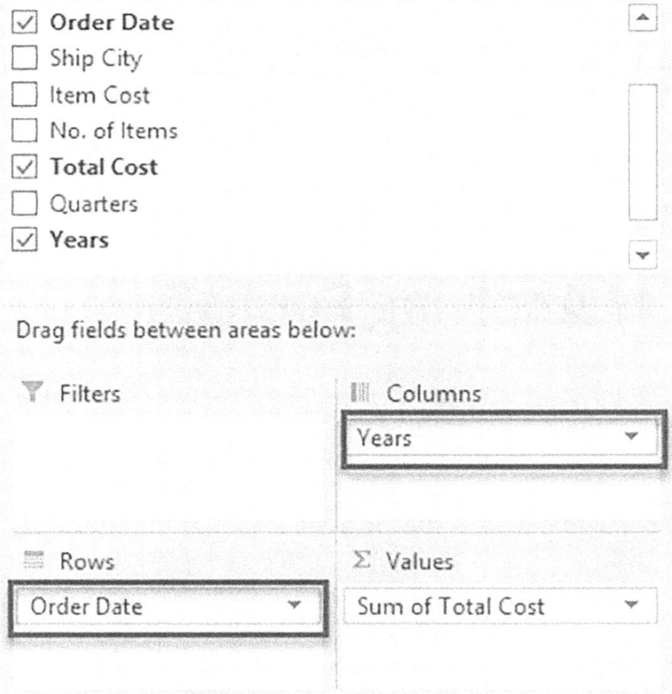

This combination will produce the following results.

Sum of Total Cost	Column Labels		
Row Labels	2016	2017	Grand Total
Jan	39569	7772	47341
Feb		22819	22819
Mar	5502	1854	7356
Apr	22724	57618	80342
May	3105	14510	17615
Jun	24021	596	24617
Jul	16060		16060
Aug	316	12141	12457
Sep	42763	9615	52378
Oct	16752		16752
Nov	34347	9756	44103
Dec	18896		18896
Grand Total	224055	136681	360736

Applying Formatting

As you can see, we can dynamically change how we want to view our data with just a few clicks. When you're happy with your summary, you can apply formatting to the appropriate columns. For example, you could format any currency field as **Currency** before any formal presentation of the data.

The good thing about Excel PivotTables is that you can explore different types of summaries with the pivot table without changing the source data. If you make a mistake that you can't figure out how to undo, you can simply delete the PivotTable worksheet and recreate the PivotTable in a new worksheet.

Filter and Sort a Pivot Table

On some occasions, you may want to limit what is displayed in the PivotTable. You can sort and filter a PivotTable just like you can do to a range of data or an Excel table.

To filter a PivotTable:

1. Click the AutoFilter (down arrow) on the Row Labels cell.

   The pop-up menu provides a list of the row headings in your PivotTable. You can select/deselect items on this list to limit the data displayed in the PivotTable.

2. Uncheck **Select All.**

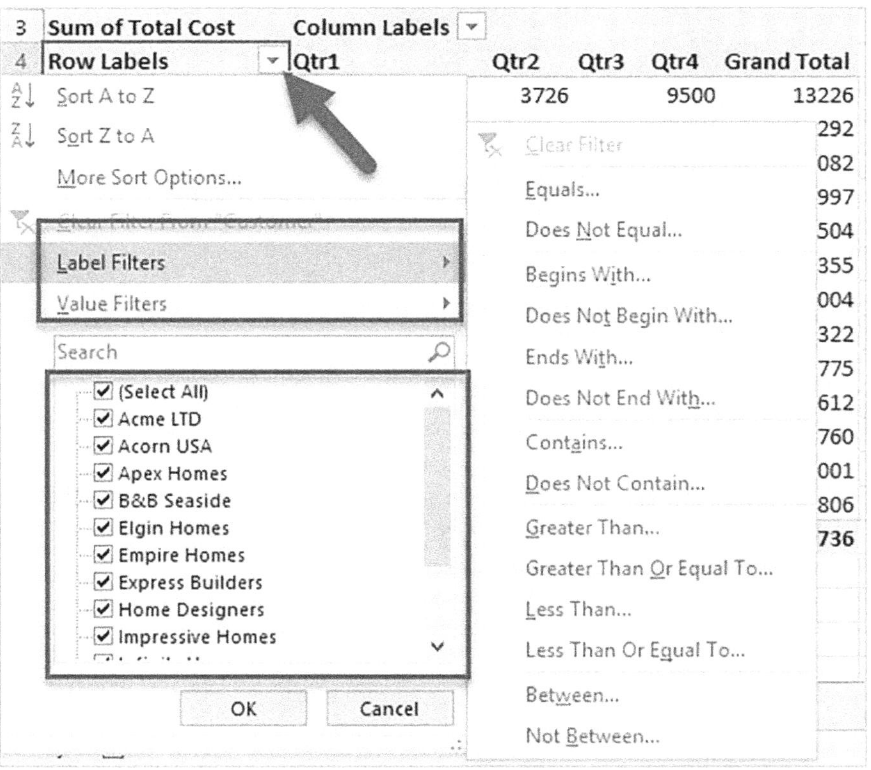

3. Scroll through the list and manually select the items you want to display.

4. Click **OK**.

The PivotTable will now show only the selected columns.

Applying a Custom Filter

You can also use the **Label Filters** and **Value Filters** menu commands to apply a custom filter to your PivotTable the same way you would for a range or table. Please see **Filtering Data** in chapter 4 for detailed steps on how to apply a custom filter.

Sorting PivotTable Data

To arrange the order of your data in a PivotTable, you use the same sorting methods you would use for a range or table.

- Click the **AutoFilter** button on the column named **Row Labels**.

- Click **Sort A to Z** (to sort in ascending order) or **Sort Z to A** (in descending order). If your column headings are dates, you'll get **Sort Oldest to Newest** (for ascending) and **Sort Newest to Oldest** (for descending).

Chapter 12

Creating Charts

Excel charts provide a way to analyze and present your data visually. As the saying goes, *a picture is worth a thousand words*. Some of us don't absorb numbers as easily as others because we're more visual, and this is where charts come in. A visual representation may sometimes create more of an impact on your audience.

This chapter covers:

- Creating a quick chart with the Quick Analysis tool.
- Manually creating a chart.
- Editing and customizing your chart with different styles and formats.
- Creating a sparkline chart.

Preparing Your Data

To prepare your data for charting, you'll need to organize it in a list with only the items you want to report on. Leave out any extraneous data and grand totals you don't want on the chart. Ideally, you should have column headings. The example below has **Product Name** and **Total Sales** as column headings. Excel's charting tools will use the column headings when labeling your chart.

	A	B
1	**Product Name**	**Total Sales**
2	Chai	$1,800.00
3	Beer	$3,400.00
4	Coffee	$4,600.00
5	Green Tea	$200.00
6	Tea	$1,400.00
7	Chocolate Biscuits Mix	$900.20
8	Scones	$1,000.00
9	Brownie Mix	$1,200.49
10	Cake Mix	$1,500.99
11	Granola	$400.00
12	Hot Cereal	$500.00
13	Chocolate	$1,200.75
14	Fruit Cocktail	$3,900.00
15	Pears	$100.30
16	Peaches	$1,000.50

Creating a Chart with the Quick Analysis Tool

The Quick Analysis tool appears as a button on the bottom-right of your selection when selecting a range of data in Excel. The Quick Analysis button offers a host of features for quickly adding conditional formatting, totals, tables, charts, and Sparklines to your worksheet.

To generate a chart using the Quick Analysis tool:

1. Select the range you want to use for your chart. The Quick Analysis button is displayed at the bottom-right of the selection.
2. Click the Quick Analysis button and then click **Charts**. You'll get a list of recommended charts.

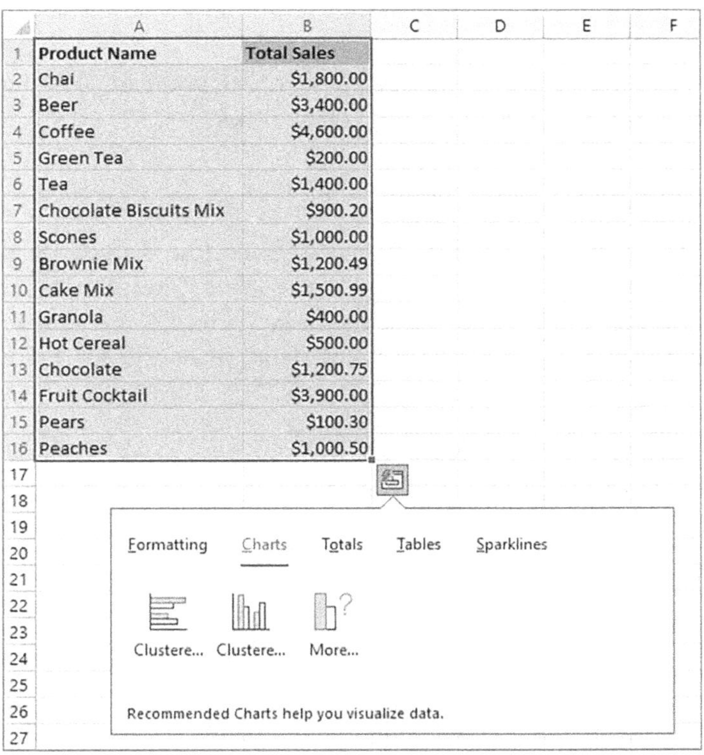

3. Click the second option to generate a column chart.

A floating chart will be created in the same worksheet as your data. You can click and drag this chart to another part of the worksheet if necessary.

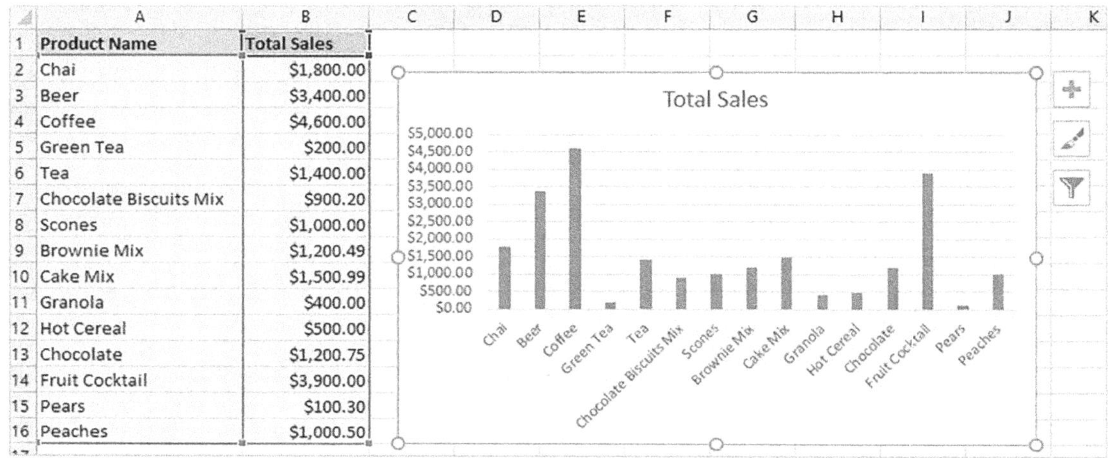

Product Name	Total Sales
Chai	$1,800.00
Beer	$3,400.00
Coffee	$4,600.00
Green Tea	$200.00
Tea	$1,400.00
Chocolate Biscuits Mix	$900.20
Scones	$1,000.00
Brownie Mix	$1,200.49
Cake Mix	$1,500.99
Granola	$400.00
Hot Cereal	$500.00
Chocolate	$1,200.75
Fruit Cocktail	$3,900.00
Pears	$100.30
Peaches	$1,000.50

To create another type of chart, for example, a pie chart, you can click the **More** option on the Quick Analysis menu to show a list of all chart types.

Tip

Another way to create a quick chart is to select the data and press the **F11** key to generate a chart of the default type on a new chart sheet. The default chart created would be the column chart unless you've changed the default chart. To create an embedded chart using this method (in the same worksheet as the data), press the **Alt** + **F1** keys together.

Creating a Chart Manually

The **Charts** group in the **Insert** tab has several commands to create different types of charts. You can click a chart type, for example, the pie chart icon, to display a list of chart options available for that chart type.

Alternatively, you can open the **Insert Chart** dialog box that shows a list of all the chart types you can create in Excel.

To create a chart from the Insert Chart dialog, do the following:

1. Select the range of data for your chart.
2. On the Ribbon, click **Insert** > **Recommended Charts** > **All Charts**.

   Excel displays the **Insert Chart** dialog box.
3. Select the type of chart you want to create from the list of charts on the left.
4. Click **OK**.

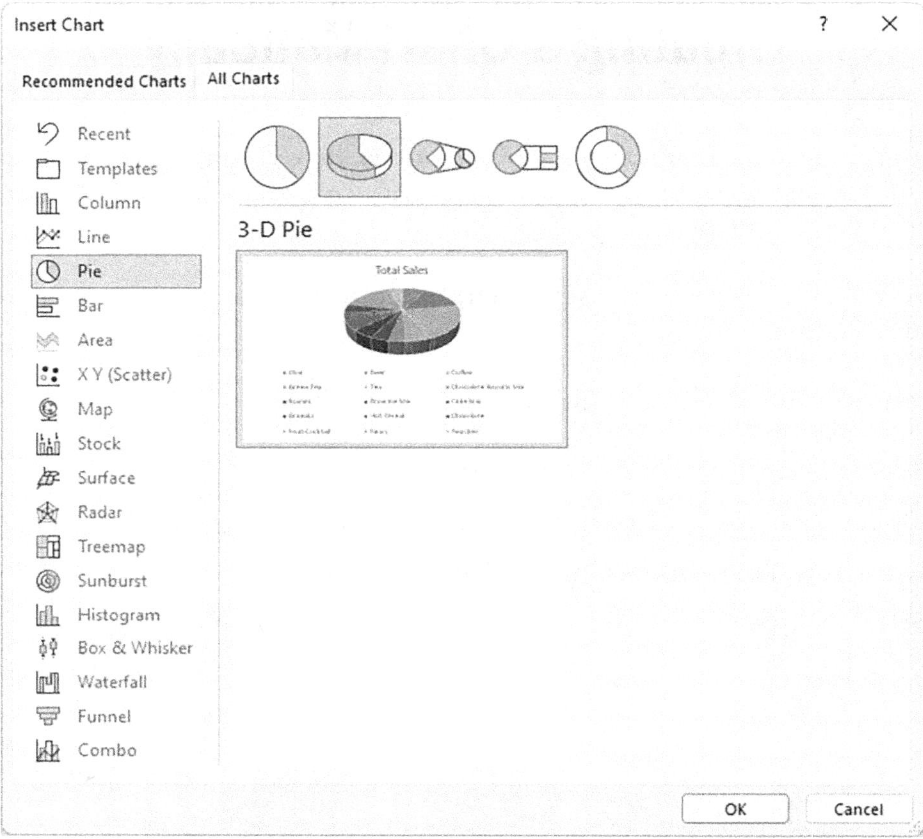

Excel creates a floating chart in the same worksheet as your data. You can click and drag this chart to another part of the screen if necessary.

To delete a chart, simply select the chart and press the **Delete** key.

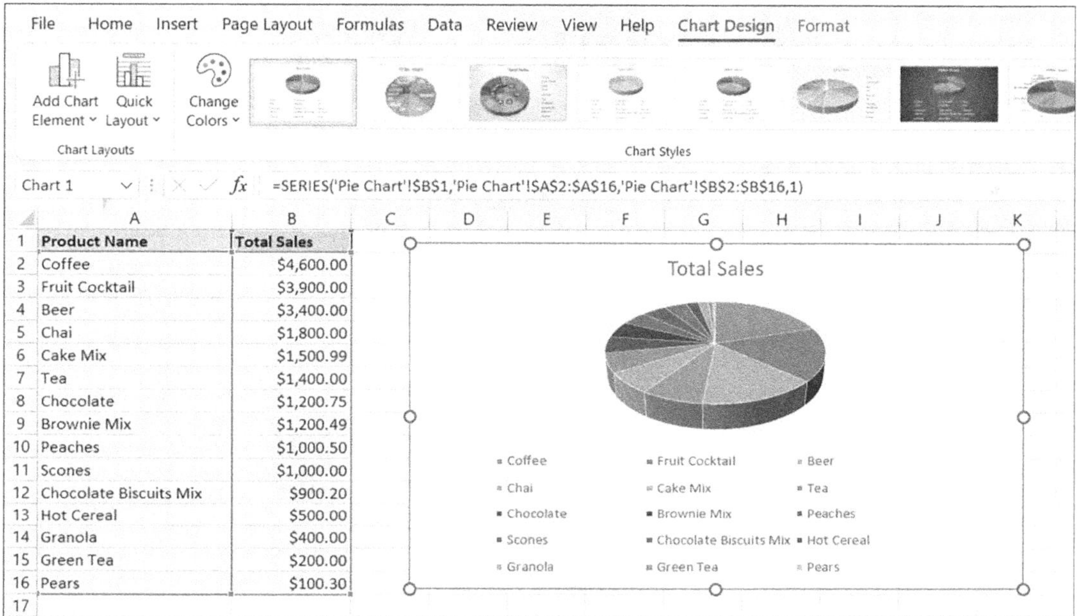

When you select a chart by clicking it, Excel displays the **Chart Design** tab on the Ribbon. This tab provides many options for editing and styling your chart. The next section will cover editing the chart axis labels and style.

Customizing Charts

After creating a chart, Excel provides several commands for customizing the chart to your liking. For example, you can swap the axis, change/adjust the data source, update the chart title, adjust the layout, apply a chart style, and apply a theme color to your chart.

To demonstrate some of these options, let's say we need to create a chart with four quarters of sales, as shown in the image below.

	A	B	C	D	E
1	Sales by Quarter				
2	Product	QTR1	QTR2	QTR3	QTR4
3	Chai	300	300	200	400
4	Beer	300	200	400	300
5	Coffee	350	400	500	500
6	Green Tea	250	150	100	300
7	Tea	100	400	100	500
8	Chocolate Biscu	320	200	100	300
9	Scones	250	500	200	100
10	Brownie Mix	350	400	550	200
11	Cake Mix	200	370	300	200
12	Granola	250	100	200	400
13	Hot Cereal	350	500	300	200
14	Chocolate	350	200	500	500
15	Fruit Cocktail	200	230	250	200
16	Pears	100	200	300	450
17	Peaches	200	300	200	600
18					

To create the chart:

1. Select the range with the data, including the column headers and row headers.
2. Select **Insert** > **Charts** > **Recommended Charts**.

   Excel displays the **Insert Chart** dialog with several chart recommendations for your data.
3. Select the **Clustered Column** option.

4. Click **OK**.

A chart will be created and added to your worksheet.

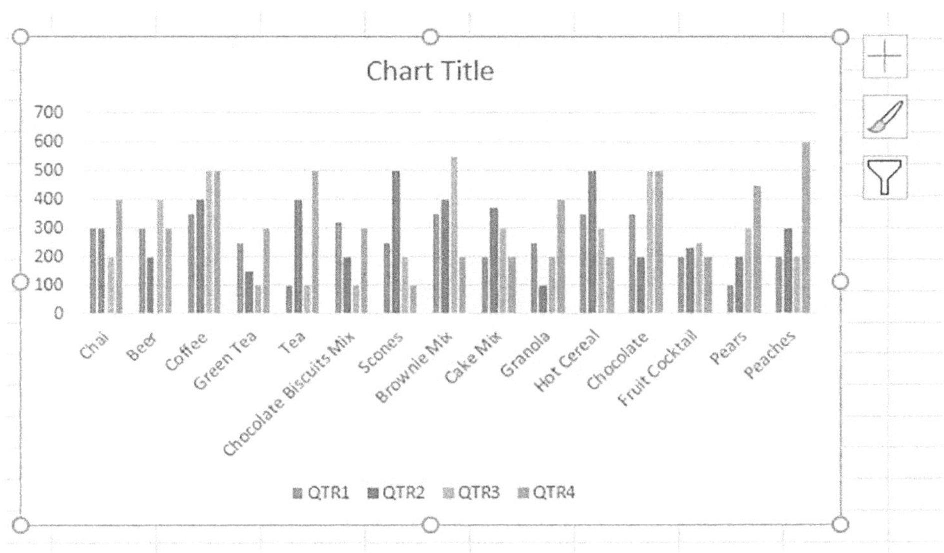

Switching the X and Y Axes

You can switch the values Excel applies to the vertical axis (also called the y-axis) and horizontal axis (also called the x-axis).

To switch the values applied to the axes:

1. Select the chart.
2. Click **Chart Design** > **Switch Row/Column**.

Excel swaps the values applied to the vertical and horizontal axes.

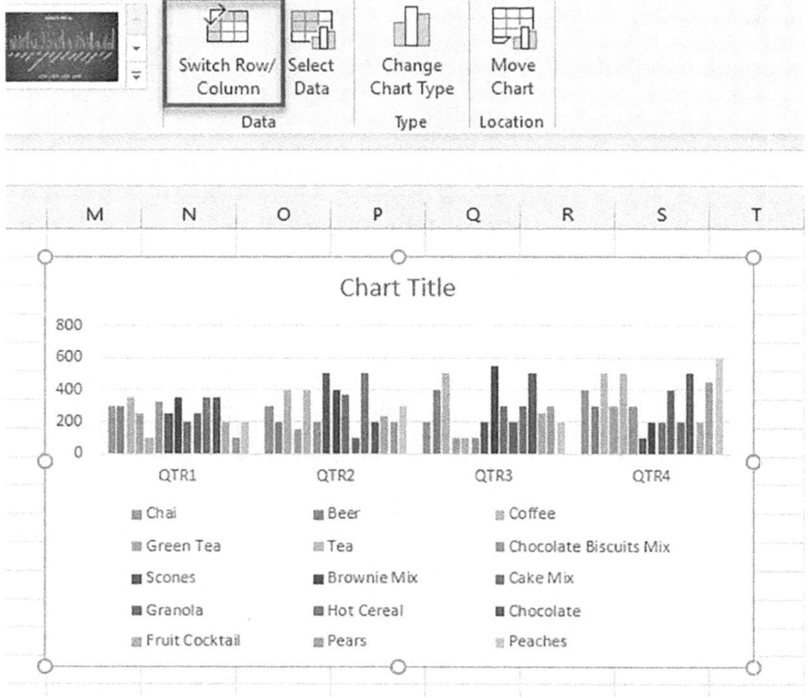

To swap the values back, simply click the **Switch Row/Column** button again.

Change the Data Source

To change the data used as the source of the chart, do the following:

1. Click the Chart to activate the **Chart Design** tab.
2. In the **Data** group, click **Select Data**.

   Excel displays the **Select Data Source** dialog.

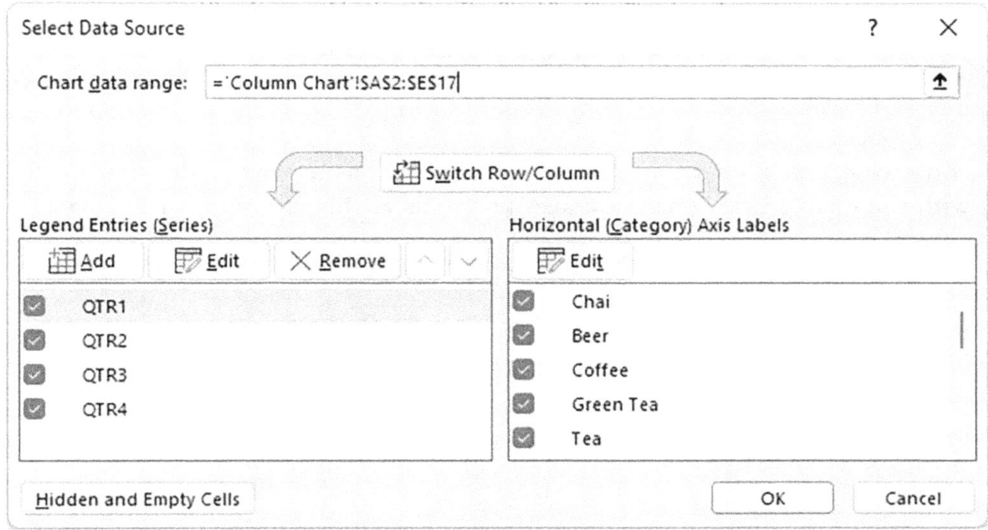

3. Click the Expand Dialog button (up-arrow) on the **Chart data range** field.
4. Select the cells you want in the worksheet area and click the Collapse Dialog button (down-pointing arrow) to return to the **Select Data Source** dialog box.
5. Click **OK** to confirm the change.

The new data source will now be used for the chart.

Adding Axis Titles

When you create a new chart, you'll see "Chart Title" as a placeholder that needs to be edited with the chart's title. There are also no labels at the axis, and we may want to add them to the chart.

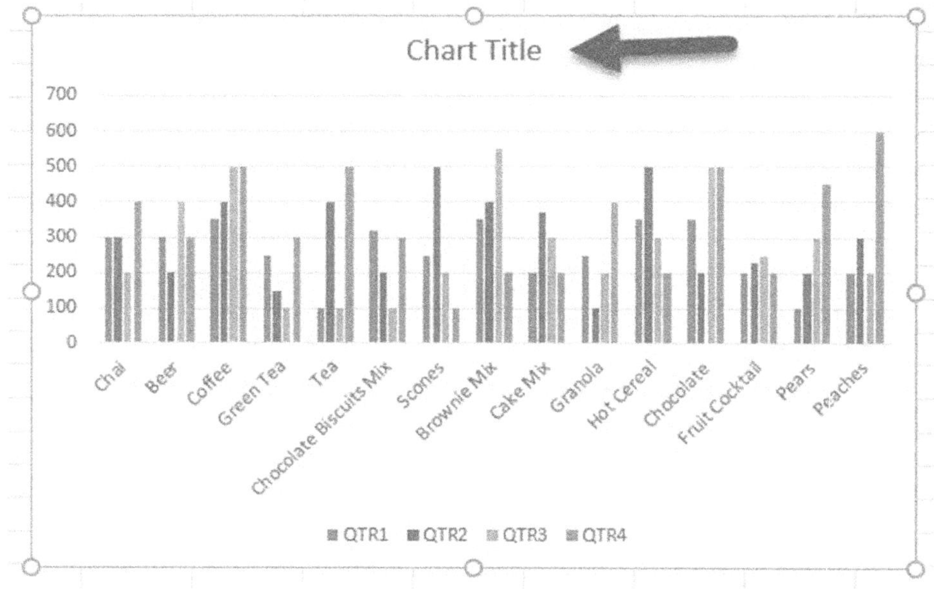

To change the **Chart Title**, you can simply click it and type in the title. Alternatively, you can select the name from a field on your worksheet. For example, to change the chart title to *Sales by quarter,* a value in cell **A1** of the worksheet, click the **Chart Title** label and enter "=A1" in the formula bar. Excel will use the value in cell A1 for our chart title.

We can also add titles down the left-hand side and at the bottom of the chart. These are called axis titles. The left side is the *y*-axis, while the bottom is the *x*-axis.

To change the layout of your chart, click **Chart Design** > **Quick Layout**.

You'll get a pop-up with several chart layouts. With the chart selected, you can hover over each layout to view more details and get a preview of how your chart will look with that layout. A few of the options provide axis titles and move the legend to the right of the chart. If you want a layout with both axis titles, then **Layout 9** is a good option.

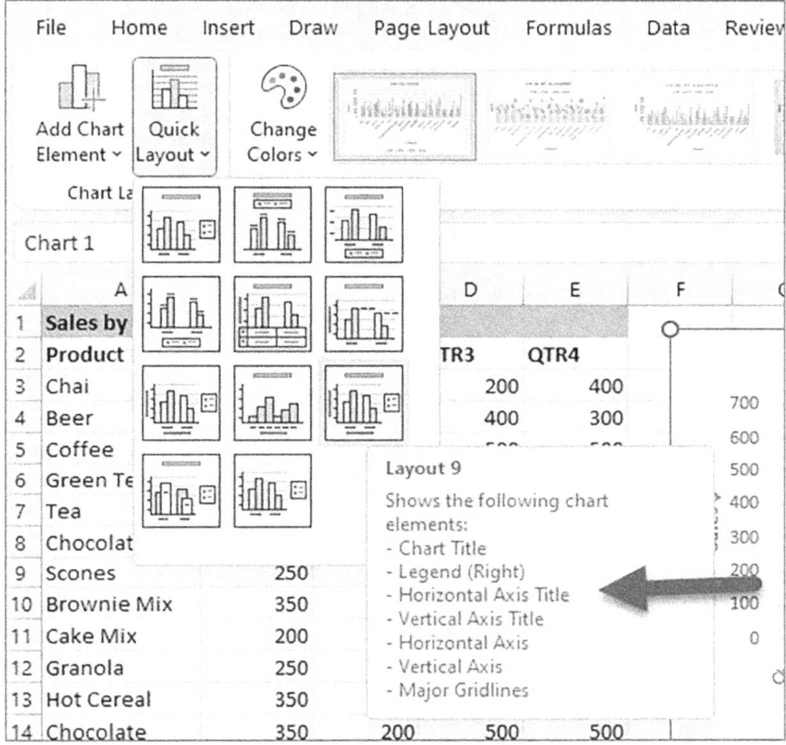

If we select **Layout 9**, we get a chart with labels that we can edit to add titles to the x-axis and y-axis.

You can edit the axis labels as described above. You can click the labels and type in the text directly or pull the text from your worksheet area by typing in a cell reference, for example, **=A1**, assuming cell A1 as the text you want for that label.

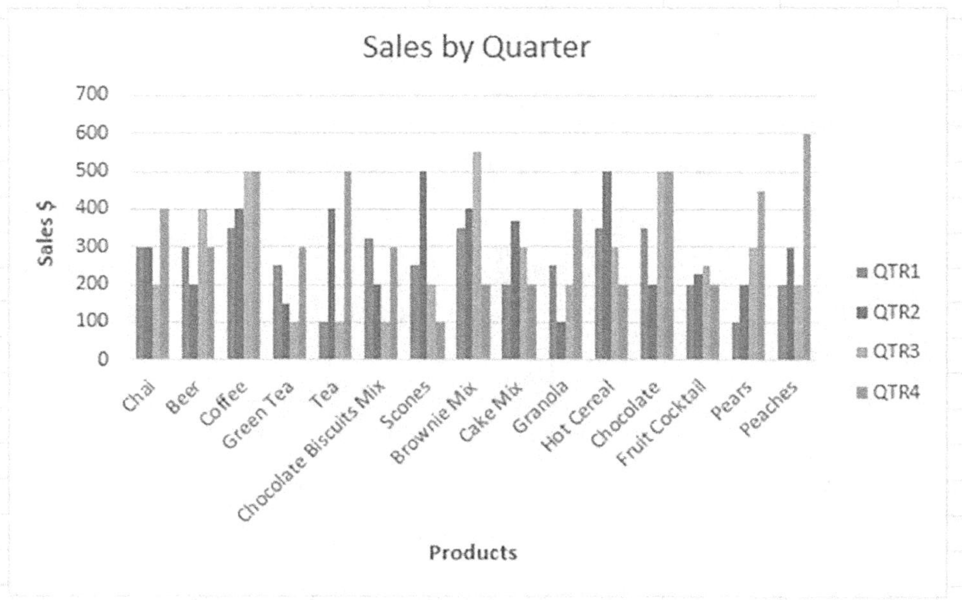
Sales by Quarter
700
600
500
400
300
200
100
0
Sales $
Chai
Beer
Coffee
Green Tea
Tea
Chocolate Biscuits Mix
Scones
Brownie Mix
Cake Mix
Granola
Hot Cereal
Chocolate
Fruit Cocktail
Pears
Peaches
Products
QTR1
QTR2
QTR3
QTR4

Chart Styles

The **Chart Design** tab shows up on the Ribbon when you click a chart. On this tab, you have various **Chart Styles** you can choose from to change your chart's overall look and color.

To change your Chart Style, do the following:

1. Click the chart to select it.
2. On the **Chart Design** tab, in the **Chart Styles** group, click the down arrow to expand the list of predefined styles.
3. You can hover over each style to preview how your graph will look with that style.
4. When you find the one you want to use, click it to apply it to your graph.

To change the color of the plot area:

1. Click the plot area to select it (this is the center of the chart).
2. On the Ribbon, click the **Format** tab, and in the **Shape Styles** group, click the drop-down button to expand the list of Theme Styles.
3. Hover over each style to see a preview of what your chart would look like if selected.
4. When you find the style you like, click it to apply it to your graph.

To change the colors of the bars on the graph, do the following:

1. Click the chart to select it.
2. On the **Chart Design** tab, in the **Chart Styles** group, click **Change Colors**.
3. Hover over the color combinations to see how your graph will look with an option. When you see the one you like, select it to apply it to your graph.

Creating Sparkline Charts

Sparklines are mini charts you can place in single cells to show the visual trend of your data. Excel allows you to quickly add Sparkline charts to your worksheet in a few steps. Sparklines are an excellent visual representation that can be viewed alongside the data. The following example uses the Quick Analysis tool to add sparklines to a dataset.

Adding a Sparkline:

1. Select the data you want to create a Sparkline chart for. You'll see the **Quick Analysis** tool on the lower-right edge of the selection.
2. Click the Quick Analysis tool to open a pop-up menu of Quick Analysis options - **Formatting**, **Charts**, **Totals**, **Tables**, and **Sparklines**.
3. Click **Sparklines** and select one option from **Line**, **Column**, or **Win/Loss**.

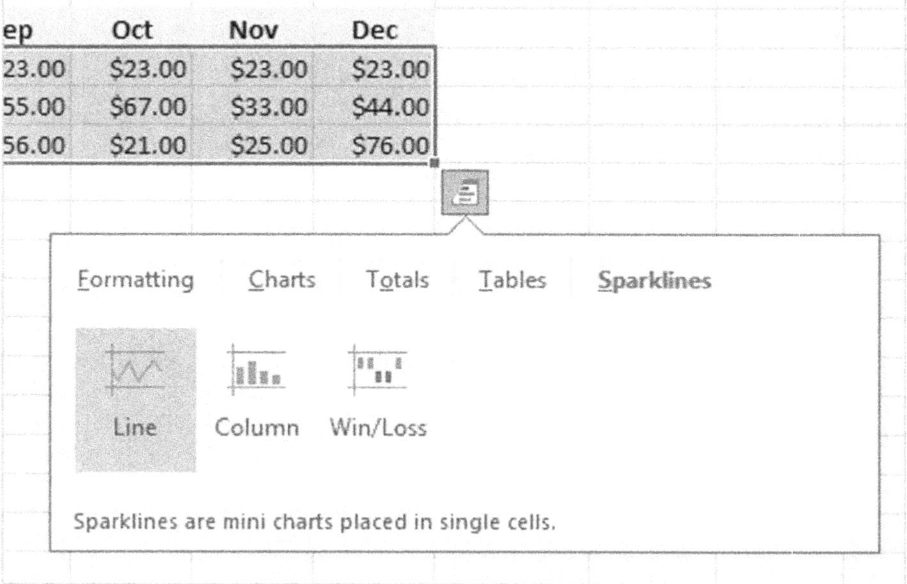

This example uses the **Line** option. The sparklines will be created in the cells immediately to the right of the selected values.

Notice how it's easier to see the data trend with the sparkline than with the figures.

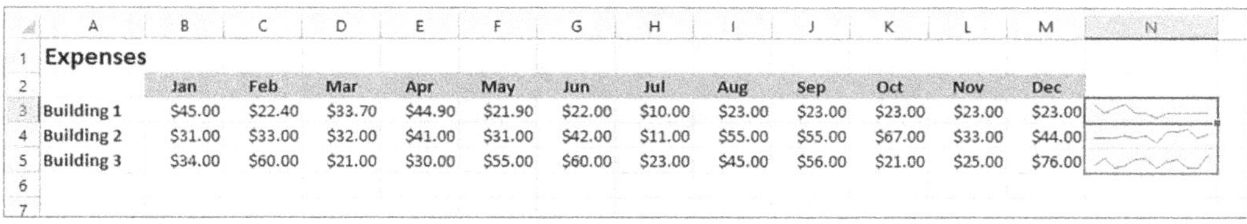

	A	B	C	D	E	F	G	H	I	J	K	L	M	N
1	Expenses													
2		Jan	Feb	Mar	Apr	May	Jun	Jul	Aug	Sep	Oct	Nov	Dec	
3	Building 1	$45.00	$22.40	$33.70	$44.90	$21.90	$22.00	$10.00	$23.00	$23.00	$23.00	$23.00	$23.00	
4	Building 2	$31.00	$33.00	$32.00	$41.00	$31.00	$42.00	$11.00	$55.00	$55.00	$67.00	$33.00	$44.00	
5	Building 3	$34.00	$60.00	$21.00	$30.00	$55.00	$60.00	$23.00	$45.00	$56.00	$21.00	$25.00	$76.00	
6														
7														

Formatting a Sparkline Chart

Select the chart to display the **Sparkline** contextual tab on the Ribbon. The Sparkline tab provides various options to edit, format, and style your sparkline chart.

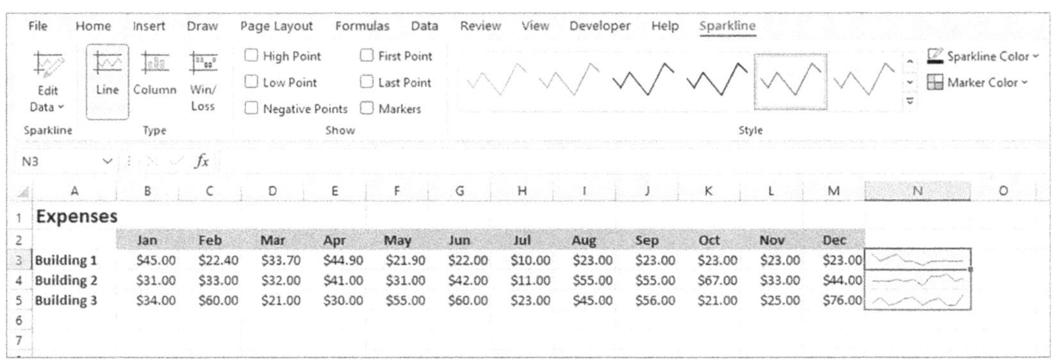

	A	B	C	D	E	F	G	H	I	J	K	L	M	N	O
1	Expenses														
2		Jan	Feb	Mar	Apr	May	Jun	Jul	Aug	Sep	Oct	Nov	Dec		
3	Building 1	$45.00	$22.40	$33.70	$44.90	$21.90	$22.00	$10.00	$23.00	$23.00	$23.00	$23.00	$23.00		
4	Building 2	$31.00	$33.00	$32.00	$41.00	$31.00	$42.00	$11.00	$55.00	$55.00	$67.00	$33.00	$44.00		
5	Building 3	$34.00	$60.00	$21.00	$30.00	$55.00	$60.00	$23.00	$45.00	$56.00	$21.00	$25.00	$76.00		
6															
7															

You can use the following options on the Sparkline tab to format and design your sparkline:

- In the **Type** group, you can use the **Line**, **Column**, or **Win/Loss** buttons to change the chart type.
- The **Show** group provides options to add Markers that highlight specific values in the Sparkline chart.
- You can select a different **Style** for the Sparkline.

- You can change the **Sparkline Color** and the **Marker Color**.
- Click **Sparkline Color** > **Weight** to change the width of the Sparkline.
- Click **Marker Color** to change the color of the markers.
- Click **Axis** to show the axis if the data has positive and negative values.

Chapter 13

Printing Your Worksheet

Even though we live in an increasingly digital world, on some occasions, you may need to print your worksheet on paper as part of a report or present it to others. Excel provides several features that allow you to print your data.

This chapter covers:

- Configuring your print settings in Page Setup.
- Setting the Print Area.
- Previewing and printing your document.

Page Setup

Before you print your document, you may need to change some settings to get the page layout the way you want it. The Page Setup dialog lets you configure several page layout settings in one area.

To open the Page Setup dialog box, click the **Page Layout** tab, and in the **Page Setup** group, click the dialog box launcher.

Excel displays the Page Setup dialog.

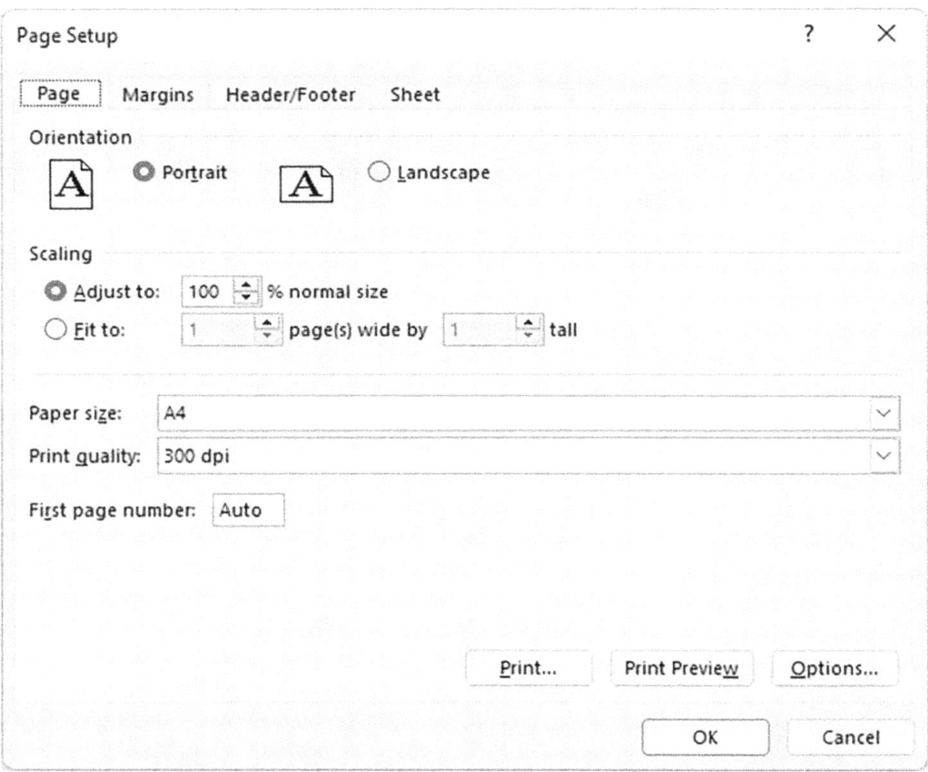

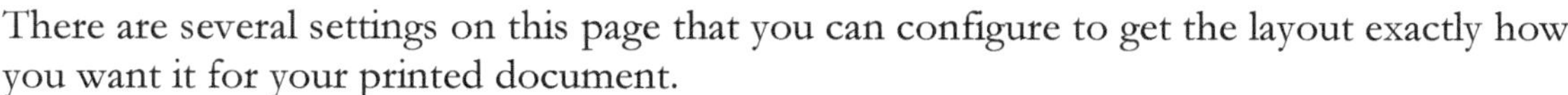

There are several settings on this page that you can configure to get the layout exactly how you want it for your printed document.

❒ Orientation

On the **Page** tab, set the orientation to **Landscape**. Landscape is usually the best layout for printing worksheets unless you have specific reasons to use Portrait.

❒ Scaling

Under scaling, you have two options:

- **Adjust to:** This option enables you to scale the font size of your document up or down. 100% means it will print in normal size. For example, if the normal size of your content is larger than one page, but you would like it to print as one page, you would reduce the percentage to less than 100%.

- **Fit to:** This option lets you choose the document's width (number of pages across) and how tall (number of pages down). For example, you may choose to fit the width on one page and make it more than one page tall.

❒ Paper Size

The default paper size is A4. However, if you are printing to another paper size, you can change it here.

❒ Margins

On the Margins tab, you can change the size of the Top, Bottom, Left, and Right margins, including the size of the Header and Footer.

❒ Header/Footer

You can insert a header or footer on this tab. For example, you can insert a document header that'll appear on all pages and a page number in the footer. You can either select an option from the dropdown list or enter a custom header/footer by clicking the **Custom Header** or **Custom Footer** buttons.

Click **OK** to save your changes and close the Page Setup window when you're done.

Setting the Print Area

You need to set the Print Area so that unpopulated parts of the worksheet are not included in your print, as this could lead to blank pages. You can set the print area in the Page Setup dialog, but it is easier to use the **Print Area** command on the Ribbon.

To set the print area:

1. Select the area in the worksheet that contains the data you want to print.
2. On the **Page Layout** tab, click the **Print Area** button.
3. Select **Set Print Area**.

Note To clear the print area at any point, click the Print Area button and select **Clear Print Area**.

Preview and Print Your Worksheet

Click **File** to display the Backstage view, then click **Print** from the menu on the left.

Excel displays the Print page. You can adjust several settings here to change the page layout, many of which are also available in the Page Setup dialog.

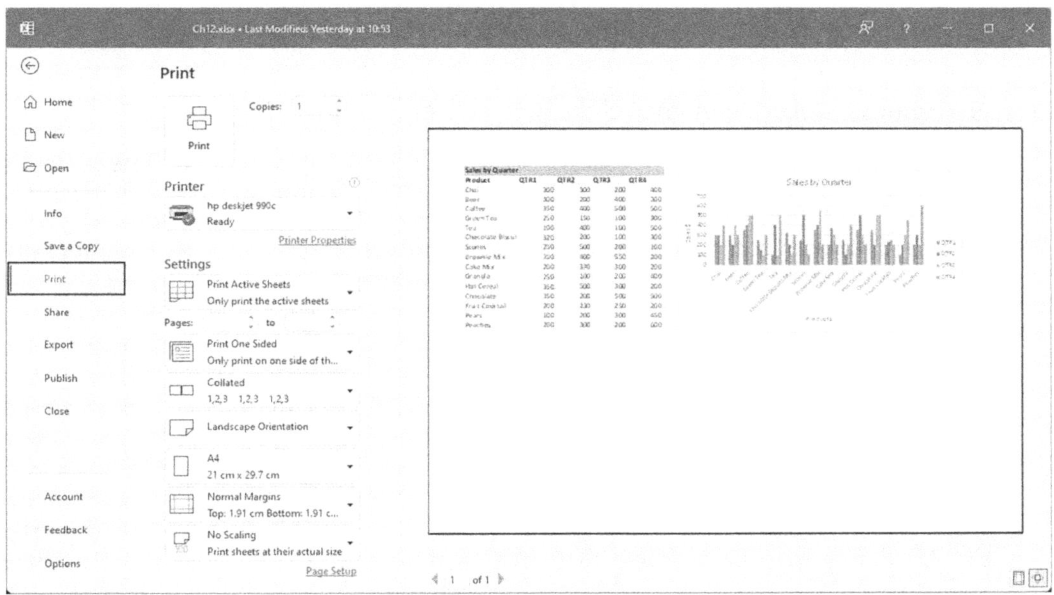

The options on this screen are self-explanatory and similar across Microsoft 365 applications. However, we'll touch on the ones you'll most likely need to set.

Printer

This option allows you to choose the printer to which you want to print. If your printer has been configured on the computer, it will be available for selection here. You also can print to an electronic document like PDF, OneNote, Microsoft XPS Document Writer, etc.

Settings

Print Active Sheets is the default. Leave this option selected if you want to print only the active worksheet. If your workbook has more than one worksheet and you want to print the entire workbook, then click the drop-down list and select **Print Entire Workbook** from the list. If you have selected a range and want to print only those cells, use the **Print Selection** option.

The last option on this page is **scaling**. If you have not set the scale in the Page Setup dialog box, there are four predefined scaling options to choose from here:

- **No Scaling**: The document will be printed as it is, with no scaling.
- **Fit Sheet on One Page**: All columns and rows in the print area will be scaled into one page.
- **Fit All Columns on One Page**: All the columns in the print area will be scaled down to fit one page, but the rows can carry on to other pages.

Tip This is the recommended option if you have many rows of data but a few columns. Always try to scale the columns into one page, if possible, so that you can see a full record on one page.

- **Fit All Rows into One Page**: All rows in the print area will be scaled to fit one page, but the columns can carry on to other pages.

Previewing Your Document

The right side of the screen shows a preview of how your printed document would look. If you have more than one page, use the navigation buttons at the bottom of the screen to view the other pages.

Note Always preview your document before printing to ensure you're happy with the layout. You'll save yourself a ton of ink and paper!

The other settings on the Print page are self-explanatory.

When you're happy with your settings and the preview, click the **Print** button to print your document.

Chapter 14

Securing Your Workbook

Excel enables you to protect your workbook with a password to prevent others from editing your data, deleting worksheets, or renaming worksheets in the workbook.

⚠ **Important** Before you protect your workbook with a password, ensure you have the password written down and stored in a safe place where it can be retrieved if necessary. Without an advanced password cracking tool, it is impossible to gain access to an Excel file that has been password-protected if the password has been forgotten.

How to set a password for your Excel workbook:

To set a password on your Excel workbook:

1. Click **File** > **Info** > **Protect Document** > **Encrypt with Password**.

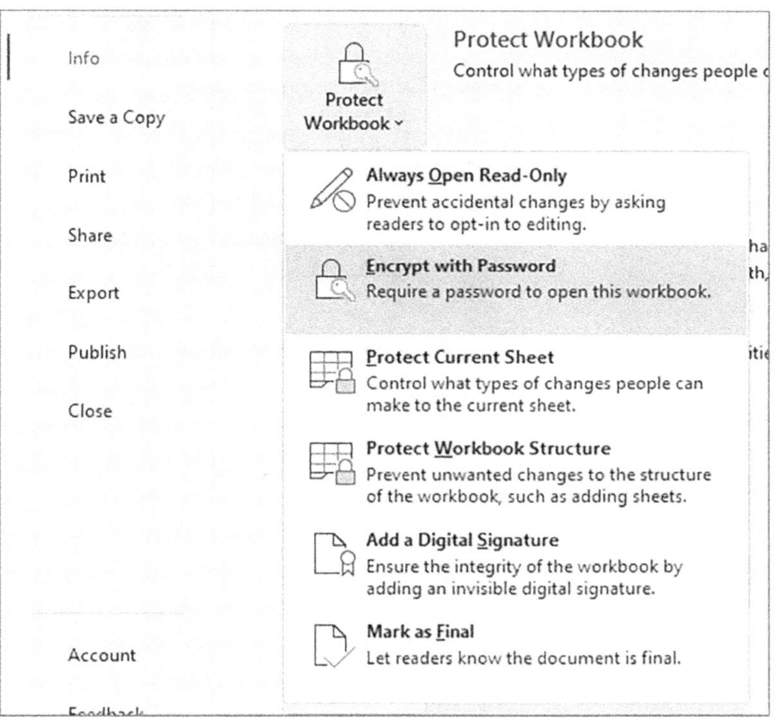

2. At the prompt, enter your password, then confirm it.

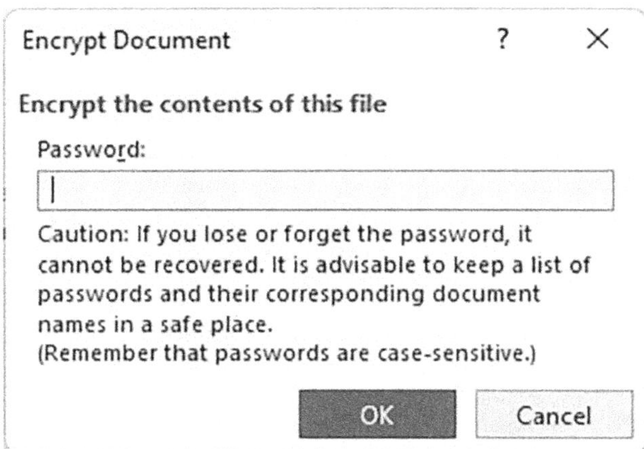

Encrypt Document
?
Encrypt the contents of this file
Password:
Caution: If you lose or forget the password, it cannot be recovered. It is advisable to keep a list of passwords and their corresponding document names in a safe place.
(Remember that passwords are case-sensitive.)
OK
Cancel

3. Click **OK** after confirming the password.
4. Save and close the workbook.
5. When you reopen the workbook, Excel will prompt you for the password.

Removing a Password from an Excel Workbook

On some occasions, you may want to remove a password from an Excel workbook. The process of setting a password encrypts the workbook, so you'll need to remove the encryption. Carry out the following steps to remove the password.

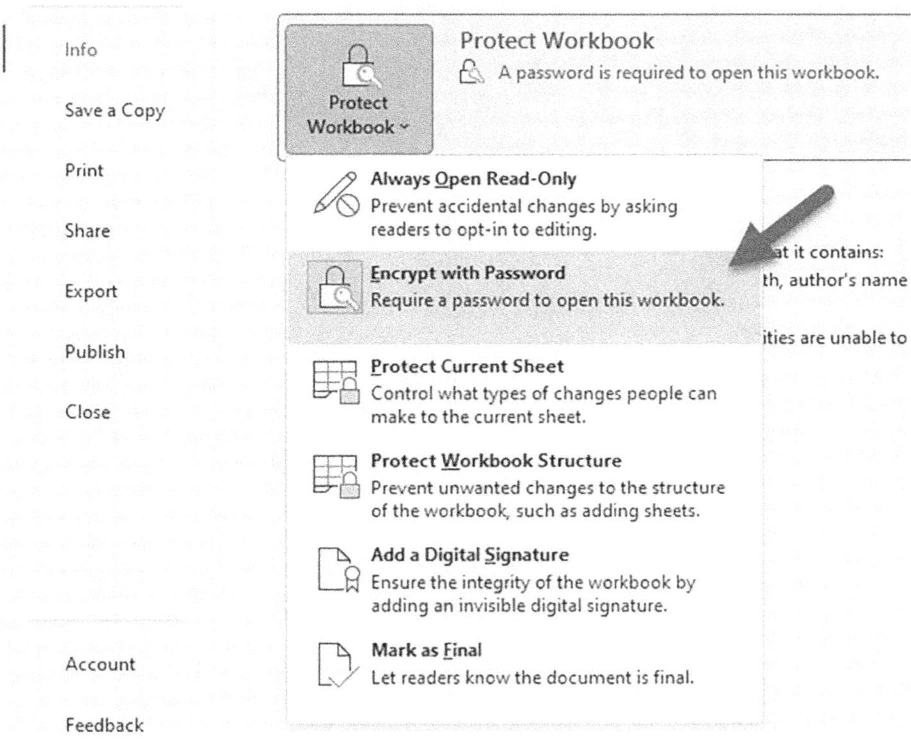

1. Open the workbook and enter the password in the **Password** box.
2. Click **File** > **Info** > **Protect Workbook** > **Encrypt with Password**.

   Excel displays the Encrypt Document dialog box.
3. Delete the contents of the **Password** box.
4. Click **OK**.

5. Save the workbook and close it.

When you reopen the workbook, Excel will not challenge you for a password.

Appendix A: More Help with Excel

For more help with Excel, you can visit Excel's official online help site.

https://support.office.com/en-gb/excel

This website is a comprehensive help center for Excel. Although not an organized tutorial like this book, it is useful when you're looking for help on a specific topic. You'll also find resources like Excel templates that you can download and use as the starting basis for your worksheets.

You can also visit our website for many free Excel tips and techniques.

https://www.excelbytes.com

Appendix B: Keyboard Shortcuts (Excel for Windows)

The Excel Ribbon comes with new shortcuts called Key Tips. Press the **Alt** key when Excel is the active window to see Key Tips.

The following table lists the most frequently used shortcuts in Excel.

Keystroke	Action
F1	Opens Excel's Help window
Ctrl+O	Open a workbook
Ctrl+W	Close a workbook
Ctrl+C	Copy
Ctrl+V	Paste
Ctrl+X	Cut

Ctrl+Z	Undo
Ctrl+B	Bold
Ctrl+S	Save a workbook
Ctrl+F1	Displays or hides the Ribbon
Delete key	Remove cell contents
Alt+H	Go to the Home tab
Alt+H, H	Choose a fill color
Alt+N	Go to the Insert tab
Alt+A	Go to the Data tab
Alt+P	Go to the Page Layout tab
Alt+H, A, then C	Center align cell contents
Alt+W	Go to the View tab
Shift+F10, or Context key	Open context menu
Alt+H, B	Add borders
Alt+H,D, then C	Delete column
Alt+M	Go to the Formula tab
Ctrl+9	Hide the selected rows
Ctrl+0	Hide the selected columns

Access Keys for Ribbon Tabs

To go directly to a tab on the Excel Ribbon, press one of the following access keys.

Action	Keystroke
Activate the Search box.	Alt+Q
Open the File page, i.e., the Backstage view.	Alt+F
Open the Home tab.	Alt+H
Open the Insert tab.	Alt+N
Open the Page Layout tab.	Alt+P
Open the Formulas tab.	Alt+M
Open the Data.	Alt+A
Open the Review.	Alt+R
Open the View.	Alt+W

To get a more comprehensive list of Excel for Windows shortcuts, press **F1** to open Excel Help and type in "Keyboard shortcuts" in the search bar.

Glossary

Absolute reference

A cell reference that doesn't change when you copy a formula containing the reference to another cell. For example, $A$3 means the row and column have been set to absolute.

Active cell

The cell that's currently selected and open for editing.

Alignment

The way a cell's contents are arranged within that cell, which could be left, centered, or right.

Argument

The input values a function requires to carry out a calculation.

AutoCalculate

An Excel feature that automatically calculates and displays the summary of a selected range of figures on the status bar.

AutoComplete

Completes data entry for a range of cells based on values in other cells in the same column or row.

Backstage view

The screen you see when you click the **File** button on the Ribbon. It has several menu options for managing your workbook and configuring global settings in Excel.

Cell reference

The letter and number combination representing the intersection of a column and row. For example, B10 means column B, row 10.

Conditional format

A format that's only applied when certain conditions are met by the cell content.

Conditional formula

A conditional formula calculates a value from one of two expressions based on whether a third expression evaluates to true or false.

Dialog box launcher

You'll see a diagonal down-pointing arrow in the lower-right corner of some groups on the Excel Ribbon. When you click the arrow, it opens a dialog box containing several additional options for that group.

Excel table

A cell range that has been defined as a table in Excel. Excel adds certain attributes to the range to make it easier to manipulate the data as a table.

Fill handle

The Fill handle is a small square on the lower right of the cell pointer. You can drag this handle to AutoFill values for other cells.

Fill Series

A feature that allows you to create a series of values based on a starting value and any rules or intervals included.

Formula

An expression used to calculate a value.

Formula bar

The area just above the worksheet grid that displays the value or formula in the active cell. You can enter a formula directly in the formula bar.

Function

A function is a predefined formula in Excel that just requires input values (arguments) to calculate and return a value.

Named range

A group of cells in your worksheet given a name that is then used to collectively refer to that range of cells.

OneDrive

A cloud storage service provided by Microsoft which automatically syncs your files to a cloud drive, hence providing instant backups. You get OneDrive automatically with a Microsoft 365 subscription.

PivotTable

An Excel summary table that lets you dynamically summarize data from different perspectives. PivotTables are highly flexible, and you can quickly adjust them depending on how you need to display your results.

Quick Access Toolbar

A customizable toolbar with a set of commands independent of the tab and Ribbon commands currently on display.

Relative reference

Excel cell references are relative references by default. When you copy a formula to another cell, the references will change based on the relative position of columns and rows.

Ribbon

The top part of the Excel window containing the tabs and commands.

Sort

A sort means to reorder the data in a worksheet in ascending or descending order by one or more columns.

Sparkline

A small chart that visually represents data in a single worksheet cell.

Validation rule

A test that data must pass to be a valid entry in a cell.

Workbook

The Excel document itself, which can contain one or more worksheets.

Worksheet

A worksheet is like a page in an Excel workbook.

x-axis

The horizontal axis of a chart where you could have time intervals etc.

y-axis

The vertical axis of a chart, which usually depicts value data.

Index

P

Q

R

S

T

U

V

W

X

About the Author

Nathan George is a computer science graduate with several years' experience in the IT services industry in different roles which included Access development, Excel VBA programming, end-user support of Access power users, and Access training. One of his main interests is using computers to automate tasks and increase productivity. As an author, he has written several technical and non-technical books.

Other Books by Author

Excel 2019 Functions

70 Top Excel Functions Made Easy

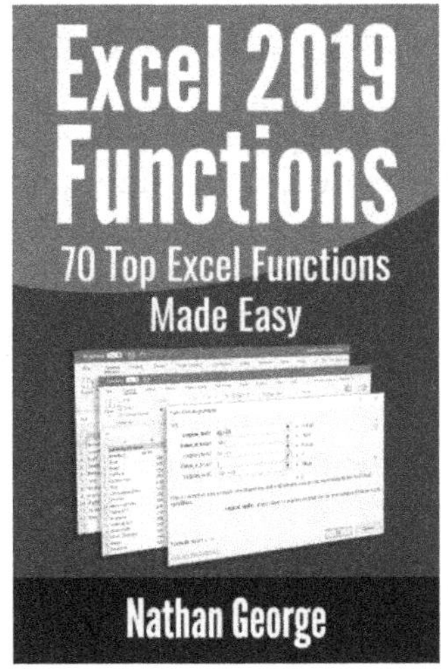

Leverage the full power of Excel functions in your formulas!

Excel 2019 Functions is a practical guide covering 70 of the most useful and relevant Excel functions from different categories, including logical, reference, statistical, financial, math, and text. Excel functions are predefined formulas that make creating answers to your questions easier and faster.

This guide comes with Excel sample files for all examples in the book available for download online. You can copy and use the formulas in your own worksheets. *Excel 2019 Functions* will be a great resource for you whether you're a beginner or experienced with Excel.

For more information, visit:
https://www.excelbytes.com/excel-books

Excel 2019 Macros and VBA

An Introduction to Excel Programming

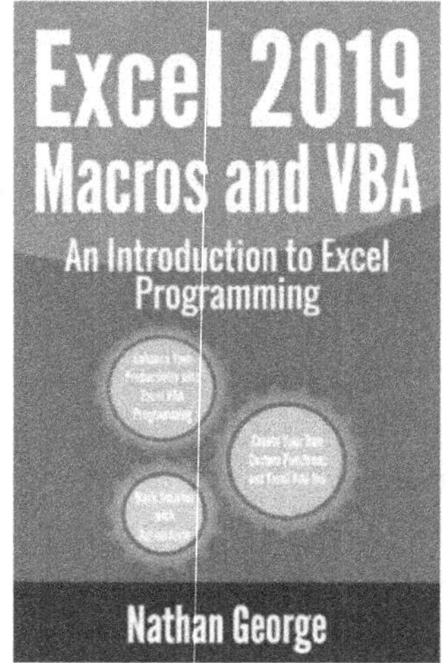

Take your Excel skills to the next level with macros and Visual Basic for Applications (VBA)!

Create solutions that would have otherwise been too cumbersome or impossible to create with standard Excel commands and functions. Automate Excel for repetitive tasks and save yourself time and tedium.

With *Excel 2019 Macros and VBA,* you'll learn how to automate Excel using quick macros as well as writing VBA code. You'll learn all the VBA fundamentals to enable you to start creating your own code from scratch.

For more information, visit:
https://www.excelbytes.com/excel-books

Mastering Access 365

An Easy Guide to Building Efficient Databases for Managing Your Data

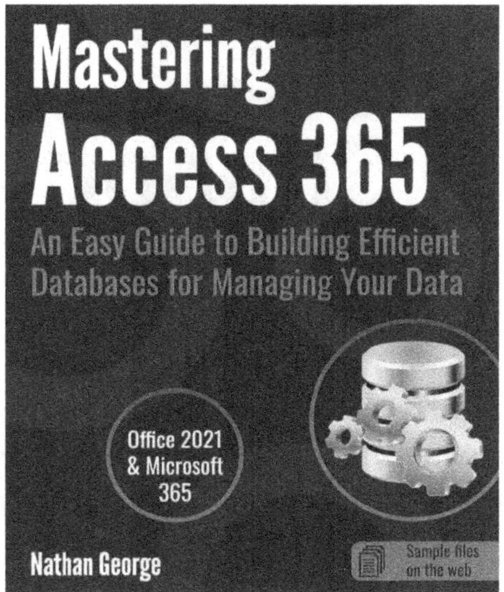

Has your data become too large and complex for Excel? If so, then Access may just be the tool you need.

Whether you're new to Access or looking to refresh your skills on this popular database application, you'll find everything you need to create efficient and robust database solutions for your data in this book.

Mastering Access 365 offers straightforward step-by-step explanations with practical examples for hands-on learning. This book covers Access for Microsoft 365 and Access 2021.

Available from many book retailers. Visit our website for more info:

https://www.excelbytes.com/access-book

Support and Feedback

Thank you for buying this book. The topics have been kept at the beginner to intermediate level to ensure you're not overwhelmed if you're new to Excel. If you have any questions or comments, please feel free to contact me at **support@excelbytes.com**.

Feedback

If this book has been helpful to you, I would be very grateful if you could spend just five minutes leaving a review on this book's Amazon page (it can be as short as you like). Go to the page below and click the appropriate link to this book's reviews page on your local Amazon store.

https://www.excelbytes.com/excel-365-basics-feedback

Thank you very much!

Errata and Support

Every effort was made to ensure the accuracy of this book and the supplementary content. But if you discover an error, please submit it to us using the link below.

https://www.excelbytes.com/submit-errata

All reported issues will be investigated, and any necessary changes will be incorporated in future editions of this book.

For additional book support and information, please visit:

https://www.excelbytes.com/contact

www.ingramcontent.com/pod-product-compliance
Lightning Source LLC
Chambersburg PA
CBHW081805200326
41597CB00023B/4151

9781915476043